THE AUTHOR Ian C. Robertson, part-editor and contributor to José Hermano Saraiva's *Portugal: A Companion History*, is the author of four editions of *Blue Guides* to both *Spain* and *Portugal*; also of *Portugal: A Traveller's Guide* (Murray, 1992), and *Wellington at War in the Peninsula*. He has edited or provided Introductions to reprints of Joseph Baretti's *Journey from London to Genoa* (across Portugal and Spain), Richard Ford's *Hand-Book for Spain* and *Gatherings from Spain*, and Larpent's *Private Journal*, among other important works concerning travel in and aspects of the history of Spain and Portugal.

SERIES EDITOR Professor Denis Judd is a graduate of Oxford, a Fellow of the Royal Historical Society and Professor of History at the University of North London. He has published over 20 books including the biographies of Joseph Chamberlain, Prince Philip, George VI and Alison Uttley. His most recent book is the highly praised *Empire: The British Imperial Experience from 1765 to the Present*. He is an advisor to the *BBC History* magazine and reviews and writes extensively in the national press.

Other Titles in the Series

THE TRAVELLER'S HISTORY SERIES

'Ideal before-you-go reading' *The Daily Telegraph*

'An excellent series of brief histories' *New York Times*

'I want to compliment you ... on the brilliantly concise contents of your books' *Shirley Conran*

Reviews of Individual Titles

A Traveller's History of France

'Undoubtedly the best way to prepare for a trip to France is to bone up on some history. *The Traveller's History of France* by Robert Cole is concise and gives the essential facts in a very readable form.' *The Independent*

A Traveller's History of China

'The author manages to get 2 million years into 300 pages. An excellent addition to a series which is already invaluable, whether you're travelling or not.' *The Guardian*

A Traveller's History of India

'For anyone ... planning a trip to India, the latest in the excellent Traveller's History series ... provides a useful grounding for those whose curiosity exceeds the time available for research.' *The London Evening Standard*

A Traveller's History of Japan

'It succeeds admirably in its goal of making the present country comprehensible through a narrative of its past, with asides on everything from bonsai to *zazen*, in a brisk, highly readable style ... you could easily read it on the flight over, if you skip the movie.' *The Washington Post*

A Traveller's History of Ireland

'For independent, inquisitive travellers traversing the green roads of Ireland, there is no better guide than *A Traveller's History of Ireland*.' *Small Press*

A Traveller's History
of Portugal

A Traveller's History
of Portugal

IAN C. ROBERTSON

Series Editor   DENIS JUDD
Line Drawings   JOHN HOSTE

Interlink Books
An imprint of Interlink Publishing Group, Inc.
New York • Northampton

First American edition published in 2002 by
INTERLINK BOOKS
An imprint of Interlink Publishing Group, Inc.
99 Seventh Avenue • Brooklyn, New York 11215 and
46 Crosby Street • Northampton, Massachusetts 01060
www.interlinkbooks.com

The front cover shows a detail from an eighteenth-century azulejos *illustrating the* Fables of La Fontaine *on the walls of the cloisters of São Vicente de Fora, Lisbon. By permission of Brian Gibbs/Ancient Art & Architecture Collection.*

946.9
ROB

Library of Congress Cataloging-in-Publication Data
Robertson, Ian, 1928–
    A traveller's history of Portugal/by Ian Robertson.—1st American ed.
      p. cm.—(The traveller's history series)
    ISBN 1-56656-440-9
    1. Portugal—History.   2. Historic sites—Portugal   I. Title.
II. Traveller's history
DP538 .R53 2002
946.9—dc21

                        2001006742

Printed and bound in Great Britain

To order or request our complete catalog,
please call us at **1-800-238-LINK** or write to:
Interlink Publishing
46 Crosby Street, Northampton, MA 01060
e-mail: info@interlinkbooks.com • website: www.interlinkbooks.com

Contents

Preface

Portugal was one of the greatest maritime powers of the late medieval and renaissance age of discovery. From relative obscurity, the country suddenly became one of the prime movers in that extraordinary expansion of Europe that, by the end of the nineteenth century, was to culminate in the subordination of nearly every region of the world to European imperial rule and control. Hitherto a modest medieval state at the continent's westernmost Atlantic edge, the Portuguese cashed in on their geographical position by sending their ships down to the west coast of Africa, round the Cape of Good Hope and beyond. Great leaders, mariners and explorers like Prince Henry the Navigator, Vasco da Gama and Bartholomew Diaz became household names, their praises sung by poets and minstrels.

As a result of their daring, their naval and military skills, and their persistent probing at the peripheries of European geographical and cartographical knowledge, the Portuguese helped permanently to transform the world and to leave it in a shape easily recognisable today. Portuguese is the language of Brazil, and is understood in many other former Portuguese colonies; large numbers of territories were brought under Portuguese rule, two of them, Angola and Mozambique among the last to achieve independence in the late twentieth century. Elsewhere a phenomenal number of countries and lands were reached, named and controlled, even if temporarily, by the Portuguese: among them was Ceylon, Tristan da Cunha, the Guinea coast, the Cape Verde islands, Mombasa, Goa, Macão, Ormuz, Java, and so on. Not confining themselves to tropical or temperate climates, Portuguese explorers arrived on the coast of Newfoundland just a couple of years after John Cabot, and also surveyed the coast of Greenland.

The daring and initiative that brought Portugal such commercial and imperial success pulled the country out of its relative backwardness, and made it a European power to be reckoned with. During its time as a not always enthusiastic partner of the Spain of Philip II, Portugal played an important part in various European campaigns, including the disaster of the Spanish Armada in 1588. When in 1640, after eighty years, Portugal finally achieved its freedom from Spain, it managed to survive a series of wars fought on its territory and to stagger towards the twentieth century as an independent and free-standing state although not one that counted for much in the European or indeed the global balance of power.

Fighting as one of the Allies during the First World War, Portugal thereafter gradually relapsed into a mild version of fascism yapping at the side of the far greater tyranny of Franco's Spain. The army led revolution of 1974 was the means by which Portugal was able to cleanse and rehabilitate itself as a 'normal' western European state. Its empire was finally abandoned – although especially in southern Africa the withdrawal was painful and bloody – and it achieved membership of the European Economic Community in 1986.

Nowadays Portugal is a stable state, and one increasingly benefiting from the income from the great new staple trade of tourism. It is for these travellers that this fascinating, well researched and very readable book is written. Within its pages the reader will find clear and ample detail and information that will surprise them, and episodes of which they may only have been dimly aware. As a result, English-speaking visitors to Portugal will know precisely how John of Gaunt fits into the picture, and why the Portuguese princess, Catherine of Braganza, journeyed to England to become the Queen of that cynical, worldly and inconstant monarch, Charles II.

One thing is clear from a reading of this comprehensive and lively book: Portugal is today a country where a rich and complex past provides a solid background to a holiday experience which can encompass sun drenched beaches, wild mountains, inexpensive and delicious sea food, the architectural glories of Lisbon and other towns, and abundant fine wine. No wonder it attracts so many visitors and travellers.

Denis Judd
London, 2002

Introduction

Although any condensed survey is inevitably inadequate, in the following pages I have attempted to give a new dimension to the historical background of Portugal, which may interest and stimulate the prospective traveller. Aldous Huxley once remarked that 'For every traveller who has any taste of his own, the only useful guidebook will be the one he himself has written. All others are an exasperation – they make him travel long miles to see a mound of rubbish; they go into ecstasies over mere antiquity.' Perhaps something very similar might be said of history books, for it is impossible for even the most objective of historians to provide an entirely balanced version of a country's development. While endeavouring to maintain continuity and the whole wide canvas in perspective, inevitably the flow of the narrative will be erratic; his selection of which subjects deserve more detailed examination must be idiosyncratic; he will concentrate on those periods and aspects of a country's past which – in his opinion – were of significance or which retain their intrinsic interest; and, involuntarily, he will impose on his readers his own interpretation of historical events, for them to accept or question. While certain phases of Portugal's history may well have got out of focus in the telling, I trust that this overview will retain a sense of proportion and explain it intelligibly to both the armchair traveller and to the visitor curious to know more about a beautiful and captivating country.

It is not generally appreciated that the frontiers of Portugal have remained virtually unchanged for longer than those of any other European country, and it is mainland Portugal which will be the subject of this *Traveller's History*, while at the same time some account

1

must be given of her considerable impact on her former extensive overseas empire.

I should emphasize that until the beginning of the twelfth century there was no distinction between Spain and Portugal. Thus some Peninsular history in general, not specifically relating to Portugal, will be included in the first few chapters; and throughout, I have tried to avoid burdening these pages with more than is essential concerning the eastern two-thirds of the Peninsula. Inevitably, there will be numerous lacunae in what is a concise history, and I have therefore included a selective list of books covering a very much wider range of subjects impinging on Portuguese history and culture, to which one may refer, and which themselves contain bibliographies.

There are inconsistencies in most books as to the spelling of Arab names, such as Umayyad, Ummayad, Ummaiyad, etc. I have also chosen to retain the more familiar names Almoravids and Almohads – described briefly in the Glossary – rather than the more politically and academically correct *Murabit* and *Muwahhid*, which merely compound the chances of misunderstanding. The reader should not expect entire consistency in the spelling of names, whether of people or of places, particularly before the late medieval period, after which there is more general agreement about usage. Most personal and topographical names remain in Portuguese (or Spanish), although I have preferred such common anglicizations as Braganza (for Bragança), Busaco (Buçaco), Lisbon (Lisboa), Oporto (Porto) and Tagus (Tejo in Portugal; Tajo in Spain), among others. I have listed in the index most of the Roman and some Arabic place names in the text, together with their present names, for usually it is only on the first occasion one is mentioned that the latter is also included in brackets. Precisely when, over the centuries, one will have developed or changed to another may be obscure, and occasional overlapping is unavoidable. Wellington is referred to by that name only in the Historical Gazetteer, although he was known as Sir Arthur Wellesley until August 1809.

Portugal's long history has been well served in recent decades by British historians among other writers describing the country and aspects of its culture. While it may be invidious to mention specific names, my indebtedness to the late David Francis, Harold Livermore and Peter Russell cannot go unacknowledged, while the late Charles Boxer's experiences while researching aspects of the former Portuguese empire – a subject he made his own – deserve scrutiny also. Many other authors, whose studies have been found invaluable, are listed in the section on Further Reading.

I greatly appreciate the encouragement and material assistance received from Andrew Hewson, Arthur Boyars, Birgitta Rosén and, especially, Kim Taylor, without whose sound judgement this concise history for travellers to Portugal would have been much the poorer: any errors of fact among other infelicities and misinterpretations the following pages will undoubtedly retain, are my own. I must also thank Lucinda Phillips, and Jorge de Alarção for permission to adapt a map from his *Roman Portugal*.

CHAPTER ONE

The physical environment and prehistory

Portugal is situated at the south-western extremity of Europe, covering an area of 88,550 square kilometres (34,200 square miles), approximately one-fifth of the Iberian Peninsula, which she shares with Spain. The country is only 218km (or 137 miles) at its widest, and 561km (or 350 miles) from north to south. Its mainland population is now approximately ten million, but very unevenly distributed, for over one-third of it is crowded into the *distritos* of Lisbon and Oporto alone. The southern and eastern districts, although making up 70 per cent of the area of Portugal, contain merely 30 per cent of the population.

Although Portugal's coast is long, forming a buttress against the surging Atlantic ocean, which for centuries has had an important influence on its history, it is provided with comparatively few good harbours. The 1,215km (762-mile)-long land frontier is flanked to the north by the granitic mountainous massif of Galicia, with its seaward reaches formed by the Minho, while its eastern border is either partially formed by or fractured by three of the four major rivers of the Peninsula flowing into the Atlantic: the Douro (in Spain, the Duero), with Oporto by its mouth; the Tagus (Tajo in Spain, Tejo in Portugal), with Lisbon near its capacious estuary; and the Guadiana (the Roman *Anas*, and Arabic *Wadi-Anas*), dividing the southernmost province of the Algarve from western Andalucía. Further east, at Cádiz, is the mouth of the Guadalquivir, formerly the *Baetis*. However, these rivers rarely provide ways of communication, as might be expected, but rather separate the country into three characteristic regions. Yet in Portugal, a comparatively small and homogeneous country, there is little emphasis

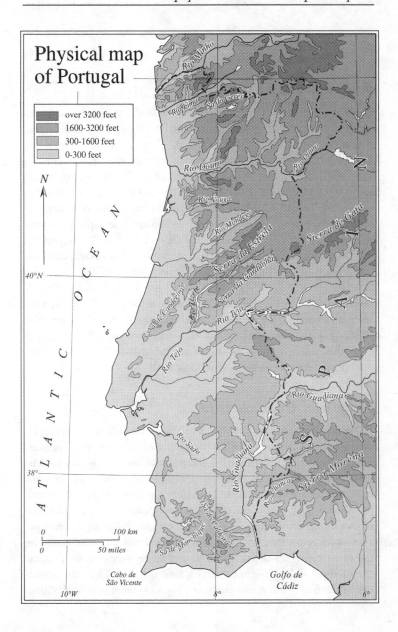

Physical map of Portugal

- over 3200 feet
- 1600-3200 feet
- 300-1600 feet
- 0-300 feet

N

Rio Minho

Rio Lima

Sª do Gerês

Rio Douro

Rio Douro

Rio Vouga

Rio Mondego

Sierra de Gata

Serra da Estrela

ATLANTIC OCEAN

Sª da Gardunha

40°N

Sª de Candeeiros

Rio Vicente

Rio Tejo

Rio Tejo

Rio Guadiana

Rio Sado

Rio Guadiana

38°

Sª de Caldeirão

Rio Chança

Sierra Morena

Sª de Monchique

Cabo de São Vicente

Golfo de Cádiz

0   100 km

0   50 miles

10°W   8°   6°

on regionalism; such nationalistic groups as the Basques or Catalans in Spain do not exist.

Provinces and Districts

The former nine provinces have been divided into smaller administrative *distritos*, named after their capitals: the Minho, to the north-west, is now the districts of Braga and Viana do Castelo; Duoro Litoral is that of Oporto, to the north-east of which extends the upland Trás-os-Montes (Vila Real and Braganza). South of the Douro, and spreading across the country, lies the Beira, once divided into Alta (abutting the high-lying Trás-os-Montes), Litoral, and Baixa or Lower, extending south to the Tagus where it enters from Spain. The capitals are now Aveiro, Viseu, Guarda, Coimbra and Castelo Branco. The capitals of the former coastal province of Estramadura, which also extended to the south bank of the Tagus opposite Lisbon, and that of the Ribatejo (straddling the lower Tagus valley) are Leiria, Lisbon and Santarém. Setúbal administers an area further south, once part of the Alentejo (Alto and Baixo), an extensive region now composing the districts of Portalegre, Evora and Beja. The Guadiana flows through the latter to form the eastern frontier of the present district of Faro, the former province of Algarve, whose coast basks in the sun.

Individual Characteristics

There are considerable physical variations and differing population densities between one part of Portugal and another. The seaboard province of Minho, with a high density, had been settled by the barbarian Suevi, as had Galicia; the conservative and prolific Minhotos still have much in common with their Gallegan cousins and, like them, provided a high proportion of emigrants – once to Brazil, but now more frequently to northern Europe. Its high rainfall allows intensive cultivation, and where it is not cultivated it is thickly wooded except on the steep upper hill-slopes of the several ranges rising from the transverse valleys of the Lima and Cávado, among others. Here the vines of *vinho verde* trail over granite props, trellises and fences of small-holdings or *minifúndios*, and even up into the trees. Still to be seen are lyre-horned oxen, yoked together in pairs by ornamented *cangas*, slowly dragging creaking carts along the narrow lanes, their wooden axles emitting an excruciatingly shrill whine. Along the roads stand *espigueiros*, small granaries built on piles like the *hórreos* of adjacent Galicia. The Minhotos are traditionally both superstitious and pious, and the ecclesiastical capital of Braga was long a centre of reaction to Republican and Left-wing reforms.

Further east, beyond the Serra da Peneda-Gerés, extend the bare and rugged uplands of the backward and thinly populated Trás-os-Montes (literally across the mountains), an extension of the Castilian *meseta*, to reach the upper valley of the Douro at Miranda. The river, dammed, and here turning south, forms the frontier as far as Barco de Alva, where it again bears west. Its steep schistose banks are terraced with port wine vineyards, which provide the Trásmontanos with some seasonal employment.

The countryside south of the Douro is more attractive and the climate milder. Beyond the valley of the Mondego rises the transverse massif of the Serra da Estrêla, the highest range in Portugal, with an altitude of 1991m (6,530ft) at Torre, only occasionally snow-clad. The river descends from near high-lying Guarda and past Coimbra to reach the sea at Figueira da Foz, north of which, at the estuary of the Vouga, lies Aveiro, its lagoon studded with high-prowed *moliceiros*, seaweed-gathering craft. To the south extend pine forests partly planted to fix the coastal dunes.

Through broken country beyond the southern flank of the Serras da Estrêla and da Lousã winds the Zêzere, with its several dams. Further south, beyond Tomar, the Tagus bears south towards its wide estuary at Lisbon. On its left bank extend low-lying *lezirias*, where bulls are bred; west of Santarém, on its right bank, rises the Serra de Montejunto, which is extended by lower ranges towards that of Sintra.

The Alentejo, the granary of Portugal, and that part of the country which was longer under Muslim occupation than most others, is a vast undulating plain, partly covered by forests of cork-oak, heaths with a maquis of cistus and extensive estates (*herdades* or *latifúndios*). The owners of these estates – like those of Spanish Extramadura and

Andalucía further east – over the centuries, have exploited the peasantry who became the most communistically inclined in Portugal. South of Beja, near both Aljustrel and Mértola, are anciently exploited copper mines, an extension of those at Tharsis and Río Tinto further east beyond the Spanish frontier.

The Algarve (*al-Gharb* in Arabic, the westernmost part of what was Muslim-occupied al-Andalus) was the last area of what is present-day Portugal to be wrested from the Muslims, and after its reconquest, the sovereign was first described as 'King of Portugal and the Algarves'. The Serra de Monchique, among others, divides it from the Alentejo. At its far west end projects the Cabo de São Vicente and that of Sagres, 'where the land ends and the sea begins', in the words of Camões; from its small ports many ships set sail on their voyages of discovery. Inland, further east, extends hilly country (similar to the Spanish Sierra Morena), through which cuts the Guadiana. The southern slopes of these ranges have a scanty rainfall compensated for by Atlantic humidity, in which citrus groves and a variety of semi-tropical fruits and flowers flourish. It still has a large fishing community, although this sunny coast, with its extensive beaches and occasional lines of cliffs, picturesquely carved by the cold Atlantic, has been also much exploited by the tourist trade in recent decades. Colonies of villas and hotels have not added to its natural attractions, yet it was described only seventy years ago as being 'so seldom visited by strangers, that the traveller will find himself an object of the greatest interest, and will probably walk about a town with a tail of twenty of thirty of the inhabitants'!

Any tendency to regard Portugal as merely a geographical extension of Spain should be avoided entirely, for the differences between the two countries are many and profound, and it would be invidious to make comparisons. Perhaps one of the most striking of these is the change in vegetation: far more flowers and bushes are to be seen throughout Portugal and there are more trees, including extensively – but controversially – planted eucalyptus, which are noticeably absent on the parched, high-lying and windswept Castilian plateau. When not using the few *auto estradas* now traversing Portugal, one may still find many tree-shaded roads, providing pleasanter driving through softer, greener and less austere landscapes.

Prehistory

PALEOLITHIC

Several Paleolithic sites have been discovered within the frontiers of Portugal, the earliest being at Vilas Ruivas. Other early sites have been located above the north bank of the Tagus south-west of Castelo Branco; also near the Spanish frontier east of Vila Velha de Ródão; at Fratel, to the west; and further downstream near Alpiarça (south of Santarém). Concentrations of human habitation from the Mesolithic period are to be found near the mouths of the Tagus and its tributary, the Muge, and the Sado (south-east of Setúbal); along the Atlantic littoral; and in isolated places inland. Characteristic survivals are shell middens or *concheiros*, dating from *c*. 7000 BC, notable among which is that at Cabeça da Arruda, near Muge (south of Santarém), of *c*. 5400– 3200 BC.

NEOLITHIC

It was only in the Neolithic or New Stone Age period that settled communities developed, of which much more evidence remains. Early examples of megaliths are to be found in the vicinity of Reguengos de Monsaraz (south-east of Evora), among them being several dolmens, the menhirs of Bulhôa and Outeiro, and the cromlech do Xerez, surrounded by a circle of standing stones. Most of the earlier sites have been found in the Alentejo and Algarve, and in caves in Estremadura. Neolithic tholoi, rock-cut tombs, among other grave types, together with pottery and other artefacts have been discovered further north also, near the mouth of the Mondego.

CHALCOLITHIC

The Neolithic era was followed by the Chalcolithic (*c*. 2500–1700 BC). Southern Portugal was rich in seams of copper, with which axes, daggers and various other implements were fashioned. Settlements became fortified by thick concentric walls, some bastioned, examples of which survive at Zambujal (near Torres Vedras), Vila Nova de São Pedro (west of Santarém), among several sites west of the Tagus, and near Torrão (south-east of Alcácer do Sal), on a tributary of the Sado,

Aerial view of the cromlechs of Almendras, west of Evora

then navigable. The Copper Age merged with the Bronze Age (1800–700 BC), bronze being an alloy of copper and tin, substantial deposits of which were exploited in the centre and north. Later metallurgical refinements led to an increase in trading in weapons and other manufactures, among them pottery. Pastoral and agricultural societies, although still warlike, had by now spread over most of the country, their communities often living within walled hill-top settlements for protection, some being occupied subsequently by Iron Age peoples.

IBERIANS

The indigenous inhabitants of much of the Peninsula – predominantly along the Mediterranean coast, up the Ebro valley and what is now Andalucía – were later given the name Iberians. Their ancestry is unclear and their two related non-Indo-European languages remain undeciphered. They were related neither to the Basques, already in possession of the western Pyrenees, nor to the Celts, the first wave of whom had crossed the Pyrenees early in the first millenium BC and had settled in the northern *meseta*, the north-west of the Peninsula and along the Atlantic coast. The Celts intermarried and eventually dominated the 'Iberians' by now in the upper Ebro valley and Aragón, and also those nearer the centre of the Peninsula, who were then referred to by early writers as the Celtiberi. (The Roman poet Martial, born in AD 40 near Calatayud, south-west of Zaragoza in Spain, was proud of his Iberian and Celtic pedigree.)

CELTS

From the evidence of place names, it would seem that there was also a Celtic enclave in the Alentejo, although the influence of these 'Celti' was at first comparatively slight, when compared to the powerful Turdetani tribe further east. Widely distributed throughout the north-west of the Peninsula are *citânias* or *castros*, fortified hill-top villages containing round houses, built by these Celts, whose culture is associated with that of the La Tène or second Iron Age culture of western Europe at this period. In Portugal, over 800 surviving *citânias* have been counted north of the Douro, although doubtless there were many more. Notable examples among them are those of Briteiros (south-east of Braga), Sanfins (near Paços de Ferreira, south-east of Santo Tirso), and the Castro de Carvalhal (near Barcelos).

The Celts, who cremated their dead, were also skilled ironworkers and goldsmiths. It is possible that the sophisticated culture known as that of Tartessos, which flourished in the lower reaches of the Guadalquivir and Guadiana during the eighth to sixth centuries BC, may have stemmed from both Celtic and Phoenician 'orientalizing' influences on the local population (predominately the Turdetani tribe), who controlled the rich mineral resources of the region, notably the silver and copper mines of Río Tinto and Nerva. They traded to their mutual benefit with the Phoenicians (and later, Greeks), who had been forming coastal settlements, such as Cádiz (Phoenician Gadiz, Roman Gades), then an island; Huelva (Onuba) and the site of La Joya; Faro (Ossonoba); Alcácer do Sal (Salacia); and further north along the Atlantic seaboard, including Lisbon (Olisipo). Also but less frequently, they had settlements some distance inland (as confirmed by the rich

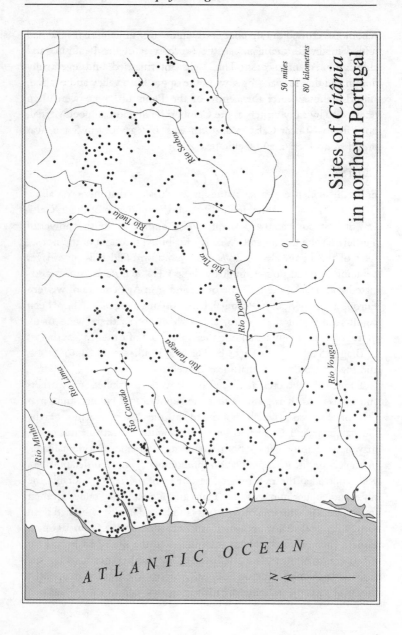

Sites of *Citânia* in northern Portugal

Phoenician tomb of *c.* 625 BC found at Aliseda, west of Cáceres). Their influence may be seen also in the manufactures, ornaments, funerary sculpture and religious practices of the Turdetani. The collapse – for no known cause – of the Tartessian culture appears to have taken place towards the end of the sixth century BC.

CHAPTER TWO

The Romans in Iberia:
Lusitania part of the Empire

Carthaginians

After their defeat by the Romans in the First Punic War (247–241 BC) the Carthaginians sought to make up for their losses elsewhere, and established several trading-posts along the southern and eastern coasts of the Peninsula, notably at Qart Hadasht (Roman Carthago Nova, now Cartagena), a convenient harbour close to rich mineral deposits. Their activity beyond the Mediterranean and in southern Portugal is obscure, although it is known that a force commanded by Hasdrubal was stationed later near the Tagus estuary. In 226 BC the Carthaginians made a treaty with Rome, making the Ebro, the only river of consequence flowing into the Mediterranean, the boundary between their spheres of influence in the Peninsula. Seven years later Saguntum was attacked by Hamilcar Barco, the Carthaginian general (d. 228 BC), and the father of Hannibal. Although south of that river, it was allied to Rome, who made it a *casus belli*. With the destruction of Carthage at the end of the Second Punic War (218–212 BC), the Romans remained the dominant power in Hispania, their name for the Peninsula.

Romans enter the Peninsula

The western part of the Peninsula was then largely inhabited by tribes of Celtic descent, among which, in what is now Galicia, were the Gallaeci (abutted to the east by the Astures and Cantabri). A sub-group, the Bracari, dwelt between the Minho and the Douro, while in the highlands to the east were the Banienses. In the Beira Litoral were the Turduli Veteres, with the Lusitani (originally a pastoral pre–Celtic tribe)

Partial view of the site of Conimbriga

further inland in the Beira; they later, under their leader Viriatus, were to make their name by long resisting the Roman invaders. Nearer the Tagus valley and in the Alentejo were the Celtici, with the Conii in the southern Alentejo and Algarve. The Celtic suffix '-briga' (hill-fort or citadel) to Conimbriga (south-west of Coimbra), would suggest that the latter tribe had formerly occupied that region before being driven further south and becoming subject to the Celtici, as evident from the names Caetobriga (Setúbal) and Mirobriga (Santiago de Caçem).

It was the southern part of the country which was the most culturally advanced and least bellicose when the first Roman incursions took place, largely due to the commercial influence of the Phoenician, Greek and Carthaginian colonists. It was shortly after the end of the Second Punic War that the Roman occupation of the Algarve and Alentejo took place without any serious opposition, but few accounts of its pacification survive in comparison with those devoted to the Lusitanian wars fought further north. Notable among Luso-Roman bases is the Castro da Cola (south-west of Ourique, near the river Mira). The Ribatejo, controlled from Scallabis (Santarém), and the coastal lowlands as far as the Mondego were next subdued, and Olisipo (Lisbon) was occupied in 205 BC.

PROVINCES OF HISPANIA

By 197 BC, Hispania had been divided into two Roman *provinciae*; that of Citerior composed the eastern seaboard as far south as Cartagena, and was gradually extended inland up the Ebro valley. By 133 BC the western frontier of the province ran south-west from the Basque coast to near present-day Zamora, and then south-east to Avila and south across the central reaches of the Tagus to meet Hispania Ulterior. From near Sisapo (now Almadén) the frontier of the two provinces formed a line south-east to Cartagena. To the north-west, Ulterior then extended as far as the estuary of the Tagus, the river forming a natural boundary.

LUSITANIAN WARS

In 155 BC, in retaliation for raids by the Lusitanians, Roman *praetors* or governors, foremost among whom was treacherous Servius Sulpicius Galba, coordinated a series of campaigns against them and their allies during a prolonged guerrilla war, which were not always successful. It was not until 138 BC, the year after Viriatus, a Lusitanian chieftain, had been assassinated with Roman connivance, that Decimus Junius Brutus (proconsul in 138 BC) was able to check residual Lusitanian resistance, at least temporarily. His legions advanced from Olisipo up the Tagus valley to Moron (near Alpiarça), where a fort was built. A fortified camp was then established at Viseu (the so-called Cava de Viriato), from which the proconsul continued north after crossing the Douro at Cale, renamed Portucale (Oporto) and probably entering Braga (later Bracara Augusta). He reached the banks of the Limia eventually, but had difficulty in urging his troops across. Having marched far enough through unknown and hostile territory, they assumed that it must be the Lethe, the River of Oblivion, its beauty having the effect of making one forget home and country. Wading into the stream, standard in hand, Junius Brutus exhorted his reluctant men to follow, which they did. Ponte de Lima, the village which grew up beside the later Roman bridge, was named Forum Limicorum, known as Lemici by 394, in which year it was the birthplace of Hydatius, the Suevic bishop and annalist. After making a raid across the Minho into Gallaecia, the proconsul turned south to terminate his campaign of pacification, although the Lusitani were by no means entirely subjugated in this mopping-up operation.

Civil War

SERTORIUS

In 83 BC, during a confused period in which civil war in Rome had extended into the Peninsula, the Lusitani approached Quintus Sertorius, *praetor* of Citerior, to lead them against the supporters of Sulla. Troops commanded by Pompeius or Pompey (after whom Pamplona in Navarre is named) eventually forced Sertorius on to the defensive, but even after he had been assassinated at Osca (Huesca) in 72 BC, the intractable Lusitani continued sporadically to harass the Romans' hegemony.

JULIUS CAESAR (102–44 BC)

In 61 BC Julius Caesar, when governor of Hispania Ulterior, raised Olisipo to the rank of *municipium*, with the official title of Felicitas Julia. He was more successful in bringing the Lusitani to heel, after which he also made a descent on Brigantium (either Betanzos or La Coruña) on the coast of Gallaecia before returning to Rome. Meanwhile, Roman colonists were settled at Scallabis and Bracara Augusta, and Pax Julia (Beja) was founded.

AUGUSTUS (63 BC–AD 14)

Julius Caesar's successor was Augustus, the first Roman emperor, who continued Caesar's policy of planting *coloniae* of Roman citizens. Emerita Augusta (Mérida) on the Guadiana was founded partly by veterans of the Cantabrian War. In 26 BC the emperor and his generals had commenced the definitive conquest of the Astures and Cantabri. From Asturica (Astorga) Augustus advanced north-west to take the Cantabrian redoubt of Bergidum (Villafranca del Vierzo) and ascended into the highlands of Gallaecia to capture Lucus (Lugo), which together

ASTURES CANTABRI

Lucus
Augusti

Asturica
Augusta

Legio

GALLAECI

CEL

Bracara
Augusta

T A R R A C

VACCAEI

Portucale

Salmantica

VETTONES

Segovia

A T L A N T I C

Aeminium

Conimbriga

Alcantara

Toletum

LUSITANI

L U S I T A N I A

Scallabis

Emerita
Augusta

C A R T

Olisipo

CELTICI

Ebora

B A E T I C A

O C E A N

Pax Julia

Corduba

Mirobriga

BAETURIA

Myrtilis

Hispalis

TURDETANI

Gades

The Iberian Peninsula
under the Romans

M A U R

GALLIA

VASCONES

TIBERI

ONENSIS

Caesar
Augusta

Tarraco

Saguntum

HAGINENSIS

Carthago Nova

MEDITERRANEAN SEA

MEDITERRANEAN

ETANIA

0 ——— 250 km
0 ——— 200 miles

	Principal Roman roads in the western part of the Peninsula
----	Provincial boundaries
o	Principal towns

with Astorga was to become an important military base, as did Legio Septima (León, that of the 7th Legion), further east. In 24 BC Augustus returned to Rome to celebrate a triumph, although it was not for another five years that a further revolt was put down and the region, together with the Peninsula as a whole, was substantially under Roman domination, diplomatically referred to as the '*Pax Augusta*'.

With the pacification of Hispania, between 16 and 13 BC Augustus readjusted the provincial boundaries. To facilitate administration of the huge area, the provinces were subdivided into several judicial districts, each known as a *conventus* and each with its capital. The province of Citerior – also referred to as Tarraconensis, its main city being Tarraco (Tarragona) – was much enlarged. It included most of the north-west of the Peninsula, including what is now Portugal north of the Douro. Part of the former province of Ulterior, with Corduba (Córdoba) its capital, was renamed Baetica after its main river (later known to the Muslims as the Guadalquivir). Its western boundary almost precisely coincided with that of present-day Portugal, and its northern frontier ran south of but parallel to the Guadiana, from a point on a bend in that river near Juromenha.

Roman Capital Towns

Beyond this, as far as the Douro, was Lusitania, which also extended east to include Salmantica (Salamanca) – and the modern Spanish province also – and most of Spanish Estremadura. Emerita Augusta was the capital of an easterly *conventus* and other capitals were Scallabis and Pax Julia. Mérida stood at the highest navigable point on the Guadiana, but a high waterfall – the 'Pulo do Lobo', north of Mértola (Myrtilis) – precluded access to the sea, and the latter town, also near rich mineral deposits, remained the main river port.

Each *conventus* was sub-divided into several *civitates*, their boundaries often approximately those of pre-Roman tribes, and each had their own administrative capital or *oppidum* and magistrates. The more important of these might be promoted to the rank of *municipium*.

Among these regional 'capitals' – some now merely villages – identifiable within present-day Portugal were Igaeditana or Egitana

(Idanho a Velha, north-east of Castelo Branco); Bobadela (near Oliveira do Hospital); Marialva (north-east of Trancoso); Aeminium (Coimbra); Conimbriga (near Condeixa a Velha, south-east of Coimbra); Sellium (Tomar); Olisipo, Ammaia (São Salvador de Aramenha, near Marvão); Ebora (Evora); Salacia (Alcácer do Sal); Mirobriga; Myrtilis; Ossonoba (Faro); and Balsa (Tavira).

ROMAN REMAINS

In several of these places there are Roman remains, notably at Conimbriga, Mirobriga (which has the only hippodrome found in Portugal) and Evora (with its early second-century temple, so-called 'of Diana'), while the cryptoporticus at Coimbra is also impressive. These buildings, together with those the Lusitanian capital of Mérida (with its temples, circus, theatre, amphitheatre and aqueduct) must have greatly impressed the 'natives'. Several architectural features at Mérida were made with or clad by marble from the quarries of

The Temple of Diana at Evora

Borba, Vila Viçosa and Estremoz, some being transported as far afield as Conimbriga.

ROMANIZATION

The towns mentioned above were partly settled by Roman citizens. Forming a social hierarchy, they set examples of the Roman way of life to the indigenous population, who were not slow to appreciate at least some of the advantages of Romanization, particularly as the Romans tolerated their customs, ancient cults, languages and laws. These inevitably became greatly modified over the years by the dominant culture, with the Romance languages of Castilian and Gallego-Portuguese developing, with growing devotion to Classical and Imperial gods, and with submission to Roman standards and education and to their forms of justice and taxation, which were not yet too oppressive. In the main it was a painless co-existence.

Although Roman civilization penetrated deeply into the southern half of Portugal, integration was slower in the physically intricate northern regions, where hardly any villas or remains of Classical sculpture survive. Making up for this lack are the curious granite figures of armed warriors, described as Gallaeci or Lusitani, clasping their round shields protectively before them, examples of which may be seen at Guimarães. The inhabitants of the nearby *citânia* de Briteiros remained perched on their hilltop dwellings until *c.* AD 350, before descending to less austere accommodation in the valleys.

Villas, Agriculture and Local Industries

In addition to the growth of urban communities, numerous Roman villas were established, particularly in the undulating plains of the Alentejo and in the Algarve, notable among them those of São Cucufate, Torre de Palma, Pisões, Milreu and Cero da Vila (near Vilamoura). The Romans employed the rural population, although some labour was provided by slaves acquired during the wars of pacification. There was a gradual improvement in agricultural methods. Some estates cultivated cereals, olive-groves or vineyards were planted on others, or cattle or pigs raised. Several reservoirs demonstrate new forms of irrigation. Near the coast, fish was salted for export, and at Tróia and Caetobriga on the Sado estuary with its salt pans, the production of *garum* was a flourishing industry. This sauce or condiment, a nauseous-sounding confection of tuna, mackerel and anchovies placed in brine and sun-dried – a form of 'gentlemen's relish' – was much appreciated by jaded Roman palates. Some estates, often with fortified villas, exploited their mineral deposits; others on the banks of the Sado manufactured amphorae for the transport of *garum* and oil; while numerous tile and brick-kilns were busy baking along the Algarve shore.

Roman Roads and Bridges

The early empire saw the completion of a comprehensive system of roads, which over the decades had been laid out largely by local slave labour, several of them connecting the capitals. Not infrequently, Roman soldiers – by now their legions contained a high proportion of local men – superintended their construction and maintainence, which continued well into the reign of the Emperor Hadrian (AD 117–138). An important highway, later improved, was the *Via Lata* (the Camino de la Plata or Silver Road), which led from Emerita Augusta to Asturica Augusta. It was thus named as it provided a highway along which silver and gold from the mines of the Asturias and those of Las Médulas (south-west of Ponferrada) might be transported south to Hispalis (Seville), where the road met the western end of the Via Augusta, which led to Cádiz. From there, the precious cargo was shipped to Rome. While the *Antonine Itinerary* mentions a few routes, many more must have traversed the country, and much archaeological work has still to be done before the network can be accurately described. Few Roman roads in the convoluted hilly terrain common throughout large areas of Portugal were as straight as it is generally assumed Roman roads should be. They deteriorated over the centuries, although several continued to be used in the medieval period. One should not be surprised that Joseph Baretti (an intimate of Dr Johnson), when travelling across Portugal in the mid-eighteenth century, referring to their condition, stated that he would 'submit to eat thistles' if other visitors – fancying that travelling there was an easy thing – did not change their minds when experiencing the reality.

One of the principal highways was that from Lisbon to Bracara via Scallabis (there joined by the road from Emerita Augusta) via Sellium, Conimbriga and across the Douro at Cale, but the precise line has not yet been mapped with certainty. A series of milestones from there onwards provide a route which is fairly sure, although some milestones may have been moved from their original positions. From Braga, for example, several roads started, among them to Tudae (Tuí) on the Minio (Minho); another crossed the hills to Aquae Flaviae (Chaves) – from which a branch led to Asturica – before continuing east to Castro de Avelas (near Braganza) to meet the *Via Lata* at Arrabalde (Zamora); while a third forked off the latter to climb north-east to the Portela do

The Roman bridge at Alcántara

Homem in the Serra da Peneda-Gerês, leading eventually to Aquae Urentes (Orense) and on to Lucus.

Along these roads several imposing bridges were built: the Guadiana was spanned at Mérida, where there was also an aqueduct; the Tagus was crossed at Alconétar (north of Cáceres), and further west at Norba Caesares (later Alcántara, from the Arabic al-Qantara, the bridge); and the Esla was crossed at Benavente. Among such bridges surviving entire in present-day Portugal are those at Vila Formosa, and Chaves (partly built by troops of the 7th Legion). There are notable remains at Ponte de Lima, and the reconstructed Ponte de Pedra (north-west of Mirandela), although a medieval bridge, probably rests on Roman foundations, as was probably the case with several later bridges.

Late Roman Hispania

In AD 171–3 Baetica suffered serious raids by Moors (Mauri) from Mauretania. Further raids some decades later caused insecurity in the region. Lusitania was not much affected until 260–80 when there was an incursion into the Peninsula by Franks and Alans. In 298 the Emperor Diocletian (284–305) subdivided Tarraconensis into three parts by making the separate provinces of Carthaginensis, south of the Ebro valley, and Gallaecia in the north-west, with its eastern boundary running inland from the coast near Noega (Gijón) to include Legio and along the Esla to its confluence with the Douro. Bracara Augusta was now the capital of Gallaecia.

It was in Gallaecia principally that an ascetic early Christian heretical doctrine developed and flourished, although its founder, Priscillian, bishop of Abila (Avila), died a martyr in 385. Paganism was prohibited throughout the empire only seven years later by Theodosius, who was also a native of the Peninsula. Among early bishops and chroniclers were Orosius of Emerita and Hydatius (bishop of Aquae Flaviae from 428), born in Bracara and Lemici respectively. Both recorded the events which were to precipitate the disintegration of Roman power in the Peninsula during the ensuing decades. AD 357 is the earliest date recorded for a bishop in Olisipo (Lisbon).

CHAPTER THREE

Invasions and early reconquests

Alans, Suevi and Vandals

Taking advantage of a period of turmoil in the Peninsula during the reign of Theodosius's son, Honorius (393–423), caused by the usurpation of imperial power there by the pretender Constantine III (407–411), migratory hordes of Alans, Suevi, and Hasding and Siling Vandals, having crossed the Rhine two years previously, rampaged through Gaul and in the Autumn of 409 poured through the Pyrenees. Although relatively few in numbers and unequally distributed, these so-called 'barbarians' were soon able to carve up the whole Peninsula, for the Hispani-Romans could not put up any substantial opposition; by 411, Roman Spain ceased to exist.

Approximately 80,000 Suevi (Swabians) and 40,000 Hasding Vandals veered west into Gallaecia – the largest group in the least prosperous area; 30,000 Alans overran Lusitania and Carthaginensis; some 50,000 Siling Vandals occupied Baetica. One should not imagine that this confederation of invading tribes was composed merely of uncivilized hairy heathen causing mayhem wherever they went. Apart from the Suevi, a central European farming community living beyond the Imperial frontiers, in terms of their material culture they had much in common with those of the provincial Romans elsewhere in the empire and the Hispani-Romans among whom they were to establish themselves. They were able to dominate them largely because Roman authority had caved in.

Naturally, contemporary chroniclers recorded their excesses. Tarraco, a strategic seat of residual Roman power, was pillaged and certain other capitals (among them Bracara) were ravaged in civil disturbances or clashes with the foreign forces garrisoning them. It has been suggested that in some areas subversive groups had collaborated with the invaders as a means to ensure their freedom from what had been tantamount to slavery under the Roman yoke. While undoubtedly there had been some real distress, with expropriations of property and redistribution of land taking place, in many respects the occupation was accepted as a *fait accompli*, and life continued its usual course under the change of administration and regime; the natives would merely be toiling for different masters.

Visigoths

In 410 Alaric the Visigoth sacked Rome in retaliation for the new Roman government's failure to honour agreements made by its predecessor. On his death, he was succeeded by Athaulf, who, allied with Rome, undertook to reimpose their control over the lost provinces. In 416 the Teutonic Visigoths entered Spain, defeated the Alans and almost exterminated the Siling Vandals before withdrawing to Gallia Aquitania, centred on Toulouse. The surviving Siling Vandals were absorbed by the Hasding Vandals, who, after quarrelling with the Suevi, migrated south and settled in the areas their cousins had occupied. The Vandals captured Hispalis in 428, and in the following year they crossed to North Africa, appropriating the Roman provinces there, which remained in their hands until 554. Although their occupation of Baetica had been short, in North African memories it remained al-Andaluz, the land from which the Vandals came.

It may be mentioned here that many Berbers – both sedentary and nomad – in north-western Africa (thus Barbary) had become Christianized. It is not usually realized that such eminent Fathers of the Church as Tertullian (b. *c.* 150–160), Cyprian (200–258) and Augustine (354–430) were Berbers, as was the Emperor Septimius Severus (193–211), although the majority of them long remained unsophisticated tribesmen. At a later date, before being converted to Islam, they became allies of the Byzantines.

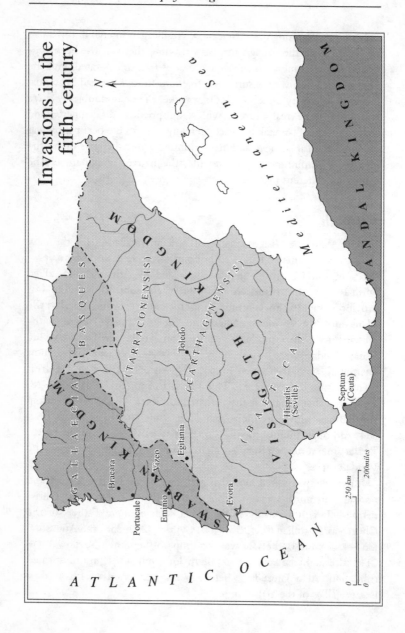

THE SUEVIC EXPANSION

The vacuum created by the Vandal migration was taken advantage of by the Suevi, who from Gallaecia steadily increased their hold of Lusitania and Baetica. In 439 'King' Rechila (d. 488) took Emerita, which he made his capital, and then Myrtilis, and within two years had occupied Hispalis. Nevertheless, in spite of this territorial expansion, the Suevic base, where their roots had struck deepest, still remained between the lower reaches of the Minho and the Douro, as is evident from the predominance of Germanic toponyms there. Rechila died a pagan, but his son Rechiarius converted to Christianity, the orthodox religion of the Empire, and expanded the Suevic kingdom towards the Mediterranean coast, then still under residual imperial rule – but then his luck ran out.

THEODORIC II

In 456, as part of a wider agreement with Rome, Theodoric II (453–66), king of the Visigoths in Gaul, crossed the Pyrenees and defeated Rechiarius near Asturica. The Suevi retreated north-west, leaving the Visigoths to take over and garrison the land they had briefly controlled, while Hydatius recorded that Braca was slighted and Rechiarius, captured at Cale, was later put to death. By the mid-470s, under Theodoric's brother, Euric (466–84), the Visigoths, probably further reinforced by another migration, had occupied the rest of the Peninsula, forming a small but martially and politically dominant minority. They were unlikely, at any time, to have been more than 10 per cent of the Peninsula's total population. Euric's troops had also suppressed an attempt on the part of the Suevi to break out of their Gallaecian enclave. Conimbriga was razed and the Suevi were expelled entirely from Lusitania. It may perhaps be emphasized here that the Suevi, longer established in the Peninsula than the Visigoths, and more assimilated with the Hispano-Roman population than the latter, as far as Germanic stock and distinct influences are concerned, may be thought of as the 'barbarians' of Portugal, and the Visigoths those of Spain.

At the battle of Vouillé (507), the Franks and their Burgundian allies defeated Euric's son, Alaric II (484–507) and overran Visigothic Gaul.

The Visigothic votive crown of Reccesuinth

The Visigoths then transferred their base of government south of the
Pyrenees, eventually making Toletum (Toledo) their capital. While
they adopted many forms of Roman legislation, they also promulgated
their own codes of law, notably under Euric and Leovigild; those of
Chindasuinth and Reccesuinth (654) deprived the Hispano-Romans of
most political, executive and ecclesiastical power. However, although
the political stabilization of the kingdom became progressively more
apparent, in 552 the Visigoths were to experience a setback.

The imperial ambitions of the Byzantine emperor Justinian were
such that he set out to recover the former African provinces of the
Roman Empire and, from Ceuta, the Byzantines invaded Baetica,
which under Athanagild had rebelled against Agila, then the Visigothic
king, and also occupied coastal and some interior districts of western
Carthaginensis. These were not finally reconquered by the Visigoths
until the second decade of the following century.

LEOVIGILD

Meanwhile, in 585, Leovigild (569–86) had subjugated and annexed Gallaecia, which, a decade before, had been formally converted to Catholicism by Bishop Martinho of Braca, but only after the conversion of Reccared (586–601) from Arianism, which the Catholic Hispano-Romans regarded as heresy, was there ecclesiatical stability. John of Biclarum, a native of Scallabis, wrote a *Chronicle* of Leovigild's reign. At a later date, Fructuoso of Dumium (Dume, the royal seat adjacent to Braga), of which he was bishop from 656, was responsible for the foundation of numerous churches within his diocese, notable surviving examples being the chapel of São Fructuoso de Montélios on the outskirts of Braga and São Pedro de Balsemão, near Lamego. Several of these, particularly in the Bierzo, became the sites of monasteries, among which that at Santo Comba Bande at Celanova is a fine example of the Mozarabic style.

The Christian church regarded usury – the lending of money at interest – as sinful and trade as exploitation; accordingly this was left in the hands of the flourishing Jewish community. Although favoured under the Arians, this mercantile class was discriminated against by Reccared and more so in 616 by the more fanatical Sisebut, when many lost their property or were banished. Further legislation against them was issued by King Ervig in 681 and in 694 their enslavement was ordered by King Egica, all of which provoked Marranism (a form of concealed Judaism) in what is now Portugal.

The Muslim Invasion

Civil war erupted at the death of King Wittiza in 710, with Roderick 'the Goth' seizing power at Toledo. (It is recorded that Count Ulyan or Julian, the governor of Ceuta, outraged on learning that his daughter, when completing her education at Toledo, had been ravished by Roderick, sought the help of the local Muslim commander in avenging the crime perpetrated by the upstart king, whose rule was resented already by a proportion of the nobility.) Taking advantage of the ensuing chaos, after some fruitful preliminary incursions, a major Muslim invasion took place in 711. The Arabs, who under Musa ibn

Nusayr had completed their aggressive expansionist conquest of Ifriqiya (Mediterranean Africa) by 694 (only sixty-two years after the death of the prophet Muhammad), reinforced by a large contingent of Islamized Berbers commanded by Tariq Ibn Ziyad, determined to or were invited to cross the straits of Gibraltar.

In the subsequent battle of the Guadalete, Tariq routed the Visigothic army sent to counter the invasion and, virtually unopposed, swept rapidly north to take Toletum, overrunning Baetica and the Tagus valley in 713 and the Ebro valley in the following year. By 720 most of the Peninsula had succumbed. The Visigothic nobility had been virtually destroyed in futile attempts to stem the tide and there was no other military class to resist the invaders. It has been estimated that the first wave of Muslims numbered approximately 40,000.

Adminstration passed into the hands of the 'Moors', who transferred the capital to Seville and then Córdoba. The Algarve and Lusitania were thinly occupied – like the Visigoths before them, numerically the Moors were a very small minority of the population they were to dominate, which remained largely unaffected by the change in masters – and Muslim control over distant Gallaecia and the rugged Cantabrian mountain ranges along the Biscay coast lasted for a few decades only.

By the mid-eighth century the southern coast of what is now Portugal had been partly settled by Egyptian Muslims in the region of Shalb (Silves), Ossonoba and Pax Julia (Beja), and by Syrian Muslims further east along the coast, the area being known as al-Gharb al-Andalus (the western part of Andalucía). The more numerous and more independent Berbers were dispersed further north, around Mérida, in the Tagus and Mondego valleys, and in the vicinity of Coimbra and Astorga, among other areas. Unlike the Visigoths, who to a large extent had married among themselves, the Berbers intermarried with the indigenous female population, whether they remained Christian or agreed to convert to Islam, in which case they were referred to as *Muwallads*.

Authoritative estimates of the number of Arab and Berber warriors – as distinct from camp-followers – who settled in the Peninsula in the first few decades after their invasion, put the figure at between 150,000 and 200,000. It is not known whether they were accompanied by their wives, families and servants; if these followed later, the figure should be multiplied between four and six times. However, it is just as likely that a high proportion came unattached and later acquired women and slaves, in which case a figure of about four million may be a plausible estimate of the population of the Peninsula just prior to the invasion.

The Berbers were dissatisfied with what they felt was condescending treatment at the hands of the aristocratic city-bound Arabs, and at receiving an inferior share in the spoils and poorer regions to exploit, and this caused them to revolt in 740. To restrain the Berber troops from marching on Córdoba, a contingent of Syrian warriors, which had recently quelled a similar rebellion in North Africa, were ferried over. They then settled in the Guadalquivir valley. A complex situation developed between opposing groups of Arabs, but eventually 'Abd-al-Rahman I, a member of the Umayyad family, was able to crush all opposition and in 756 he set up an emirate at Córdoba independent of the Caliph in Damascus, which survived until 929, and subsequently as a caliphate until 1031.

Christian Resistance

Residual resistance to the Muslim invasion had manifested itself *c.* 722, when a small group of Christians commanded by Pelagius (Pelayo) ambushed and defeated a Muslim unit sent to smoke them out, near Covadonga, in the Asturian highlands, a symbolic episode later much exaggerated. The Berbers, having over-extended their communications in the north-west, had withdrawn south, making it easier for the Christians to concentrate their forces within their mountain fastnesses and to make forays across what had become a wasted and depopulated no-man's land into Muslim-controlled territory. An additional reason for the depopulation had been a famine in 750, which prompted numbers of Berbers to return to North Africa.

Meanwhile, in 741 the Asturian King Alfonso I (739–57) had seized Lugo, and by 753 Tuí, Braga, Oporto and Viseu, and in 754 raided as far south as Mérida and Coria. After causing as much devastation as possible in the *meseta* south of the Douro, he returned home with as many Christians as wanted to accompany him. Naturally, these raids caused retaliation, but his son, Fruela I (757–68), was able to defeat at least one of the punitive expeditions against Gallaecia launched by the Emir Hisham I (788–96).

During the long reign of Alfonso II (791–842), who had raided as far south as Olisipo (by then Al-Ushbuna; later Lishbona) in 798, the Asturian capital was established at Oviedo and there was a further consolidation of Christian power.

SANTIAGO OF COMPOSTELA

Christianity was opportunely reinforced *c.* 830 by the miraculous discovery of a tomb at Iria Flavia (Padrón), purporting to contain the relics of St James the Greater. These were later transferred to Compostela, where a chapel was erected. Their presence was zealously propagated by the ecclesiastical authorities, who for centuries were to profit by pilgrimages to the site. The relics – supplemented by those of St Eulalia, among others, rescued earlier from Mérida – would surely protect them in their struggle against the Infidel. Later, the patron saint was referred to as Santiago '*Matamoros*', the Moor-slayer. Al-Mansur, the new Muslim leader, must have heard of this phenomenon by 997, for in that year, having recruited additional Berber troops from North Africa, who had no scruples about pillaging a 'foreign' country, he ravaged the north-west of the Peninsula. Although the shrine itself was spared desecration, the sanctuary at Compostela was destroyed and, to further humiliate the Christians, its bells were carried off to Córdoba and hung in the mosque there.

The policy of Ramiro I (842–50), Alfonso II's successor, was largely defensive, for the intermittent retaliatory raids or *sa'ifa* launched by 'Abd al-Rahman II (822–52) frustrated any attempt to occupy León, and it was only under his more enterprising son Ordoño I (850–66) that the city was resettled definitively. Its Roman walls were rebuilt and resisted a punitive Muslim expedition in 882. Resettlement accelerated during the reign of Alfonso III (866–910), notably between the Minho and the line of the lower Douro.

CALE RE-OCCUPIED

In 868 Cale or Portucale was re-occupied by Vimara Peres, prompted by Alfonso III. He strengthened its defences and brought the surrounding districts under cultivation. Vimaranes, later Guimarães (north-east of Oporto) was probably named after him. This whole area, which was gradually extended south to the river Vouga, became known as the 'territorium Portugalense'.

This newly conquered land was administered by a series of counts, among whom were Gonçalo Mendes and his wife Mumadona, one of whose descendants, Mendo Gonçalves, tutor to young Alfonso V (999–1027), ruled with some autonomy but was killed in a Viking raid (1008). This was by no means the first of such raids: in 968 a flotilla of long-ships had entered the *rías* of Gallaecia, when both their commander and the bishop of Santiago were killed in skirmishes. It was at this period that the fishing-port of Vila de Conde and the monastery of Lorvão (east of Coimbra) were founded.

Alfonso V met his death in 1028 while laying siege to Viseu, which was not taken until thirty years later. Meanwhile Montemor, which commanded the north bank of the Mondego between Coimbra and the Atlantic, was captured in 1034, Lamego in 1057, and Coimbra was definitively re-occupied in 1064 by Fernando I (1037–65) after a six-months' siege. Together with the region immediately north of the Mondego, Coimbra was to be administered by Sisnand ibn David or Davidiz, a Mozarab, probably of Jewish descent, from Tentúgal (between Montemor and Coimbra), who had formerly been employed by the Arabs at Seville. The predominant Muslim community at Coimbra was largely replaced by Mozarab citizens, but Muslim institutions were observed for some time, the governor being still referred to as the *alcaide*. It was a curious amalgamation, with many of the inhabitants bearing a mix of Arabic and Christian names, such as Pelagius Abu Nazar.

From 1037 Fernando I had been king of Castile, an extensive area containing numerous castles, which he had inherited from Sancho III of Navarre (1000–35), himself half-Castilian. During previous decades Sancho had been single-mindedly annexing territories abutting those of the royal house of Navarre, among them those of the enervated neo-Gothic Asturo-Leónese monarchy, by then on its last legs.

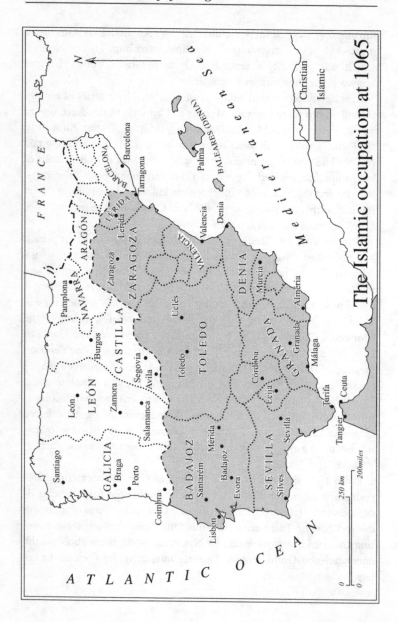

The Islamic occupation at 1065

The Taifa Kingdoms

The first three decades of the century were a period of confusion and civil war throughout al-Andaluz and other Muslim-settled land in the Peninsula, with Córdoba itself being sacked in 1031. This brought about the end of the Umayyad dynasty or Caliphate, which virtually disintegrated. Its place was taken by a number of independent *taifa* or party kingdoms, among the more important of which – as far as Portuguese history is concerned – were those of Badajoz (with that city its capital rather than Mérida); Seville, which included Beja and Shalb in the Algarve; and Granada. As smaller entities, they were also less capable of defending themselves against stronger Christian incursions.

On Fernando's death in 1065, the kingdom was divided up, with Castile going to Sancho II, León to Alfonso VI, and Galicia to García, who was of little account and soon deposed, while Urraca and her sister Elvira were provided with several monasteries. Neither Sancho nor Fernando recognized the autonomy of the county of Portugal. These two elder brothers were soon at each other's throats and, in the fratricidal war, Urraca took Alfonso's part and defied Sancho, who in 1072, while besieging her at Zamora, was assassinated. Alfonso now ruled the joint kingdom of León-Castile. During his long reign (until 1109) he was spasmodically supported by the Cid (whose campaigns up to his death in 1099 are not relevant to this history). Extensive inroads were made on Muslim territory, by then further broken up into petty *taifas*.

The Almoravids enter the Peninsula

In 1085 Alfonso VI (1065–1109) captured Toledo and this had important repercussions. His extortionate demands for tribute from the *taifas* caused Al Mu'tamid, emir of Seville, the foremost among them, in concert with the emirs of Badajoz and Granada, to summon aid from Yusuf ibn Tashufin, but with grave misgivings. Yusuf was then the killjoy leader of a fundamentalist sect, the Almoravids, founded among the nomad Berber tribes of the Sahara. By 1084 their policy of territorial expansion over an area in which they would enforce their tenets had taken them as far as the Mediterranean coast at Tangier and Ceuta. They would be invited across the Straits of Gibraltar on condition that they re-embark for North Africa once Alfonso had been defeated.

Alfonso was taken off his guard and Al Mu'tamid, together with Yusuf's troops (including a Negro contingent) and the Christians were scattered in the ensuing battle, which took place at Sagrajas (or Zallaqa), near Badajoz. Yusuf did not exploit his victory and returned to Ceuta, leaving a large detachment of cavalry in Al-Andaluz.

CHAPTER FOUR

The early Burgundians and Dom Afonso Henriques

Burgundian Intervention

EUDES OF BURGUNDY

In desperation, under pressure from the Muslims, Alfonso VI turned for help to Eudes, Duke of Burgundy, the natural brother of his wife, Constanza. In the following Spring (1087) Eudes crossed the Pyrenees with an army, but by then Yusuf was no longer in evidence. Alfonso had reservations about having such a large force on his territory, so Eudes, cold-shouldered but not wanting to withdraw his troops without striking a blow for Christendom, marched on Zaragoza. In the event, however, the expedition petered out.

RAYMOND OF BURGUNDY   (d. 1107)

Of more consequence to the future history of Portugal was the fact that Eudes's cousin, Count Raymond of Burgundy, who had remained at Alfonso's court, became betrothed to the king's six-year-old daughter, also named Urraca, and the marriage took place in 1090. The Burgundian connection was to be reinforced further by the Benedictines of Cluny, who were in the process of establishing a chain of monasteries along the main routes through France to Santiago.

But Yusuf recrossed the Straits, in both 1089 and 1090, in the latter year with the intention of appropriating by force the *taifas* of Granada and Seville among others. The emir of Badajoz, expecting to be deposed, had ceded the towns of Santarém, Sintra and Lisbon to Count Raymond, in return for Christian protection against the Almoravid aggression. In a document of February 1094 Raymond, as Alfonso's son-in-law, is referred to as 'Count of Coimbra and all Galicia', and in August of the following year as 'lord of Galicia and Santarém'. Although he had garrisoned the three towns (Sintra is still overawed by the Castelo dos Mouros), he was unable to hold them against Yusuf's cousin, who had already seized Badajoz, and Raymond was forced to retreat to the line of the Mondego.

HENRY OF BURGUNDY

In 1095 Raymond's cousin, Henry of Burgundy (d. 1112), had entered the Peninsula and appears to have superseded Raymond, for by 1097 he is styled Count of Portugal. Although Queen Constanza, Henry's aunt, had died in 1093, Henry consolidated his place in the royal family by marrying Teresa, Alfonso's other, but illegitimate, daughter. Count Henry made a pact with Raymond, whereby he would support the latter's claim to succession on condition that he was given either Toledo or Galicia as a *quid pro quo*. Meanwhile, he set up his court at Guimarães, near Braga. By 1096 his jurisdiction had extended into the Trás-os-Montes. Although Braga had been restored as a see in 1070, with the Cluniac Gerald as its bishop, it was not until 1118 that it was able to get its metropolitan rights confirmed by the Pope. Gelmirez, the militant bishop of Santiago, had struggled hard for Santiago's supremacy meanwhile – to the extent of carrying off by force the relics of both St Fructuoso and St Victor from Braga to Santiago in 1102, for which he received papal reproof.

Alfonso had remarried, this time to a Muslim, daughter of the deposed emir of Seville, and Sancho, his heir-apparent, was born in 1097. This caused consternation among the two Burgundian counts and their wives, who had a family conference at Santiago in the following year. However, in 1108 the young prince was killed at the battle of Uclés, the last against the Almoravids by Alfonso, who himself died shortly after this defeat. Count Raymond had died in 1107, and so his infant son, Alfonso Raimúndez, was declared heir to the throne by Alfonso, to the great dissatisfaction of Count Henry. The pact he had made with his cousin was thus rendered valueless, as the king was not prepared to make any territorial concessions.

URRACA

Urraca (1109–26) became regent for her son, but as it was essential that a ruler wielded a sword in those turbulent days, she was prevailed upon to marry the formidable Alfonso 'the Battler' of Aragón (1104–34), who assumed the title of Emperor, while young Alfonso VII Raimúndez (1126–57), under the guardianship of Pedro Froilaz, was proclaimed king of Galicia. This further angered Henry, who searched without much immediate success for military support for his own territorial pretensions. Meanwhile, Urraca had quarrelled with her new husband, who then offered to help Henry, and although he defeated a Castilian force in 1110, he was later induced by Urraca to change sides. Henry then demanded a partition of territory in his favour for having supported her, which provoked the queen to a brief reconciliation with her husband before returning to her supporters in Galicia. 'The Battler' retaliated by winning Henry over by granting him the towns of Astorga and Zamora. In 1112 negotiations were resumed between Henry and Teresa and her half-sister Urraca, soon after which Henry died.

The Forming of Portugal

AFONSO HENRIQUES   (1128/39–85)

Henry left a five-year-old son, known as Afonso Henriques, who with his mother sought some security in Coimbra, as Astorga and Zamora were again in Urraca's hands. Dona Teresa, Countess of Portugal (among other titles she flourished), was allied to Pedro Froilaz, who sent his son Fernão Peres de Trava to defend Coimbra against an Almoravid attack in 1117. By 1121 Fernão's intimacy with Teresa had produced a daughter, and he was now described as Lord of Oporto and Coimbra. On Urraca's death in 1126, Alfonso VII made peace with Teresa and her consort, and confirmed his aunt in possession of her territories, but as she refused to do homage, he invaded and forced her to do so. Teresa and her consort were blamed for this loss of face by the Portuguese barons, who now ranged themselves behind Afonso Henriques. In April 1128 Afonso Henriques confirmed the charter his father had granted to Guimarães without making any reference to his mother, and in the following month appointed Paio Mendes as Archbishop of Braga. Teresa and Fernão, not tolerating this presumptuous behaviour on the part of her son, in July marched on Braga where in a confrontation on the field of São Mamede, near Guimarães, her forces were beaten. Afonso Henriques captured both his mother and her favourite, expelled them to Galicia and remained in sole possession of the county of Portugalense.

In 1135, his step-father 'the Battler' having died, Alfonso VII was crowned emperor at León and received the homage of all the Christian sovereigns in the Peninsula with the exception of Afonso Henriques. Perhaps this was a calculated snub, but certainly it was an assertion of the fact that he considered himself entirely independent. This caused friction and minor skirmishing between the two cousins until in *c.* 1139 they agreed to bring an end to their rival claims. The title of Afonso Henriques first appears as *rex* in documents of that year. With Alfonso VII's acquiescence, in 1143 Afonso Henriques approached the Holy See to obtain the Pope's recognition of his independence, provisionally as *dux Portugalensium*, until 1179, when the title *rex* was confirmed, as was his and his successors' right to possess all the territory he had conquered. In 1146 Afonso Henriques married Mafalda, daughter of Amadeus III of Maurienne and Savoy. Their first son died in infancy and his eventual successor, Sancho, was born in 1154. His capital, Coimbra, was described by the contemporary Muslim geographer Idrisi as 'flourishing and well populated, rich in vineyards and orchards of apples, cherries and plums. Its fields are very fertile … and the inhabitants, who are among the bravest of the Christians, possess many cattle, great and small: the Mondego moves many mills and bathes many vineyards and gardens.'

In 1135, Afonso Henriques had marched south to establish a forward bastion by constructing a castle at Leiria, which he then had to rebuild after it had been razed in a Muslim counter-attack. In 1139, he pressed further south to win the major battle 'of Ourique', probably fought at Chão de Ourique near Santarém, after which the Muslims obtained a truce and resumed the payment of tribute.

The Almohad Invasion

In about 1143 a certain Ibn Qasi, a native of the flourishing river-port of Shalb in the western Algarve, claimed that he was the Mahdi, sent to throw off the Almoravid yoke, but he was soon put in his place by Ibn Wazir of Evora. Ibn Qasi then approached the new leader of the Almohads at Fez to lead a crusade against the Almoravids. The Almohads, or Unitarians, were a strictly orthodox and far more puritanical Islamic cult than the Almoravids, whom they considered both decadent and heretical. It was founded among the Berber tribes of the Atlas mountains by Ibn Tumart (who died in 1130) and was becoming a serious threat to the Almoravids, who at an earlier date had drawn support from a rival tribe. Ibn Tumart's successor agreed to intervene in the Algarve, where Ibn Qasi had been proclaimed governor, and Almohad troops overran Silves, Mértola, Beja, Evora and Badajoz during the Summer of 1146. They then turned on their tracks to march on Seville when they heard that Alfonso VII was threatening Almería, much further east.

LISBON CAPTURED

It was an opportune moment for Afonso Henriques to press south again. Shantariya (Santarém) itself fell to him and was sacked in 1147. Afonso Henriques had already made a probing attack on

View of the Arabic fortress dominating Silves

Lisbon in 1140, when he razed its suburbs; it was now the time to capture it entire. Providentially, only two months after Afonso Henriques had captured Santarém, a fleet of 142 vessels which had assembled at Dartmouth *en route* to the Holy Land with a complement of 13,000 Crusaders, anchored off the Douro estuary. Among them, apart from Germans and Flemings, was an expeditionary force of English under their constables, Hervey de Glanvill, Simon of Dover and a certain Andrew of London, whose reputation as 'plunderers, drunkards and rapists, men not seasoned with the honey of Piety' had apparently preceded them. However, they listened patiently to Bishop Pitões of Oporto, who – perhaps dreading that they might well sack the place – proposed that they would find it worth their while to join forces with Afonso Henriques, who was intending to attack Lisbon at any moment. They lurched back to their ships, fortified 'with good cheap wine and other delights' (as a 'war correspondent' of the time described the event – either he or the recipient of the report was a certain Osbert of Bawdsley in Sussex) to follow up what certainly sounded like a profitable escapade. As a precautionary measure they took both Pitões and João Peculiar (archbishop of Braga) with them as hostages.

They met Afonso Henriques the day after disembarking in the Tagus estuary to discuss allied operations, when he agreed that the spoils of the city would go exclusively to them and, additionally, that any Crusader wishing to remain would be given land. Although the suburbs were taken with ease, the walled citadel was able to hold out for six weeks against bombardment from catapults and mangonels, until a movable wooden tower had been constructed and hauled into position, from which an assault on the parapets could be made. The Muslims and Mozarabs were almost starving, for their stores of grain had been discovered tunnelled into the hillside. They asked for a brief truce and were allowed to leave, having handed over all their possessions to the besiegers. One must draw a veil over the scenes of pillage and debauchery which must have followed before the expeditionary troops set sail. The mosque served as a church, and an English priest, Gilbert of Hastings, was consecrated bishop. He was to establish the Sarum Use, which continued to be observed there until 1536. Several foreigners accepted the offer of land in or in the vicinity of Lisbon in preference to crusading in more distant climes.

Sintra, now isolated, soon capitulated, as did the fortress of Palmela, and the vanquished fled south-east to Alcácer do Sal and Evora. The immediate problem was to re-occupy and repopulate the thinly inhabited territory south of Leiria and Porto de Mos and as far as Lisbon, and the Templars were given several important areas to defend, notably the line of the Tagus. By 1153, Burgundian Cistercians had taken over land around Alcobaça; by 1157 Alcácer had fallen to the Portuguese; by 1162 Gualdim Pais had founded Tomar. Both Evora and Beja submitted to Afonso in 1159, but were then recaptured by the Almohads.

On the death of Alfonso VII in 1157, Sancho III (his eldest son) and Fernando II (the youngest, who inherited Galicia and León) threatened to partition Portugal. The plan came to nothing as Sancho died prematurely in the following year, leaving Castile to the infant Alfonso VIII. In 1160 Afonso Henriques made what was to be a brief alliance with Fernando, who married his daughter Urraca in 1165.

Geraldo Sem Pavor

In the Autumn of 1166, Evora was taken by surprise by an adventurer banished from the Portuguese court known as Geraldo Sem Pavor (the Fearless), who went on to occupy Cáceres and Trujillo, some distance to the north-east, and Serpa (south of Beja). However, when his motley troops laid siege to Badajoz in 1169, its Muslim citizens appealed to Fernando II, as they were under his protection, while Geraldo turned to Afonso Henriques for help. Unfortunately, the latter broke a leg at Badajoz, was captured by his son-in-law and only ransomed after undertaking to abandon all claims to Galicia. Fernando also occupied both Trujillo and Cáceres. No longer able to ride, Afonso Henriques knighted his sixteen-year-old son Sancho at Coimbra in 1170 and began to share the problems of government with him.

In 1171 Abu Ya'qub Yusuf, the Almohad caliph, led his troops north to occupy several important sites along the frontier with Portugal, including Cáceres and the Roman bridge over the Tagus at Alcántara, but failed to take Fernando's new south-western base of Ciudad

Rodrigo. Both Fernando and Afonso Henriques then came to terms with the caliph, the latter making a truce. Once that had ended, the Christian armies, now commanded by young Sancho, began a series of campaigns against the Almohads, attacking Beja while *en route* to raid Seville, but another seven decades were to pass before that city fell to them. The contest was also carried on at sea, with Lisbon being attacked by an Almohad fleet from Ceuta, which was then raided in reprisal. In the Summer of 1184 the caliph laid siege to Santarém, where he was mortally wounded. The Almohads withdrew their forces and five years passed before the Holy War was resumed under his successor.

In December 1185, full of years and after a fifty-seven-year reign, Afonso Henriques died and was buried in the church of Santa Cruz in Coimbra, his capital.

CHAPTER FIVE

The Afonsin Dynasty

It was left to Sancho I (1185–1211) to carry on his illustrious father's intentions, which were to drive the Almohads from the southern Alentejo and Algarve, apart from consolidating the rest of the kingdom. Indeed, he was to gain the epithet *Povoador*, a person who encouraged land settlement, notably with the repopulation of Trás-os-Montes and the inland parts of Beira, including the resuscitation of Guarda (which received its charter or *forais* in 1199), Covilhã and Idanha, which would serve as bastions to protect the land frontier with León. Christian settlers migrated to such cities as Lisbon, Santarém and Evora, and the administration set up for these extensive reconquered areas guaranteed the security of their Muslim or Mozarab communities.

In the Summer of 1189 another fleet of Crusaders sailed into the Tagus estuary. They agreed to assist Sancho with the conquest of Shalb in the Algarve, which was then besieged and sacked. Appeals were made to the Almohad caliph, who, having made a provisional truce with Castile and León, was able to build up a respectable offensive force, which was able to overrun all the Portuguese gains south of the Tagus, with the exception of Evora. In this campaign, the Templars, under Gualdim Pais, had almost lost Tomar when the caliph retired. However, once the truce had expired, the caliph turned on the Castilians, who under Alfonso VIII, together with a Portuguese contingent, were routed at Alarcos (south-west of Ciudad Real) in July 1195. Thereafter, the Almohads were able to cause much havoc although they captured no major towns.

The next few decades, notably during Afonso II's reign (1211–23), were years of conflict with León, with the papal authorities and with

The gradual reconquest of present Portuguese territory

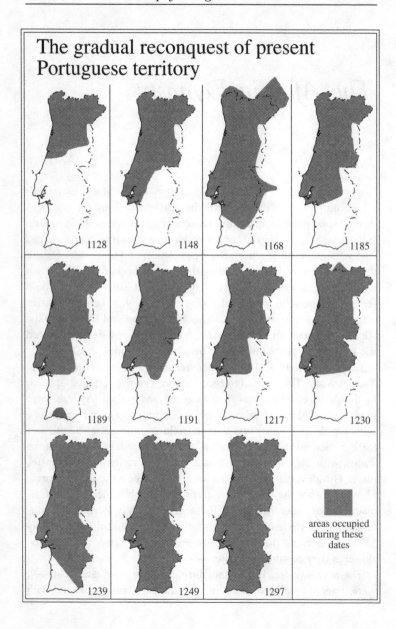

1128　1148　1168　1185

1189　1191　1217　1230

1239　1249　1297

areas occupied during these dates

the Portuguese nobles, and Afonso (who in 1208 had married Urraca, daughter of Alfonso VIII of Castile and Eleanor Plantagenet) died an excommunicated leper. However, in July 1212 the new Almohad caliph, Muhammad II al-Nasir, when advancing north through the defile of Despeñaperros in the Sierra Morena at the start of an offensive campaign, found his way blocked by the combined armies of his Christian adversaries and was routed near the village of Las Navas de Tolosa. The battle marked a watershed in the reconquest of the Peninsula as a whole, leaving the Almohads in complete disarray.

By 1230 Alfonso IX of León had recaptured Cáceres, Mérida and Badajoz. Fernando III of Castile had taken Baeza four years earlier, which was followed by the fall of Ubeda in 1233, Córdoba in 1236, Jaén in 1246 and Seville in 1248. The Almohad 'empire' in Spain had collapsed; little now remained other than the Nasrid Kingdom of Granada. This was only able to hold out with substantial military aid provided by the Banu Marinid sultans then in power at Fez. Although the latter were crushed at the battle of Salado – south-east of Cádiz – by the combined forces of Alfonso XI of Castile and Afonso IV of Portugal in 1340, it was not for another century and a half of sporadic skirmishing on its frontiers that the inexorable advance of the Christians had brought them to Granada itself, which capitulated eventually to Isabel of Castile and Fernando of Aragón – the 'Catholic Monarchs' – in January 1492.

Sancho II

Meanwhile, Sancho II (1223–c. 46), easily dominated by rival groups, was also at odds with the papacy; his younger brother Afonso had denounced Sancho's marriage to Mécia López de Haro in 1241 as uncanonical and Pope Innocent IV had taken Afonso's part. Sancho was eventually deposed after a civil war. This arrogation of supremacy over kings by meddling popes was not lost on either Fernando III or the recalcitrant Frederick II Hohenstaufen, who had commented to the Castilian on how the pope 'wielded his sickle in the cornfields of other men'.

Afonso III

The papal candidate, Afonso III (*c.* 1246–79), also had the support of the Portuguese Church, the barons and the military Orders, the Knights of Santiago (founded in 1170) and the Templars (at Tomar) among them. Already, in 1169, the latter had been promised one-third of all territories reconquered south of the Tagus.

Mértola and Tavira had been captured in 1238 and 1239 respectively by the Knights of Santiago, pushing south from Alcácer and Aljustrel during Sancho II's anarchic reign. As a *quid pro quo* for their crusading activity, the Knights obtained a papal bull confirming their occupation of Palmela, Alcácer do Sal, Mértola and Tavira, among other towns. From Crato (founded by them after Sancho's donation in 1232) the Hospitallers occupied and were granted property rights over Moura and Serpa. The Muslims were isolated within a triangular enclave hemmed in by the Atlantic. Faro capitulated in 1249, but as Shalb was under Castilian 'protection' (due to a former treaty covering future conquests), the Pope had to intervene again in 1253 to prevent war between Afonso and Alfonso X of Castile, who was also jealous of his neighbour's recent territorial acquisitions.

However, with Niebla falling to Alfonso X (1252–84) in 1262 after a long siege, and with Afonso (his first wife having died) marrying Alfonso's illegitimate daughter Beatriz in 1263, their differences were patched up. By 1267 Alfonso had formally agreed that the lower reaches of the Guadiana were an obvious line of demarcation between the two kingdoms, with the Portuguese retaining sovereignty over the western Algarve. Unfortunately, this territory could only be thinly settled – the population for the whole kingdom at that time has been estimated at only 400,000 – and it long remained an isolated and sparsely inhabited area, largely devoted to cattle- and sheep-rearing on large estates. The Muslims and Mozarabs along the coast and its hinterland were left to continue their pursuits undisturbed.

In *c.* 1260 Afonso transferred his capital from Coimbra to Lisbon, which began to increase in wealth and population. The king's later years were blighted by further wrangling with his prelates and with the papacy, and Dinis, his eighteen-year-old heir, was already excommunicate when he began his long reign. However that did not stand in his way when he married Isabel of Aragón in 1282.

Dinis, 'O Lavrador'

Dom Dinis (1279–1325), whose progressive schemes of re-afforestation were to earn him the epithet of 'O Lavrador' (the husbandman), did not bother to reach a concordat with Rome for another decade, and then to his advantage. (The Pope had more immediate problems with which to deal; by 1309, driven from Rome, he had settled in Avignon.) In 1285 Dinis convoked a *cortes* at Lisbon, and obtained their support to pass laws forbidding the sale of any more land to religious corporations, which did not endear him to the clergy.

The military Orders, formerly owing allegiance to the Holy See, were 'nationalized', and the independent Portuguese Order of São Tiago, now based at Palmela, elected its own provincial Master in 1288. The Spanish Order of Calatrava developed into a separate institution known as the Order of Avis from the town donated to it by Dinis. Taking advantage of the suppression of the Templars in 1308, with the pope's authorization, in 1319 Dinis founded the Portuguese Order of Christ, which, although based on Castro Marim, guarding the Algarve, received many former Templar properties, notably Tomar and Castelo Branco. The erection of a series of border fortresses was put in hand.

By the *Treaty of Alcañices* in 1297 the land frontier with Castile was definitively fixed, sealed additionally by the agreement that Fernando IV and his sister Beatriz would marry Dinis's two legitimate children, Constanza and Afonso. Nevertheless, the military Orders remained on a war footing, although as far as Portugal was concerned the reconquest was virtually over. It seemed wise to have them at the ready should it be necessary to defend the long frontier with Castile, in spite of the Treaty (for young Constanza had died in 1313).

But it was not only with his land forces that Dinis was preoccupied. The main reason for his programme of re-afforestation – in addition to anchoring the encroaching dunes, notably in the 'Pinhal d'el-Rei', the extensive pine forest west of Leiria – was to provide timber for the

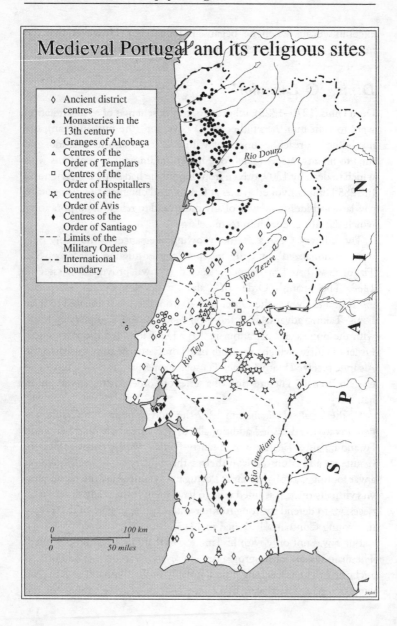

Medieval Portugal and its religious sites

◊ Ancient district
    centres
● Monasteries in the
    13th century
○ Granges of Alcobaça
△ Centres of the
    Order of Templars
□ Centres of the
    Order of Hospitallers
✿ Centres of the
    Order of Avis
◆ Centres of the
    Order of Santiago
--- Limits of the
    Military Orders
—·— International
    boundary

Rio Douro

Rio Zezere

Rio Tejo

Rio Guadiana

S P A I N

0   100 km
0   50 miles

construction of a fleet. In 1322 he appointed a Genoese as hereditary admiral of Portugal. Genoese know-how had already been influential, with the establishment in 1293 of a 'maritime exchange' for Portuguese merchants, one of the earliest of such insurance organizations in Europe. Maritime trade boomed with the designing of a new form of vessel, the caravel – the first reference to which is dated 1255 – and with the development of the cargo-carrying carrack or *não*, which grew dangerously in size over the decades. Dinis also brought the exploitation of mines under royal control and introduced a number of free fairs or markets, which contributed to the flourishing economy. In addition to his other qualities, Dinis was the talented and prolific author of Gallego-Portuguese *cantigas de amor*, poems in the *trobador* style, and other works.

Unfortunately, the last years of the reign were clouded by domestic troubles. Young Afonso stirred up rebellion in 1320, choosing to assume that he would be disinherited and the crown would go to Dinis's favourite illegitimate son, Afonso Sanches, who later left the country. Afonso rebelled against his father, whom he defeated in battle at Santarém in 1325. Although Dinis then gave Afonso the cities of Coimbra and Oporto, he remained unsatisfied. After the queen's mediation there was some reconciliation, but only shortly before the king's death.

Afonso IV

Afonso IV (1325–57) immediately confiscated his half-brother's possessions, after which Portugal became involved in a dynastic controversy. Alfonso XI of Castile had promised to marry Constanza, daughter of Juan Manuel of Castile (a grandson of Alfonso X), but when he came of age he rejected her and married Afonso IV's daughter Maria. He then abandoned her for Leonor de Guzmán, who provided him with no less than ten illegitimate children. Pedro, the heir to Portugal, had been betrothed aged eight to Blanca of Castile, but as she was of unsound mind, the marriage had been dissolved and he married the repudiated Constanza by proxy. Her arrival in Lisbon in 1340 had been delayed by four years, until peace had been concluded between the various warring factions, partly on account of another invasion from Africa.

The Banu Marinid, having extended the empire, made one more attempt to recover Al-Andaluz. After they had scattered the Castilian fleet guarding the Straits, they landed in force to attack Tarifa. Joint Portuguese and Castilian armies met the Muslim host on the Río Salado, decisively defeated them, and the Marinids fled back to Africa.

Pedro

Some time after her marriage, Constanza invited her cousin Inês de Castro to attend her court, where Pedro, on first setting eyes on this 'heron-necked' beauty, conceived an uncontrollable passion for her and she had to be sent home. However, on Constanza's death in 1345, Inês reappeared and set up house with Pedro at Coimbra; Pedro later claimed that he had married her at Braganza in 1354 to legitimize the three children she bore. The Court faction, jealous of the Castilian influence they considered she had on the heir to the throne – for nobles rebelling against Pedro I of Castile were hoping he might also claim the Castilian throne – eventually extracted from Afonso his tacit permission for her 'removal'. Those most concerned had her murdered in cold blood in 1355. Pedro raised the standard of revolt but, persuaded by the Bishop of Braga, he became ostensibly reconciled with his father, who died soon afterwards.

On his accession, Pedro (1357–67) had two of those involved in Inês's assassination hunted down and executed. He also ordered an appropriately royal tomb to be carved for her at Alcobaça; his own was to be placed opposite hers (an unusual disposition) so that at the Resurrection, the lovers would see the beloved form of the other. The tragedy also formed an episode of Luis de Camões's *Os Lucíados* and inspired many later poets and playwrights throughout Europe.

To console himself, Pedro took Teresa Lourenço as his mistress and in 1358 João, the future founder of the Avis dynasty, was born. Pedro's main concern throughout his reign was the administration of justice, which did much to reinforce the unity of Portugal and gained him the epithet of 'the Justicier'. Maritime trade flourished; already in 1353 a

The tomb of Inês de Castro at Alcobaça

treaty had been made between corporations of merchants in Lisbon and Oporto and Edward III of England, confirming the reciprocal safe-conducts and protection offered to them during Dinis's reign. However, the ravages of the bubonic plague, known as the Black Death, which had reached the Peninsula in 1348, and also the Hundred Years War, were shortly to have an injurious effect on the economy. Meanwhile, landfalls had already been made in the Canaries, but these tentative explorations were yet to bear fruit.

Fernando

Pedro was succeeded by Fernando (1367–83; his son by Constanza), who was unable to avoid being drawn into the wars of succession still distracting Castile, where Pedro 'the Cruel' was threatened by a coalition of nobles led his his bastard half-brother, Enrique de

Trastámara. Although (aided by the Black Prince) Pedro defeated Enrique at Nájera in 1367, two years later he was murdered by Enrique at Montiel, who then styled himself Enrique II. Several factions formed among the Portuguese nobility: some supported John of Gaunt, Duke of Lancaster, for in 1372 he had married Constanza, the eldest daughter of Pedro 'the Cruel', and the Castilian legitimists turned to Fernando to defend their cause; others supported the claims of the usurper. Rioting broke out in Lisbon, partly in opposition to Fernando's proposed marriage to Leonor Teles, and Enrique, taking advantage of the king's unpopularity, marched into Portugal. Fernando made a humiliating peace in March 1373, after which he turned in reprisal on the leaders of the uprising, strengthened the defences of his capital and encouraged shipbuilding by allowing timber to be cut from the royal forests without payment. He also promulgated the *Law of the Seismarias* (1375), which sought to bring more land under cultivation and to control the movement of agricultural labour.

Meanwhile, through the medium of João Fernandes Andeiro, a Galician knight, Fernando had been negotiating with John of Gaunt, who now laid claim to Castile, and concluded an Anglo-Portuguese alliance with his representative at São Salvador de Tagilde, near Guimarães, in July 1372. This was ratified in London in June the following year, but it was not until July of 1386 that Lancaster himself landed in Galicia (see next chapter). During these protracted negotiations, Andeiro had taken advantage of temporary propinquity to make the queen, Dona Leonor, his mistress. When Enrique II died in 1397, Fernando started to play a double game, promising his ten-year-old heiress Beatriz (or Brites) to the young son of the Earl of Cambridge (Lancaster's brother), who was to lead an abortive expedition against the Castilians in 1381, which only reached as far east as Elvas. When this failed, due to a mutiny by an unpaid English contingent led by Sir John de Southeray (a bastard of Edward III and Alice Perrers), Beatriz was offered to Enrique's successor, Juan I, already a widower. However, it was stipulated that should the marriage remain childless, Portugal would remain autonomous. In May 1385 Beatriz left for Castile.

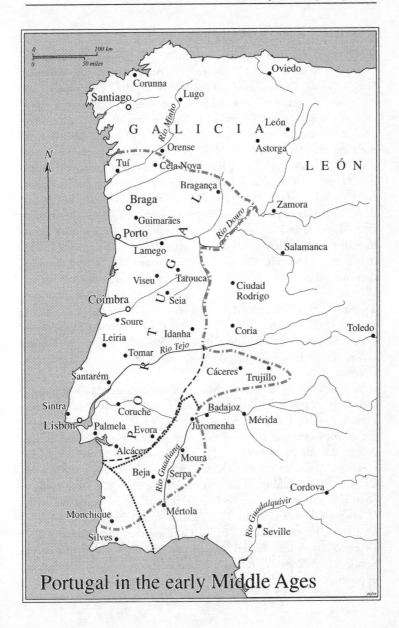

Portugal in the early Middle Ages

CASTILIAN CONTROL DEFIED

In October, on the death of Fernando, prematurely decrepit, his unpopular widow Leonor, abetted by Andeiro and the growing Galician cabal at court, assumed the title of '*regedor e governador*'. This was resented by the citizens of Lisbon, who rightly suspected a rapid erosian of the integrity of Portugal as a separate nation. Juan I arrogantly presumed a walk-over, and sent his heralds ahead to proclaim Beatriz their queen. They were mobbed in the capital, where there was consternation also on learning that Juan himself had crossed the frontier near Guarda. An influential group of nobles and merchants agreed that Andeiro had to be eliminated and this was entrusted to João, the Master of Avis (the illegitimate son of Pedro I), who on 6 December broke into the palace and stabbed him. Anti-Castilian feeling was running so high that the Castilian-born bishop was flung from the cathedral tower in the ensuing tumult. The citizens then pressed João to lead them in defending the realm against Castilian aggression, to which he agreed after some hesitation. A committee – later known as the 'House of the Twenty-Four' – was formed by representatives of the merchant guilds to share in the administration of the capital. Leonor had fled, meeting Juan at Santarém – for he had found the gates of Coimbra and Tomar locked against him – and urged him to march on Lisbon, as the centre of resistance.

In March 1384 João and the Master of Santiago sailed to England to seek help. Support for the new leader grew rapidly. Nun'Alvares Pereira, a young nobleman – one of thirty-two illegitimate children of the philoprogenitive Prior of the Portuguese Hospitallers – left to defend the Alentejan frontier. He gave confidence to the peasantry when his square of unmounted troops was able to defeat a force of Castilian cavalry, although he was not strong enough to stop further contingents from marching on Lisbon, then closely besieged and with an enemy fleet entering the Tagus estuary to blockade it. Fortunately for Lisbon, plague broke out in the Castilian lines, soon claiming 200 victims a day, which forced Juan to raise the siege and withdraw to Seville. He reckoned to return the following year to crush Portuguese opposition.

CHAPTER SIX

Aljubarrota and the century of the Discoveries

João I (1385–1433)

In Juan's absence, Nun'Alvares Pereira re-occupied most of the Alentejo, and all the castles defending Lisbon remained in Portuguese hands. A *cortes* was convoked at Coimbra in March 1385 to discuss the election of João of Avis as king. There was no legitimate claimant: some

Dom João I

considered the sons of Pedro by Inês de Castro had the best claim, but Innocent IV had refused to recognize the marriage or legitimize its offspring. Besides, the two boys were in Castile: João was on the spot and had defended the realm against the Castilians. Residual opposition evaporated and on 6 April João was proclaimed king.

Reinforced by this title, he approached Richard II, reiterating his request for military aid and suggesting an Anglo-Portuguese alliance. João and Nun'Alvares Pereira marched north to receive the submission of Guimarães and Braga before turning towards the eastern frontier, where Juan I's invading forces suffered a serious reverse at Trancoso (north of Guarda).

Juan was still intent on taking Lisbon, and after skirting Coimbra, his army continued south past Leiria, but finding its way barred by Nun'Alvares's troops strongly positioned at Porto de Mós, they swerved west towards Alcobaça. Meanwhile, João's contingent had met up with Nun'Alvares and their joint force (including a small band of English archers) was redeployed.

THE BATTLE OF ALJUBARROTA

On 14 August 1385 the two armies converged on the village of Aljubarrota. Although caution had been advised, individual hot-heads among the undisciplined Spaniards forced the issue by indulging in harassing attacks and both sides were soon engaged in a general mêlée. The Castilians were numerically far superior, predominating in cavalry, but they faltered on seeing their royal standard go down, and the whole army disintegrated, Juan himself galloping off the field. Without exaggeration, João I was able to claim that 2,500 enemy men-at-arms had been killed, apart from a high proportion of those Portuguese magnates who had previously taken Juan's side in the matter of succession. The battle of Aljubarrota was decisive in that it secured the independence of Portugal for almost two centuries.

THE TREATY OF WINDSOR

It was an opportune moment for João I to propose that Lancaster should now join forces with him to assert his own claim to Castile. Mutual interest led to the signing in May 1386 of the Anglo-

Portuguese *Treaty of Windsor* (confirming the Alliance of 1373), containing clauses of a political, military and economic nature. It emphasized the inviolable and perpetual league of friendship and alliance between the two realms and their mutual obligation to come to the assistance of each other should their peace be violated. Although renewed and modified over the years, the treaty still remains in force, making it the longest-lasting alliance between two sovereign countries.

Lancaster himself, with 5,000 men, landed near Corunna that Autumn, and conferred with João concerning their projected joint campaign, in which the same number of Portuguese troops would also fight. It was also agreed that João should marry Philippa, Lancaster's daughter by his first marriage, and that when he had made good his claim, he would cede part of Castilian territory – roughly south of the lower reaches of the Tormes and the western half of Spanish Extremadura – as a dowry.

Philippa of Lancaster (1359–1415)

Philippa reached Oporto in December and her marriage to Dom João was celebrated in its reconstructed cathedral in February 1387 with customary pomp and raucous celebration. As the chronicler Fernão Lopes reported, at the head of the procession went 'so many pipes, trumpets and other instruments, that nothing else could be heard', and behind them came noblewomen and citizen's daughters, singing. The crush was so great in the small space between the palace and church that it was well nigh impossible to marshal the crowds.

LANCASTER'S FIASCO

The invasion of Castile commenced shortly afterwards, with a force of some 11,000 Anglo-Portuguese led by Lancaster (at his insistence, and João complied) marching east from Braganza via Alcañices. Some skirmishing took place at Benavente, which they were unable to capture, and supplies were running short. They attacked the small town of Valderas and then walled Villalobos, but the Castilians had still not been brought to battle. The Allies had occupied no place of importance, nor had there been any rising in Lancaster's favour. Frustrated and discouraged, he sought a way out of his predicament – for the English contingent was getting progressively demoralized and would be prepared to accept any reasonable settlement which would be honourable to both contestants. João found it hard to understand how his father-in-law's pretension to claim Castile during the previous fifteen years could be abandoned so easily. Negotiations were opened with the Castilians and a truce was agreed; it was proposed that Juan's heir, the future Enrique III, would marry Lancaster's daughter Catherine (Catarina) and that Lancaster – now in debt to his son-in-law – would surrender all his claims on receiving substantial financial compensation. The ten-week campaign petered out ingloriously, as the Allied troops fought their way past Ciudad Rodrigo to regain the Portuguese frontier. João was then obliged to supply galleys to transport the remaining English troops from Oporto to Bayonne in September.

João had been excluded from these negotiations and it was not for some months that the first of several truces were entered into. During this period there were a number of frontier incidents, but eventually, after Badajoz and Tuí – which the Portuguese had occupied – had been exchanged for Braganza and Miranda, a more permanent peace was established in 1411. However, it was not until 1431 that Castile finally recognized the House of Avis. Catarina, widowed in 1406 when regent for her infant son, may well have been instrumental in bringing a settlement about between Castile and Portugal, where her half-sister was queen.

BATALHA

Philippa of Lancaster (Dona Filipa) died in 1415 and João in 1433. They were both buried in the founder's chapel – their effigies hand-in-hand – at Batalha, the 'Battle Abbey' which, in consequence of a vow made before João's victory at Aljubarrota, had been under construction since 1388. The carved insignia of the Order of the Garter, founded by Philippa's grandfather Edward III, is also in evidence there. Subsequently buried at Batalha were her sons Duarte (Edward); Fernando of Avis; João of São Tiago; Henrique, Duke of Viseu and Master of the Order of Christ (better known as Henry 'the Navigator'); and Pedro,

Duke of Coimbra. Their sister Isabel married Philip the Good of Burgundy; João's illegitimate daughter, Beatriz, married the Earl of Arundel; his illegitimate son Afonso married the daughter of his companion-in-arms, Nun'Alvares Pereira, and was created Count of Barcelos (and later, the first Duke of Braganza).

Since Aljubarrota, the older nobility had been largely replaced by a new landed aristocracy dependent on the king, while the queen's beneficial influence at Court, to which she introduced English culture and manners and the tradition of education for gentlemen, was unanimously acknowledged. More power had been given to the mercantile middle class and trade and ship-building prospered, although the royal treasury had difficulties keeping abreast of inflation.

CEUTA OCCUPIED

Inflation does not seem to have prevented João, only days after the death of Philippa, from insisting that he should set sail with the fleet he had prepared for a surprise attack on Ceuta, for the Magrib had been weakened by a recent civil war. This campaign was partly to support Christian pressure on the kingdom of Granada and partly to gratify some of his more bellicose knights. In the event, Ceuta fell at the first assault and was then garrisoned. While the occupation of Portugal's first toe-hold on the African continent was to prove costly, as it had to be supplied by sea, its possession helped to protect Portuguese shipping trading west of the Straits of Gibraltar.

The remaining years of Dom João's life were comparatively uneventful at home, but they were marked by the first tentative exploratory voyages along the West African coast and into the Atlantic. Landfalls were made in the Canaries, Madeira, and the Azores, which added a new dimension to European knowledge of the world.

Duarte

Dom João was succeeded by his introspective eldest son, Duarte (1433–8), author of a philosophical treatise entitled the *Loyal Councellor*. It was during his short reign that the disastrous attack on Tangier occurred. This appeared to be a natural continuation of the Portuguese policy of expansion in the Magrib, at least in the opinion of Duarte's youngest brother, Fernando, who hoped to win his spurs there, while Henrique ('the Navigator'), who had endorsed the project, as Master of the Order of Christ, would lead the invasion. Eventually, Duarte gave his approval, but in the event, the expeditionary force, which had set sail in August 1437, found itself cut off from its ships and many men were obliged to surrender, including Fernando. The Muslims stipulated the return of Ceuta before releasing their prisoner, a condition to which the Archbishop of Braga would not agree without papal consent. Henrique proposed another raid to rescue the hostage, but no decision was reached. In September 1438 the conscience-stricken king died of plague, having not yet found a way out of the dilemma, leaving young Fernando unransomed at Fez, where he died ignominiously five years later.

The crown passed to the six-year-old Afonso V (1438–81). Although Duarte had appointed his wife regent, Pedro, Afonso's uncle, claimed the regency during the minority (until 1448). However, the moment the king came of age, he arraigned his uncle for treason. As he resisted arrest, Afonso sought the help of the Duke of Braganza. Pedro was killed and his faction decimated at the battle of Alfarrobeira (1449), after which Braganza took full advantage of the dominating position he now held at Court.

Maritime Expansion

HENRIQUE 'THE NAVIGATOR'

Prince Henry (1394–1460), also known as the 'Infante de Sagres', has been the subject of a remarkable '*Life*' by Peter Russell, in which a curious and complex character is given his due as being the often obsessional driving force behind the arduous exploratory voyages then taking place, although the prince did not accompany them in person. Were they chiefly undertaken to satisfy his curiosity; to extend the horizons of the Christian world and Portuguese sovereignty; to search for gold or slaves; or to profit by trade (for he had to recoup the crippling cost of fitting out his flotilla of caravels)? We shall never know for certain, but the results were spectacular. He had brought the Majorcan cartographer Jaffuda Cresques to Portugal as early as 1421, shortly before which, under his aegis, João Gonçalves Zarco and Tristão Vaz Teixeira had rediscovered the uninhabited Atlantic island of Madeira, which was then colonized. The Canaries, the existence of which had been known for a century, were also occupied by the Portuguese in 1424, although sovereignty over them passed to Castile in 1479. In 1427 several of the volcanic islands known as the Azores were discovered and settled in 1439; the more distant were reached in 1452. The Cape Verdes archipelago was sighted *c.* 1456 and settled soon after. In the same year Alvise Cadamosto explored the estuaries of the Gulf of Guinea.

By 1434 Henriques's captain, Gil Eanes, skirting the West African coast, had sailed past Cape Bojador, until then an object of dread. In 1441 Nuno Tristão and Antão Gonçalves were sent to explore the coast and hinterland further south, the latter returning with negroes and gold dust. In 1443 the former had reached the island of Arguim (where a trading-post was soon set up) and Senegambia in the following year.

In that same year Henrique, who had established his headquarters near Sagres, at the western extremity of the Algarve, received from Pedro, then regent, the monopoly of trade in whatever lands he might discover. Henrique also leased trading concessions to several enterprising private contractors. To encourage exploration, in 1454 the crown provided a massive subsidy augmented by loans from the Braganzas, the Abbot of Alcobaça and the Jewish community. Lagos became the main port from which the caravels sailed, returning with exotic cargoes including consignments of negro slaves, sold there to remedy the labour shortage in the Algarve and southern Alentejo. By 1460, the year of his death, Henrique's captains had reached Sierra Leone.

The fall of Constantinople to the Turks in 1453 had the effect of giving impetus to the enterprise of finding new territory in Africa. This was also seen as a form of crusade and received encouragement in the form of papal bulls – carrying Christianity to the pagan natives. In the Magrib, Alcácer Seguir was captured and garrisoned in 1458 and Arzila fell in 1471. Tangier, having successfully resisted a Portuguese attack in

1463, was then abandoned by the Muslims. Now in possession of a string of fortresses along the north and north-western coasts, Afonso V became known as 'the African'.

In the last decade of his reign, Afonso became involved in a complicated dynastic dispute over Castile. From 1474 it had been in the possession of Ferdinand and Isabella ('the Catholic Monarchs'). Afonso was tempted to make a counter claim, which was rejected by his rivals. Afonso crossed the frontier, where Zamora opened its gates to him, but his forces were defeated near Toro. Disillusioned at failing to enlist French support, in 1479 Afonso agreed to the humiliating *Treaty of Alcáçovas*. Embittered, he resolved to abdicate, but before the *cortes* had met to give him their consent, he died.

The country was wasted by several epidemics or plagues during this period: especially at Coimbra specifically in 1477–9 and between the years 1480 and 1497, at Oporto in 1486 and Evora in 1490.

João II   (1481–95)

Afonso's heir, a very different character from his father, immediately abrogated the peace treaty with Castile and set about bringing his nobles to heel, in particular the overmighty Braganza, his brother-in-law who, holding some fifty towns and castles and able to raise a large private army, was a serious threat to royal authority. The duke, who was found to be in treasonable correspondence with Ferdinand, had to be brought to justice, but this was not so easy. Eventually in 1484, when the Catholic Monarchs, who might well have taken sides with Braganza, were fully occupied in their war against Granada, João arrested the duke (whose brothers had fled the country) and on 29 June, after thirty judges had found him culpable, he was beheaded at Evora.

João had proposed that his heir, Afonso, should marry Juana, the second daughter of Ferdinand and Isabella, who might have the Canaries as her dowry. This came to nothing, and although his marriage to their eldest daughter, Isabel, was celebrated with much pomp at Evora in 1490, it was not to last long, for in June the following year the Infante fell from his horse and was killed. Dom João's nearest legitimate relative, his cousin Manuel, Duke of Beja and Master of the Order of

Christ, now became heir and in 1497 married the Infante's young widow.

The voyages of exploration continued to prosper, now administered by Fernando (Dom Afonso's younger brother) whose preoccupation was to find a sea route to the 'Indies' and the land of 'Prester John', the precise position of which was uncertain, but very approximately coterminous with Ethiopia. With this in mind, Portuguese captains sailed south along the African coast, crossing the Equator in 1473. A factory was set up at São Jorge da Mina do Ouro in 1482, and in the following year Diogo Cão, sailing further, reached the mouth of the Congo. The captains carried *padrões*, stone pillars surmounted by a cross and engraved with the Portuguese arms, to mark these new territories. João sent other expeditions: one commanded by Bartolomeu Dias rounded the Cape of Good Hope and entered the Indian Ocean, but was obliged to return to Lisbon after an absence of over seventeen months. He had fulfilled his brief and had completed at last the search for the southernmost end of the vast continent of Africa. Bartolomeu Dias named the Cape the 'Cape of Storms': the king insisted that it should be named the Cape '*de Boa Esperança*', Good Hope – of the longed for sea-route to the Indies.

A land route was also investigated in 1488, when Pero de Covilhã made his way in disguise to Aden and then on to Calicut and Goa, returning via Ormuz to Cairo. From here, news was sent back to Portugal concerning his wanderings, before Covilhã travelled south to the land of Prester John. Although well-received by the emperor, he was not allowed to depart from Ethiopia, where he was seen by a Portuguese mission some thirty-six years later.

CHRISTOPHER COLUMBUS

In about 1481 Christopher Columbus (who had married the daughter of a Portuguese sea-captain and settled on one of the Madeira group of islands) urged that since the earth was spherical there was a possibility of reaching the Indies by navigating due west. The idea was rejected by the Portuguese, so he then approached the courts of England and Spain. Eventually, after the fall of Granada, the Catholic Monarchs agreed to support his project and Columbus set sail, returning to Lisbon early in 1492 convinced that he had discovered India, or at least Zipango (Japan), mentioned in Marco Polo's *Travels*. Taking immediate advantage of this news, as the landfall appeared to be south of the latitude of the Canaries, Dom João prepared a fleet under Francisco de Almeida. When the Catholic Monarchs heard of this, on the arrival of Columbus to their court, they took measures to prevent it, obtaining papal bulls from Alexander VI (a Spanish pope) confining the Portuguese to African waters south of that latitude. After much negotiation, a new settlement – the *Treaty of Tordesillas* – was agreed in June 1494, whereby the dividing line was to run from north to south, 370 leagues west of the Cape Verdes. All landfalls to the west of that line of longitude would go to Castile, all to the east to Portugal.

CHAPTER SEVEN

Vasco da Gama reaches India: The Empire expands

João II died of the dropsy in October 1495 and was succeeded by Dom Manuel I (1495–1521), aged twenty-six, who restored to the young Duke of Braganza the properties taken from his father. He also strengthened his hold over the nobles, patronizing some seventy families, who formed a powerful court circle (their coats of arms, supported by prancing stags, may still be seen on the *artesonado* ceiling of the 'Sala dos Brasões' of the royal palace at Sintra).

The Problem of the Jews

At his succession, it was proposed that Manuel marry Isabel, the eldest daughter of the 'Catholic Monarchs', but one of their conditions was that he expel the Jewish (Sephardic) community from Portugal, where they had formed a small but influential aristocracy over the centuries. They enjoyed the protection of the crown and the nobility, particularly as doctors, financiers, printers (the first eleven Portuguese incunables were in Hebrew) and artisans. Their numbers had been augmented by an estimated 60,000 co-religionists seeking refuge in Portugal after their expulsion from Spain in 1492. Six hundred wealthy families were able to purchase the right to settle; the rest were allowed to remain there for eight months only, on the payment of a fee. Before his marriage in October 1497, Dom Manuel had paid lip-service to the stipulation made by his bigoted Spanish in-laws by ordering that all Jews and Muslims who refused baptism would have to leave after a period of ten months. In practice the remaining Muslims were let off lightly, partly to avoid possible

69

reprisals against Christians in Muslim lands. Manuel had no immediate intention of parting with such a valuable community as the
Jews and encouraged their conversion, to which some 20,000 ostensibly agreed. In spite of objections made by the monastic orders,
these 'New Christians' were given two decades' grace, during which
the authenticity of their conversion would not be investigated.
Nevertheless, in 1506 there was a pogrom in Lisbon, stirred up by
two Dominicans raising the cry of heresy, when several hundred
New Christians were massacred. Numerous communities left the
country in the subsequent Diaspora, some to France, many to London or Amsterdam – among them the Espinoza family, from whom
Baruch Spinoza descended – but it has been estimated that there
were some 20,000 Marrano families still in Portugal a century later,
principally in the Beiras Alta and Baixa. (During the Second World
War, a Polish Jewish refugee identified the building of a former
synagogue in Tomar, which had survived in a recognizable state: it is
now the Museu Abraham Zacuto, named after the mathematician
who, on leaving Salamanca in 1492, was court astronomer to João II
briefly, until obliged to seek asylum in North Africa.) It was not
until 1531 that the Inquisition was installed in Portugal, which after
1547 was under the control of Cardinal Henrique, a brother of João
III, with tribunals in Lisbon, Evora and Coimbra.

In July 1498, Queen Isabel died in childbirth and the prince, Miguel,
survived only two years. Any chance of Manuel or one of his heirs
ruling over the whole Peninsula faded in 1500, on the birth of Carlos
(the future Emperor Charles V) to the Catholic Monarchs' second
daughter Juana – later known as 'la Loca' (the Mad) – who had married
Philip, son of the Habsburg Emperor Maximilian. Manuel, now a
widower, married their fourth daughter, Maria, and his heir, the future
João III, was born in 1502.

It has been estimated that the population of the Iberian Peninsula in
the early years of the sixteenth century was approximately 11,350,000
(of which over 8,300,000 were Castilians); Portugal accounted for only
1,500,000, a point not often recognized when comparing their
respective achievements.

VASCO DA GAMA (*c.* 1468–1524)

Preoccupation in producing an heir did not divert Dom Manuel from the pursuit of expanding his empire, and he appointed a new admiral – Vasco da Gama, a member of the Order of São Tiago – to follow up Bartholomeu Dias's tentative expedition past the Cabo de Boa Esperança (Cape of Good Hope) into the Indian Ocean nine years earlier. The admiral had been provided with appropriate letters of credence to both Prester John and the Raja of Calicut. (Da Gama's mother was a member of the Sodré family, descended from a certain Frederick Sudley of Gloucestershire, who had accompanied the Earl of Cambridge's expedition to Portugal in the 1380s.)

Weighing anchor at Lisbon in July 1497, Da Gama's small flotilla made a wide circle to the west and, after much buffeting in the south

Vasco da Gama

Atlantic, reached land not far north of the Cape of Good Hope, where they took on water and careened the ships. They then doubled the Cape to approach an unknown shore on Christmas Day, which he named Natal. While sailing north along the East African (or Swahili) coast, the admiral put in at Mozambique, Mombasa and Malindi, in which ports he met with an ambiguous reception, becoming increasingly distrustful of the Muslim traders, who considered the Indian Ocean to be their private preserve and resented competition. (In 1589 troops had to be sent to protect Portuguese settlements on the Swahili coast from Ottoman attack.)

It was not until May 1498 that Da Gama found a pilot to guide him to Calicut on the Malabar or south-western coast of India. But here too, the unheralded appearance of Portuguese ships was not entirely welcomed by the long-established Muslim merchants, who felt their virtual monopoly of the trade in the area was seriously threatened. As he was unable to convince the Samorim, the local ruler, of his honest intentions, in late August 1498 Da Gama decided to sail for home. The first vessel of his diminished fleet belatedly entered the Tagus estuary in the following July, after an absence of twenty-six months, bringing the news that Portugal had indeed discovered a maritime route to the real Indies – not to the false Indies of Columbus – which, post haste, Dom Manuel triumphantly announced to the Catholic Monarchs.

PEDRO ALVARES CABRAL

Only six months later, a larger fleet of thirteen ships commanded by Pedro Alvares Cabral weighed anchor at Lisbon with the intention of following up Da Gama's remarkable exploit and to establish more enduring trade relations with the Samorim. It was while *en route* that they were blown far off course and Brazil was first sighted. Whether this was fortuitous or whether there was foreknowledge of the existence of a land-mass there, east of the longitudinal line of demarcation, remains an open question. Half Cabral's ships were lost during the long voyage, including that of Bartholomeu Dias, and one strayed off course to Madagascar and later found itself in the Red Sea.

Consolidation and Further Expansion

The first two decades of the sixteenth century, which coincided with the latter part of Dom Manuel's reign, were replete with additional discoveries by a series of expeditions following in the wake of Da Gama and Cabral. The former set sail early in 1502 on his second voyage, during which he behaved in a gratuitously aggressive and piratical fashion, even bombarding Calicut in an attempt to bring the Samorim to heel. He then based himself further down the coast at Cochin, and eventually returned to Lisbon in October 1503, profitably laden with an exotic cargo of Oriental spices. He was followed in 1505 by a fleet under Francisco de Almeida, who had the title of viceroy. Both he and Afonso de Albuquerque were able to keep Muslim fleets at bay off the Red Sea and Persian Gulf. After succeeding Almeida, in 1510 Albuquerque occupied Goa (which remained in Portuguese hands until 1960) and Ormuz in 1515. In 1511 he extended his control over the spice trade based on the emporium of Malacca, apart from making footholds at Pacém in Sumatra, Ternate in the Moluccas, and in Ceylon at Colombo, where factories and forts were established. Miscegenation with local women was encouraged and, before long, Goa had become the second city 'of Portugal' in size, with a flourishing Luso-Indian Catholic population, for the Jesuits had also made it their main base of missionary activity in Asia. In 1524 Da Gama (who appears to have been an unpopular disciplinarian) sailed to India for the third and last time, and died at Cochin on the Christmas Eve of that year, some three months after reaching Goa.

Meanwhile, in 1502 Amerigo Vespucci returned from exploring the east coast of South America and was able to demonstrate that it was part of a continent, not an island, as at first assumed. Although the monopoly of cutting dye-wood in Brazil was then granted to Fernão de Noronhã, a New Christian, and sugar-cane was introduced from Madeira in 1516, some years were to pass before the country began to be exploited seriously. Parts of a great northern continent were also being discovered, with Sebastian Cabot searching for a north-west passage in 1497, following earlier tentative probes by Bristol fishermen sailing west from Iceland. The Corte-Real brothers then skirted the

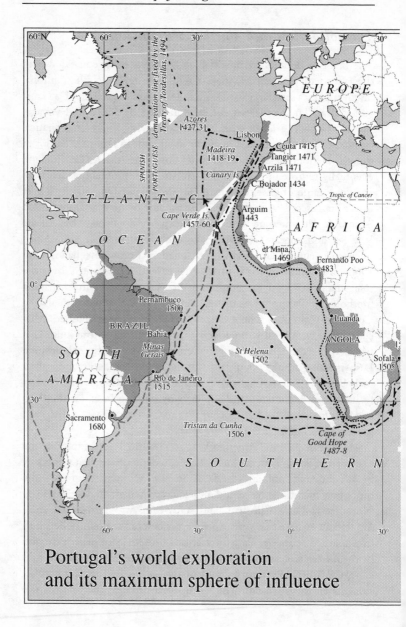

Portugal's world exploration
and its maximum sphere of influence

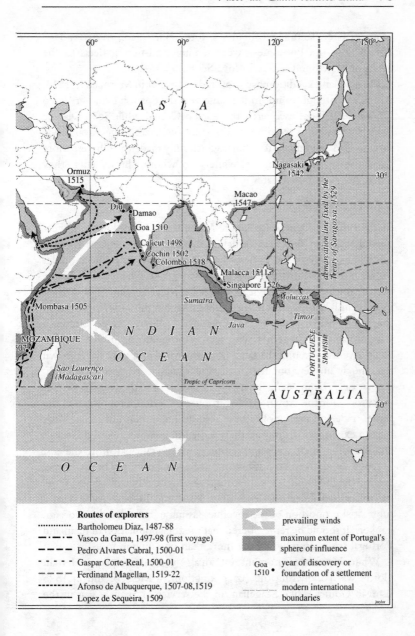

Routes of explorers

```
............  Bartholomeu Diaz, 1487-88
─ ∙ ─ ∙ ─   Vasco da Gama, 1497-98 (first voyage)
─ ─ ─ ─     Pedro Alvares Cabral, 1500-01
- - - - -   Gaspar Corte-Real, 1500-01
..........   Ferdinand Magellan, 1519-22
...........  Afonso de Albuquerque, 1507-08,1519
──────      Lopez de Sequeira, 1509
```

prevailing winds

maximum extent of Portugal's sphere of influence

Goa   year of discovery or
1510 ● foundation of a settlement

modern international boundaries

coasts of Greenland and Labrador before being lost in those icy seas. Before long the Portuguese were sending cod-fishing fleets to the banks of Newfoundland and Nova Scotia.

On land, an expedition had captured Azammur in Morocco in 1513, which was later given up. In the same year the Spanish explorer Vasco Núñez de Balboa discovered the Pacific Ocean, while João Dias de Solis had started to reconnoitre the coast of Brazil. Jorge Alvares was soon to lead an embassy to China, which only made the Chinese more suspicious of these strange foreigners, to whom, shortly after, they practically closed their gates.

MAGELLAN   (1480?–1521)

In 1518 the Portuguese Fernão de Magalhães – better known as Ferdinand Magellan, who had participated in the capture of Goa and had some knowledge of the Indies – having been given the cold shoulder on his return to Portugal, offered his services to Charles V of Spain, with a project to circumnavigate the globe. Magellan himself was killed in a skirmish with natives in the Philippines, but the surviving vessel of the five which had set out, commanded by Sebastián de Elcano, a Basque navigator, together with a crew of eighteen, limped back to Spain twenty-five months later. The known world may have grown that much smaller, but there was still much to explore. Although, dramatically, Dom Manuel may well have become the wealthiest ruler in Europe, for the crown claimed tribute on a high proportion of the Indies trade and monopolized the rest, his hubris was not to last long, for the expense of setting up these expeditions was to exceed returns, and the toll in men, ships and resources in general, apart from the cost of maintaining overseas possessions, became increasingly burdensome. During the following reign the country's economy benefited very little, for prices had fallen and enormous loans had to be repaid, with a substantial proportion of the revenue passing into the hands of foreign bankers. It should be remembered that the total population of mainland Portugal was then only slightly more than one million souls.

While Magellan's momentous voyage was taking place, Hernán Cortes was conquering the Aztec kingdom of Mexico; and in 1525 Estevão Gomes – like Magellan, in the service of Spain – was in the process of exploring the North American coast between Newfoundland and the Chesapeake. All this conspired to increase competition between the two Peninsular powers. Rivalry between them over the Spice Islands, which were being approached from the Philippines by the Spaniards and from the Indies by the Portuguese, was partly resolved in 1529 by the *Treaty of Zaragoza*, by which Portugal had paid Charles V a huge sum to withdraw the Spanish claim. Not long before, in 1525, João III had married Charles's sister Catarina, while Charles, when marrying Isabel, João's sister, had demanded and received an enormous dowry in addition.

João III   (1521–57)

Manuel's youthful successor was encumbered by debts and by the expense of supporting a surfeit of entrenched retainers and parasitical hangers-on: almost 5,000 persons drew their pay or pensions from the royal exchequer. The crown had become the honey-pot, for all honours, appointments, grants of land, permissions to trade abroad, and the like, depended entirely on the king's consent. The centralized Court became the obligatory focus of all functionaries; the penury of the populace in general was virtually ignored, for the king was no longer dependent on taxes being voted by the *cortes*. It was not until 1525, after a lapse of twenty-three years, that they were again convoked, in spite of frequent petitions. Meanwhile, there was a constant drift from the land, with a starving peasantry seeking employment in the cities – the population of Lisbon had expanded to 100,000 by mid-century – or hazarding their lives as crew in merchant fleets, if not actually emigrating; thus the contemporary maxim: 'Those wishing to stay afloat, must chose Church, Court, or Boat'. Many were to cross the frontier in the hope of seeking a living at Seville, by then the virtual 'capital' of Spanish America, thriving on the cargoes of treasure-fleets. (Among those born there of a Portuguese father in 1599 was the great 'Spanish' artist, Diego Velázquez de Silva.) Another cause for the further depopulation of the countryside was the numbers of non-productive hands who chose to enter religious communities, for monasteries proliferated.

BRAZIL

In 1534 Dom João undertook the division of Brazil's coast into several sectors, the settlement of each being supervised by *donatários*, commanders who were also responsible for protecting their areas of control from French intruders, who had become increasing prevalent. By 1549 the problem of defence had necessitated the appointment of a governor-general, Tomé de Sousa, who had his capital at Bahía, and whose administrators were directly accountable to Lisbon. In the same year, members of the Society of Jesus, among other religious Orders, entered the country to evangelize and to minister to the spiritual welfare of the colonists. Slaves from West Africa were introduced to cultivate the sugar-cane plantations, which flourished and by 1560 were exporting far more than those of Madeira; between 1570 and 1585 the number of mills had doubled. As in their other overseas territories, miscegenation between the Portuguese and the indigenous inhabitants had commenced at an early date.

MISSIONARY ENTERPRISE IN INDIA AND THE ORIENT

The first Franciscans had reached Goa in 1532, and the Jesuits followed a decade later. St Francis Xavier (1506–62), 'the Apostle of the Indies', after preaching in Portuguese India and the Spice Isles, by 1549 had reached Japan, recently discovered by the Portuguese, where he remained for two years. He died in 1552 and was buried in Goa. Fernão Mendes Pinto (*c.* 1510–83), briefly a Jesuit novice, in his *Peregrinação*, a picaresque, posthumously published autobiography, vividly described his extraordinary experiences during the two decades he spent in the Indies and Orient during this period. More famous was the epic poem by Luís de Camões (1525?–80; anglicized as Camoens) entitled *Os Lusíadas* (*The Luciades*), published in 1572, in which he retells Da Gama's discovery of the sea-route to India. He later made the same journey to Goa, spending sixteen years away from Portugal, returning poverty-stricken as did many others attempting to seek their fortune in the Indies. Among the few names in what has been referred to as the 'Golden Age' of Portuguese literature was the dramatist Gil Vicente, also a goldsmith, who in 1506 fashioned the 'Monstrance of Belém' from the first gold brought home by Da Gama. It may still be admired in the Museu de Arte Antiga at Lisbon.

ART AND ARCHITECTURE

Among artists, Nuno Gonçalves was active during the latter half of the fifteenth century as court painter to Dom Afonso V, whose remarkable 'Retablo of the Infante' may also be seen in the Museu de Arte Antiga. At a later date Frei Carlos and Antonio de Holanda, among northern masters, found employment in Portugal, influencing Jorge Afonso, Cristóvão de Figueiredo, Vasco Fernandes (better known as 'O Grão Vasco', the Great Vasco) and Gaspar Vaz. Meanwhile, there had been much building activity in the florid 'Manueline style', such as the Jerónimos monastery and the Tagus-lapped Tower at Belém, the '*Capelas Imperfeitas*' at Batalha, and at Tomar. The architects – not all of them Portuguese – included Boitac, João de Castilho, and the brothers Diogo and Francisco de Arruda at Belém; Mateus Fernandes at Batalha; Diogo de Torralva and Filippo Terzi at Tomar; and also Francisco de Holanda, who served as architectural advisor to the court after 1541; while among sculptors, Nicolas Chanterène, Philippe Houdart and Jean de Rouen were notable.

A new University was established at Coimbra in 1547, with the humanist André de Gouveia as principal and the Scottish humanist George Buchanan among the teachers – a man 'of austere countenance, but mirrie, and quick in conference and awnswres to anie questioun' – who provoked jealousy among other academics and they had him arrested and imprisoned by the Inquisition. Later, suspected of having Lutheran sympathies, the University fell into the hands of the predatory Jesuits, until they were expelled in 1772 by Pombal, who then established an enlightened system. The Jesuits had set up their own University in 1559 at Evora, fulfilling the desire of Henrique (Dom João's younger brother), by then a cardinal.

MACAU

In 1547, the last year of Dom João's long reign, a factory on the territory of Macau was granted to the Portuguese, from which they might trade with Canton. From 1565, when the Jesuits landed there (and from which Matthew Ricci was able to enter the Imperial court at Pekin eighteen years later), the thriving emporium served also as a base from which they infiltrated not only China but many other communities in the Pacific. The cosmopolitan port – the only one allowed in China until 1675 – played an important role in trade with the Orient until the 'Opium War' of 1839–44. It remained under Portuguese administration until 31 December 1999 – the last European foothold in China, as it had been the first.

From 1540, Portuguese adventurers – among them Mendes Pinto – had also settled in Japan, making Nagasaki their principal base. Here also the Jesuits were active, and the period until 1630 has been referred to as 'The Christian Century in Japan'.

Sebastião   (1557–78)

Don João's heir, who had been married in 1552 to his cousin Juana, the daughter of Charles V, predeceased him, leaving a posthumous son, Sebastião, who succeeded to the Portuguese throne aged three. Being Dom João's only grandson, and the only hope of continuity for the House of Avis, he was known even before his birth as 'O Desejado' (The Desired). Catarina, his Spanish-born grandmother, acted as regent, which caused some misgivings, as her influence was suspect. (Her brother, Charles, had by now retired to Yuste, leaving the Spanish Empire in the hands of his son, Philip II.) Henrique, Sebastião's great-uncle, took over the regency from 1562 to 1568, when the hapless youth, who suffered from such physical disabilities that it was assumed he would be unfit to marry, became of age. Sebastião spent much of his time either at his devotions – even praying by the opened tombs of his ancestors at Alcobaça – or in martial exercises, which weakened him, but he hankered to lead Portugal in another crusade against the Moors.

Mazagão, in the Magrib, had survived a siege, but the Muslim threat was increasing and the Turks invaded Cyprus, although their navy was to suffer defeat at Lepanto in 1571. The pope had appealed to Portugal also to raise a fleet, but this had been largely destroyed by storms. Although, as his mother had remarked, keeping distant India was a miracle, Sebastião preferred to seek glory closer to home, by eradicating

Islam in North Africa, where he would extend his empire. Disregarding the advice of his saner ministers, he pressed ahead obsessively with his foolhardy plan, in 1576 even meeting Philip II at Guadalupe in a vain attempt to persuade him to join in a concerted attack on North Africa.

By now, flattered by a coterie of young nobles, nothing would deter him from marshalling an army of 17,000 men, which in June 1578 embarked for Tangier to seek battle with the King of Morocco. Here at Alcácer-Quibir, his adversary lay in wait with a force of 40,000 cavalry. On 4 August the Portuguese found themselves surrounded and in the ensuing fray both Sebastião and the flower of his army were killed; those not slaughtered were taken captive. (Among those killed was Sir Thomas Stukeley, the English Catholic adventurer.) There were rumours that the king had survived and escaped, the idea of which for years ahead would sporadically surface in a manifestation of messianism: surely he would return one day. The disaster profoundly unnerved the country, aware that it could precipitate loss of independence, for there was a presentiment that Spain would take advantage of her vulnerable state.

Henrique, the Cardinal-king *(1578–80)*

The main preoccupation of Henrique, now old and failing, who succeeded Sebastião, was with his own succession; as he was childless, the crown would normally pass to his nephews, the grandchildren of Dom Manuel. Among possible claimants to the throne were Philip II of Spain, the Duchess of Braganza (a daughter of Dom Duarte), and António, Prior of Crato (an illegitimate son of the Infante Dom Luiz; his mother was Violante Gomes, engagingly known as 'the Pelican', and of *converso* descent). Philip was well aware of the opportunity thus presented of unifying the Peninsula under one crown, and had little doubt in his own mind that Portugal would fall to him like a ripe fig. A majority of the nobility and entrepreneurial classes preferred such a union, for any increase in cross-border commerce would be to their profit, and the Spanish fleet would protect Portugal's fragile trade routes. The Prior of Crato was favoured by the country as a whole, as being Portuguese at least. Henrique convoked the *cortes* at Almeirim to

Dom António, Prior of Crato

discuss the legalities of the matter, but he died before the problem was resolved. Meanwhile, Cristóbal de Moura, a Portuguese in the suite of Philip's sister Juana, who had been sent to Lisbon well supplied with silver, failed to suborn António's supporters. They declared him king at Santarém, but the final decision was taken out of their hands by events.

CHAPTER EIGHT

'The Spanish Captivity' and the early Braganzas

Philip I of Portugal   (1580–98)

The decision to crown António had been pre-empted by Philip II of Spain's army, led by the redoubtable Duke of Alba, which had marched across the frontier on 18 June 1580. Traversing the Alentejo, he scattered the Prior of Crato's hastily gathered forces near Lisbon, which was then occupied. Although António carried on residual resistance, he escaped to France in the following May, and then went to England. Only the Azores continued to hold out longer. Philip himself had entered the capital the previous December to grasp the reins of government, and a few months later, on promising that all rights and privileges would be respected and that the country would retain its internal autonomy, he was proclaimed king at Tomar by a cowed *cortes*. However, he refused to withdraw Spanish garrisons or, in spite of reducing the cost of the former administration, to reduce taxation, which with so many enormous ransoms to pay for the release of prisoners languishing in Morocco, remained irksome.

Philip returned to Spain in February 1583, leaving his nephew the Cardinal-Archduke Albert as viceroy. It has been propounded that if he had chosen to remain in Lisbon, making that port the capital of his empire rather than Madrid, as proposed by Cardinal Granvelle, the history of the Peninsula might have been very different.

Although there was a measure of political stability and economic well-being, partly stimulated by the import of sugar and tobacco from Brazil, which provided a growing source of revenue, the occupation was bitterly unpopular in Portugal. Meanwhile, her vulnerable shipping lanes – now considered Spanish – were the object of repeated assault by foreign maritime powers: corsairs from England and Holland were among the foremost in plundering well-laden galleons returning from both the New World and the Orient. This rivalry was accentuated by the fact that Elizabeth of Protestant England regarded Philip, the champion of Catholicism, who had been married to her predecessor, Mary Tudor, as a serious threat. Ever since her accession in 1558 he had been fomenting conspiracies to reinstate Mary Stuart on the throne. Mary's execution in 1587 precipitated war. A huge fleet was prepared by Philip, a high proportion assembling in the capacious Tagus estuary under the seventh Duke of Medina-Sidonia. Of the 200-odd men-of-war forming the 'Invincible Armada', which set sail in 1588 to attack England, only to be scattered, wrecked or destroyed, a mere quarter eventually limped home.

The defeat had serious repercussions and it also underlined the fact that the union with Spain had a downside as far as Portugal was concerned. While there were religious differences between Portugal and England, old alliances were covertly maintained, with Elizabeth doing all she could to 'annoy and endamage the Spaniard'. In May 1589 she sent a flotilla to Portugal under Drake in an attempt to place the Prior of Crato on the throne. Although a force commanded by Sir John Norris and Sir Roger Williams landed near Peniche and marched on Lisbon, while Drake entered the estuary of the Tagus, the expedition failed miserably, partly due to sickness among the troops, but largely because the uprising on his behalf that António had promised, never materialized. The pretender died in Paris six years later.

In 1593 Philip prohibited the Portuguese from trading with the Dutch, against whom he was campaigning in the Low Countries, and seized Dutch shipping in the Tagus, with the result that a Dutch resident who had sailed to the Indies offered to show his compatriots the route. This offer was taken up two years later with serious consequences to the spice trade, which the Dutch were not slow to appropriate, and by 1602 the profitable Dutch East India Company was launched, effectively breaking the Portuguese monopoly in India and the Orient. It was not for another thirty-eight years that the Portuguese and all other foreigners were expelled from Japan by the Tokugawa shogunate, and not until 1852 that her ports were again opened to foreign trade. Meanwhile, in 1638 the Dutch had ousted the Portuguese from Ceylon, had attacked Malacca in 1641 and Malabar in 1663.

Philip II of Portugal (1598–1621)

Philip III of Spain did not respect the conditions his father had imposed on Portugal, which were progressively eroded and violated, and he did not even bother to visit Lisbon until two years before his death in 1621. Meanwhile, he had devised a devious scheme by which the 'New Christians' (i.e. Jews) of Portugal, who had been prohibited from leaving the country, might do so on payment of a fee. This was then amended to offering them the right to remain and be admitted to office if they paid ten times the amount originally stated. Eventually in 1610, all privileges granted to them were withdrawn and the intolerable restrictions and investigations into 'purity of blood' by the Inquisition were resumed. By 1640 it was forbidden for any descendants of a person condemned by the Inquisition to hold any public office.

Philip III of Portugal (1621–40)

The economic situation had progressively deteriorated as far as the Dutch were concerned, for the Count-Duke Olivares, the forceful Spanish chief minister, chose not to renew a twelve-year truce with the Dutch, which had permitted some revival in trade. In reaction, the Dutch set up a West Indian Company, which not only preyed on Peninsular shipping but in 1624 seized Bahía and its sugar estates. Although expelled temporarily, the Dutch returned to Brazil in 1630, when they seized Pernambuco, and later sent expeditions to capture Mina and collect more slaves in Angola to work in their plantations. These flourished under Dutch administration, although the occupation was essentially military. It was not until 1654 that the Dutch retired from Brazil. Former Portuguese trading-posts had fallen to the English also, among them Ormuz in 1623. Privateering thrived, and it has been estimated that between 1623 and 1638 some 500 Portuguese vessels fell into the hands of Spain's enemies.

Meanwhile, the silver mines of Peru were becoming exhausted, causing Olivares to demand forced loans in 1628 and, among other drastic expedients, to raise taxes in Portugal without the consent of the *cortes*. This further exasperated the Portuguese, who were becoming progressively more disenchanted by the Spanish occupation, and led to rioting in Evora in 1637. Grievances against Spain were partly directed towards Miguel de Vasconcelos, who as secretary to the then governor, Margaret, Duchess of Mantua, one of Philip's cousins, was seen as the Portuguese tool implementing Olivares's machinations. A Flemish Jesuit passing through Lisbon in 1633 had noticed that while the Portuguese held the English in higher regard than any other nation, 'the Castilians they hate worse than the very devil', and that, in that very year they were expecting 'the arrival of their king Dom Sebastião who is supposed to free them from the Spaniards . . . There have been more rumours of his coming lately than in all the many years since his death.'

Spain was now engaged in a titanic struggle against France, with Richelieu at the helm. The Catalans revolted against Olivares's intransigent policies, murdered Philip's viceroy and offered their allegiance to Louis XIII. A contingent of some 6,000 Portuguese troops recruited for service in Italy were diverted to Catalonia by Olivares, who tried unsuccessfully to mobilize members of the Portuguese nobility to join them in quashing the rebellion (better occupied there than in fomenting their own revolution behind his back). Richelieu's agents in Lisbon had already offered French military support should they be planning an uprising. The perfect opportunity now presented itself and the obvious leader of such a rebellion was João, the seventh Duke of Braganza, son of the female claimant of 1580. However reluctant at first, he was persuaded by an influential group of nobles. Spanish naval losses at the battle of the Downs in October 1639 and at Pernambuco in the following month discouraged the use of Spain's naval arm against Lisbon, and her armies were pinned down by the Catalans. The conspirators had to commit themselves when Olivares attempted to lure them out of Portugal, and they decided to act on the morning of 1 December 1640. Converging on the royal palace at Lisbon, they overpowered the guards, assassinated Vasconcelos and compelled the Duchess of Mantua to guarantee the non-interference of the Castilian garrison. The *coup* went to plan; Braganza left his seat at Vila Viçosa for Lisbon and on 6 December was proclaimed king as Dom João IV amidst enthusiastic crowds. The news travelled rapidly throughout the country, and before long to Brazil, Angola and other former possessions. With one exception – Ceuta – the nation declared unreservedly its independence from Spain after sixty years' servitude.

João IV   (1640–56)

On 11 December 1640 a Council of War was set up, by which able-bodied men were recruited to defend the frontier against likely Spanish retaliation (the residual garrisons imposed soon surrendered) and governors were appointed in each province. The *cortes* were convoked to raise money by a property tax, and introduced several laws buttressing Portugal's reiterated intention to remain independent of any Spanish domination. With few exceptions – among them the Archbishop of Braga, who was to regret his attitude and died in prison, and a small clique of intransigent nobles, who were executed – João IV had the country substantially behind him. By the end of the year Sir Arthur Hopton, the English envoy in Madrid, was reporting to London that 'Portugal may be said to be entirely revolted, and not to be recovered but by conquest, for which there is at this time no good disposition on this side, nor is there any general appearance of preparations'.

Early in 1641 Dom João sent embassies to England, France, Holland and Rome (*not* received by the pope, due to Spanish influence), to seek moral and material support, for certainly the Spanish would not surrender their claim to Portugal without a fight. Sweden, also approached, agreed to trade arms for sugar and spices, etc. Negotiations with France were complicated. Richelieu, devious as ever, while not wishing to commit himself, for that might affect a future peace with Spain, by a secret article in an informal treaty arranged to send troops and artillery under the Count-Duke Frederick Hermann of Schomberg. Schomberg set about reorganizing the Portuguese forces, largely untrained, which was to prove crucial during ensuing hostilities.

The Dutch refused to evacuate northern Brazil. They had annexed

Portuguese possessions in West Africa – and were not expelled from Angola until 1648 – but did agree to a temporary truce. They promised some military aid if the Protestant Dutch were allowed freedom of worship in Portugal – a similar liberty was demanded by England – and if Dutch ships alone would be freighted in Portugal. The Dutch West India Company continued to prey on Portuguese shipping, and after Holland had made peace with Spain in 1648, became an undeclared enemy of Portugal, taking Ceylon and besieging Goa.

The Portuguese mission to Charles I was more successful, but decisions were delayed owing to England – as most-favoured nation – insisting on receiving commercial privileges. In the following January a treaty was signed which renewed the Ancient Alliance, only to be suspended by the start of the English Civil War a few months later. Not unnaturally, Dom João sided with the Royalist party. In 1650, after Charles's execution, Prince Rupert's flotilla was amicably received at Lisbon, but the Portuguese would not agree to him making it a base of naval operations against Parliamentarian merchant shipping. Cromwell retaliated by sending out Blake and Popham's fleet, by which Prince Rupert was blockaded in the Tagus estuary for several months before escaping into the Mediterranean.

In 1654, Cromwell's *Commonwealth Treaty* or *Treaty of Westminster*, reviving that of 1642 – which some Portuguese historians suggest was imposed on them in reprisal for having backed the wrong horse – not

Seventeenth-century view of the Royal Palace at Lisbon

only determined the 'privileges of an Englishman' in the Portuguese trade for almost two centuries, but raised several centuries-old concessions (which might well have been waived) to treaty rank. By this treaty, the already long-established British merchants trading and resident in Lisbon – Thomas Daniel had been importing cloth from Bristol as early as 1378 – set up what has been described as 'a kind of Chamber of Commerce-cum-Consulate', for which Thomas Maynard (Consul in 1656–89) was largely responsible. This later developed into a more formal corporative body of traders known as the *Feitoria Inglesa* or English Factory.

CATHERINE OF BRAGANZA   (1638–1705)

Any temporary frigidity between England and Portugal melted with the restoration of the Stuarts, to the extent that the former proposal by Dom João that Charles II should marry his daughter, Catherine 'of

Charles II and his queen on a Lambeth Delft charger (1669)

Braganza', was renewed in May 1660. It was confirmed in the June of the following year by a *Treaty of Alliance*, whereby in addition to a huge dowry, Charles would receive the gift of Tangier and later Bombay. The English bound themselves to defend Portugal (and her overseas territories) 'as if it were England itself' and guaranteed to supply seasoned troops. On 23 April 1662, Catherine, escorted by the Earl of Sandwich with an English fleet, set sail for England, where she remained for the next thirty years. How very different had been her father's estate at Vila Viçosa, where she had been 'bred hugely retired' and virtually uneducated, from the English Court, where only weeks later she was compelled to receive her husband's latest mistress, Lady Castlemaine. It was not until 1693, after several years of widowhood, that she returned to Lisbon. She died at her newly built palace of Bemposta in 1705, having in her last few months acted as regent for her brother, Pedro II.

FIGHTING ON THE FRONTIER

In 1641, Dom João secured the Alentejo frontier against attack and repulsed an enemy advance on Olivença. The frontier held. In May 1644 he defeated the Spanish at Montijo and Elvas was successfully defended. Another invasion was stemmed at Arronches in 1653.

Dom João died in 1656, and for the next six years the queen, Luísa de Guzmão, acted as regent for her son, Afonso VI. She adopted a more belligerent policy towards Spain, partly to show France that Portugal was an ally worth supporting, but she was unable to dissuade France from making a separate peace with Spain. In 1659, taking advantage of the termination of hostilities with France brought about by the *Treaty of the Pyrenees*, the Spaniards turned again on their neighbour. In 1662 they took Borba, among other towns near the Alentejan frontier, and in May 1663 they occupied Evora. This galvanized opposition and Evora was recovered in the following month by the Conde de Vila Flor and Schomberg at the battle of Ameixial, in which English troops under Colonel Thomas Hood distinguished themselves. It is said that on hearing of their gallantry, Dom Afonso sent a present of snuff to each company, which they threw away in disgust; Charles II ordered 4,000 crowns to be distributed among them.

In June 1665 the Spaniards, intending to capture the Braganza seat at Vila Viçosa, were decisively defeated at Montes Claros by Schomberg. Colonel Sheldon, commander of the English contingent, which had a principal share in this final battle of the war, was killed. Schomberg, who received the title of Count of Mértola for his part in this victory, had a long and varied military career, which ended with his death when commanding William of Orange's troops at the Battle of the Boyne, and he was buried in St Patrick's Cathedral, Dublin.

Philip IV of Spain died in September 1665, leaving Spain and her possessions in the hands of his feeble-minded son, Carlos II. On 13 February 1668 Philip's widow, the regent Mariana of Austria, formally recognized the independence of Portugal.

Afonso VI   (1656–83)

A complex domestic crisis in Portugal had developed during the war with Spain. By July 1661 the ambitious third Count of Castelo Melhor had coaxed Afonso – a vicious and obstreperous teenager – into terminating his mother's regency and appointing him his 'secret secretary', a position of power which he was to hold for the next five years. The queen retired to a convent, dying in February 1666. As part of a French attempt to keep Portugal within her orbit of policy – for they saw Mazarin's *Treaty of the Pyrenees* to be merely a pause in their struggle against the Spanish Habsburgs – it was proposed that both Dom Afonso and Pedro, his younger brother, should marry French princesses. Although Pedro, resenting Castelo Melhor's influence, refused the offer, Afonso found himself betrothed to Marie-Françoise-Isabelle (or Maria-Francisca), daughter of the Duc de Savoye and known as Mademoiselle d'Aumale, who reached Lisbon in August 1666. Soon afterwards, Sir Robert Southwell was to disclose that the queen's 'total disappointment in her bed' was the consequence of 'an accident, which befel the King in his childhood, of being blasted, and ever since paralytical on his whole right side, [which] did not only crack and shatter his understanding, but made him impotent as to the use of a virgin at least'. Disillusioned, but strong-minded, the queen soon came to an understanding with the virile young Pedro, round whom the nobility rallied, for rumours were rife. In the absence of a son, which would again put Portuguese independence at risk, Pedro would inherit the crown. In September 1667 the queen intimidated her mentally retarded husband into dismissing Castelo Melhor, who fled to England. In November she took refuge in the Esperança convent in Lisbon, insisting that the cathedral chapter annul, even if belatedly, the marriage on the grounds of non-consummation. Meanwhile she had written to Afonso to express her regret, requesting the refund of her dowry and permission to return to France. Afonso had little alternative but to acquiesce, having sworn that he had done his best to satisfy her; but due to their rank, no physical examination of either spouse was made, as required normally by canon law, although enough indelicate evidence was assembled to convince the chapter of his manifest incapacity. Afonso was compelled to relinquish the kingdom to his brother in exchange for a pension. In the event, he was then shipped off to the Azores in 1669, remaining there under duress until 1674, before being brought back to Portugal and mewed up in the royal palace at Sintra, where the *azulejo* floor of his chamber is said to have been worn away by his incessant pacing. There he died in 1683.

Pedro II *(1683–1706)*

In January 1668 the *cortes* declared Dom Pedro heir to the throne and he assumed the title of prince-regent. As soon as appropriate dispensation had been received, Pedro and Maria-Francisca were duly married and a daughter (Isabel-Josefa) was born to them in the following January, which assured the succession. Pedro was no great improvement on his brother in other respects. Although alcohol was anathema to him, and anyone suspected of drinking wine was banished from Court, he was to pay dearly for his other excesses. Having contracted a venereal infection as early as 1670, his palate was so damaged towards the end of his life that he required an interpreter when speaking to strangers, and even those with whom he was on familiar terms found it difficult to understand him. Although Pedro became king in 1683, his wife died only three months later. When he remarried in 1687 it was to Maria-Sophia-Isabel of Neuberg, daughter of the

Elector-Palatine, and she gave birth to the future João V in October 1689. The *cortes* had been assembled in 1697, merely to recognize the heir to the throne; it was the first meeting since 1679 and it was the last. The age of absolutism had begun.

Pedro had little to fear from Carlos II, his pathetic contemporary, the most physically and mentally degenerate victim of Spanish Habsburg inbreeding, which earned him the epithet of '*El Hechizado*', the bewitched. Like Dom Afonso, he was incapable of producing a child.

Mercantilist Policies

From 1675 the third Count of Ericeira, as superintendent of finance, promoted the revival of wool and silk production within Portugal and restricted imports; and his mercantilist policies did much to improve the country's prosperity. Maize replaced rye as the staple in the northern provinces, while the areas covered by port wine vineyards extended in the Alto Douro. In 1677 the British consul in Lisbon reported that men and women were being lured from Colchester to Covilhã by the Portuguese ambassador in order 'to teach the people to card and spin in the English way'. They then started to smuggle in their looms, which much concerned the consul, who envisaged that the export of cloth to Portugal would soon be ruined unless they were recalled. More mulberry trees were planted to stimulate the breeding of silk-worms, and glass manufactories – which in the following century flourished at Marinha Grande under the aegis of William Stephens – were established. In 1704 (by which time Ericeira's protectionist policy had been abandoned) Colonel John Richards noted that the new industries had declined, but this was partly due to the Inquisition's interference with the New Christian entrepreneurs and artisans. All the same, by the early nineteenth century some 150 looms were still in operation, manufacturing brown woollen cloth. In 1680 the firm of Quarles Harris was founded in Oporto, and in the same year Sir Robert Southwell, writing from Lisbon, was promising to send Lord Arlington in London some 'white Oporto wine'. Several Englishmen had settled in the area, among them Peter Bearsley, one of the first wine shippers to make Oporto his base. Expatriates still had their problems in relation to the

Passing barrels over the Douro rapids

Catholic Church, although generally they kept what would now be termed a 'low profile'. Thus, only one Anglican chaplain was allowed – the ambassador in Lisbon. Any Protestant unfortunate enough to die in Oporto had to be buried secretly in a common grave on the river bank at low tide; no service was allowed and no records might be kept, at least officially.

Ericeira committed suicide in 1690, after which the economy languished; but in 1699 the first shipment of gold from the rich alluvial deposits of Minas Gerais arrived in Lisbon and deliveries increased dramatically during the following two decades. Then in 1730 the Brazilian diamond mines were also discovered.

THE METHUEN TREATIES

In May 1703 another Anglo-Portuguese treaty was signed by Sir Paul Methuen, by which Portugal entered the Grand Alliance (see below), followed that December by the more famous *Methuen Treaty*, negotiated by his father, John Methuen. By this treaty, not revoked until 1842, England was to admit Portuguese wines on preferential terms, which stimulated the port wine trade, while a variety of English goods, including textiles, were now allowed into Portugal. English merchants increasingly dominated the carrying trade between Portugal and the Portuguese colonies and Europe. The unforeseen boom in Anglo-Portuguese commerce was also due in part to the influx of gold from Brazil. Portugal's dependence on Britain became more significant, causing jealousy in certain quarters.

The War of the Spanish Succession, 1702–13

Carlos II of Spain, who died on 1 November 1700, had two sisters, one married to Louis XIV of France, the other to Leopold I, the Austrian Habsburg emperor, both of whom laid claim to the Spanish throne. After a deal of indecision, under pressure from France, Carlos had finally agreed that Philip, Duc d'Anjou, Louis's grandson, would be his successor. This was unacceptable to Leopold, who declared war. Although at first England recognized Philip V's claim, the preponderance of Bourbon powers in Spain and Italy as well as in France caused her to have second thoughts, and together with Holland and the Austrians, a 'Grand Alliance' was formed in October 1701 with the intention of forcing the French from Italy and the Spanish Netherlands and placing the Archduke Charles of Austria, one of Leopold's sons, on the Spanish throne. Louis reacted by recognizing James Stuart as the English king.

In May 1702 war was declared on Louis by the Grand Alliance and negotiations were put in hand to ensure that Portugal adhered to the cause. England was already committed to defending Portuguese frontiers should Spain, in league with France, have devious designs on her, and the maritime powers would protect her shipping. It was impossible to remain neutral, so Portugal threw in her lot with the Grand Alliance, which assured her security, and this was confirmed by Sir Paul Methuen's treaty of May 1703. In exchange for allowing Portugal to be a base from which Spain could be invaded and the

Bourbons expelled, she was promised territorial concessions by the archduke. Portugal would supply a contingent of troops, some paid by Dom Pedro and some by the Allies. Portugal's relations with the court of Philip V were severed in December. The Habsburg pretender, now known as Charles III, landed in Lisbon in the Spring of 1704 and on 30 April Philip V's forces, commanded by the Duke of Berwick, took Castelo Branco, but were stopped by Allied units at Abrantes. Berwick then crossed the Tagus and captured Portalegre, but retired when the Marquês das Minas's troops advanced into Spain. On 24 July Gibraltar was captured by British troops. The combined Allied army was unable to take Ciudad Rodrigo. Not until 1705 did they enter Alcántara and Albuquerque, south of the Tagus, but they then failed to capture Badajoz. In June, Charles III transferred his activities to Catalonia, and it was not until the campaigning season of 1706 that Minas advanced on Salamanca and briefly occupied Madrid. On 1 December Dom Pedro II died. Apart from another campaign led by the Earl of Galway in 1709, which was again unsuccessful against Badajoz, Portugal took little further part in the war, which continued to drag on. Leopold died in April 1711 and Charles succeeded to the imperial throne. An armistice was agreed in November 1712, the *Treaty of Utrecht* was signed in the following year, and peace between Portugal and Spain was concluded belatedly in 1715.

CHAPTER NINE

The Eighteenth Century: João V and the domination of Pombal

João V, 'the Magnificent' (1706–50)

Dom João succeeded, aged seventeen, and in 1708 he married Maria-Ana of Austria, a sister of Karl VI, the former pretender to the Spanish throne. With peace in 1715, the country's rapidly increasing wealth was consumed in warfare no longer. It was during João V's long reign that Lisbon in particular achieved its greatest material magnificence,

Lunching outdoors

with the discovery, exploitation and influx of Brazilian gold and diamonds, although few would dispute that too much of this wealth was lavished on the meretricious embellishment of the city's numerous churches. This had the desired side-effect of the capital being endowed with the dignity of a patriarchate within a decade of Dom João's accession. Having sent a fleet which contributed largely to the Papal victory over the Turks at Matapan in 1717, Dom João presumed he would be allowed more control over ecclesiastical affairs in his kingdom, insisting that all bishops of Lisbon became cardinal-patriarchs. As this was refused, there was a twenty-year breach with Rome which lasted until 1748, when the Pope complied with Dom João's wishes and conferred the title 'Most Faithful King' on him.

JOÃO'S EXTRAVAGANCE

Dom João had put in hand a number of architectural projects, regardless of expense, among them the colossal convent of Mafra. Various estimates have been made as to its eventual cost, but it certainly was enough to hasten the financial ruin of the country. Among buildings of this period was the church of Bom Jesus near Braga, with its monumental flight of steps embellished by Baroque statuary and fountains, a grandiose folly designed by the bishop, which was praised by Alexander Jardine, author of *Letters from Barbary* (1788). More often than not critical of the extravagance of the Catholic Church, Jardine remarked that 'Where despotism has left no other power but the church that is capable of great works, the public are obliged to her when she chuses to employ a numerous poor, though in useless labour: and still more, when she employs them in works of taste.' The conceit proved infectious, for within a few years several similar staircases or *escadórios* were being constructed, among them at Lamego and, on a smaller scale, at Tibães. However, despite such monumental profligacy, in 1721 Portuguese cardinals were still in a position to convey two crates of gold bars and an immense amount of gold and silver plate with them when attending a conclave in Rome. Little thought was given to other than the souls of the lower orders; nothing was done to alleviate their poverty. Nor had the Church any intention of relinquishing its influence over the sovereign, who, while excessively pious and prodigal in his donations to the Church, showed his submission to its authority in several bizarre ways. The decisions of the Church were not seriously challenged, even as late as 1739, when the dramatist António da Silva, born of Portuguese Jewish parents in Rio de Janeiro, met his end in an *auto-da-fé* in Lisbon.

DOM JOÃO'S PROPENSITIES

Among other enthusiasms, Dom João was passionately addicted to music, church music in particular. For several years after 1721 Domenico Scarlatti attended the Court as music master to the Infanta Maria Bárbara, later to marry Fernando, the heir to the Spanish throne. It is very likely that among Scarlatti's pupils was Madre Paula Teresa da Silva, an excellent musician who, from 1718, although an inmate of a convent, had been also a royal mistress. Indeed the fashionable convent of Odivelas, not far north of the capital, was long an irregular haunt of Dom João's. Among the result of the peculiar penchant of this philo-progenitive sovereign – commonly known as the *freiratico* or nun-lover – were Dom António, born in 1714 to a French nun; Dom Gaspar, a future archbishop of Braga, born two years later to Magdalena Máxima de Miranda; and Dom José, Madre Paula's son, born in 1720, who ended his days as Inquisitor-General. Voltaire could not resist commenting on Dom João's foibles, but only a few decades later General Dumouriez remarked that he had been conforming to a common practice, and that most nuns, 'Throwing aside their professional habits, covered with rouge, with patches, and diamonds' were 'little more than cloistered prostitutes' who 'excited and practised the most refined gallantry, and passed for the most attractive favourites of the Portuguese nobility'.

As a munificent patron of culture, in 1720 Dom João founded the Royal Academy of History and erected the University Library at Coimbra (completed 1728), where his riches and magnificence were reflected in its richly gilt *talha* and 'chinoiserie' japanning. But in whatever other ways he might improvidently indulge himself, he was no bibliophile, and it was built simply in rivalry with his brother-in-law Karl VI's sumptuous Hofbibliothek in Vienna, completed two years earlier. In 1747 work commenced on the princely palace at Queluz,

north-west of the capital. On a smaller scale was the 'palace' raised at
Vendas Novas in 1729 merely to accommodate the bridal cortège of
the fourteen-year-old daughter of Philip V of Spain and Elizabeth
Farnese, Mariana Victoria, who was to marry his indolent son, Dom
José. More practical projects were the Aqueduct 'of Free Waters' in
Lisbon, completed in 1744, numerous street fountains, and hospitals.

CHANGES IN ADMINISTRATION

In spite of the above-mentioned pursuits, the king, who has been
described as 'not the most active' of monarchs, in 1738 set about
reorganizing his government by relegating most authority to secretaries
of state, who were then responsible to him. Decision-making by
Councils, in which the nobility were more able to exert their influence,
was circumvented. One of these secretaries was Azevedo Coutinho, a
former ambassador to both France and London, who in 1739 sent his
cousin Sebastião José de Carvalho e Melo – better known to history
after 1770 under the title of Marquês de Pombal – to replace him in
London, where he remained until 1744. In the following year he went
to Vienna, where he married the daughter of Marshal Daun, which
connection, on his return to Lisbon, gave him access to the queen-
mother, to whom he became increasingly indispensable. He was soon
to become the most influential of the *estrangeirados* or foreignized ones,
those enlightened members of Portuguese society who preferred exile,
some as diplomats, to remaining in a country insulated from much of
Europe by religious prejudice, with the Jesuits stifling educational
reform.

STAGNATION

Owing to innate lethargy and complacency and, after 1742, to illness,
which caused Dom João to pay frequent visits to the baths at Caldas,
affairs of state were neglected and stagnation set in. There was no plan
in evidence by which nascent industries might develop, nor systems put
in hand which might improve the quality of their management.
Without stimulus, manufactures declined and exports fell. The Portuguese share of the import of wines (including port) to England
increased from 40 to 70 per cent between the beginning of the century

and the early 1750s, and British exports to Portugal increased progressively. By this trade, Portuguese merchants profited, but not Portuguese manufacturers.

THE BRITISH FACTORY

In Lisbon, the British Factory flourished, although James O'Hara, second Baron Tyrawly, the irascible and flamboyant envoy from 1728 to 1741, referred to its members as 'a bigoted mob' and a parcel of the greatest jackasses he had ever met with, who 'attended more to their Quintas, Balls, Masquerades & Gaming than to their business', of which they were 'prodigiously ignorant'. Nevertheless, they were 'every day improving their fortunes and enlarging their dealings'. One of his non-diplomatic duties was to report to the Duke of Newcastle on the rare plants which were becoming known in Portugal, and which might be cultivated in King George II's own kitchen garden. In a dispatch of June 1733 he wrote that he did not have any other vegetables worth sending 'except tomatoes, which are a large round fruit, as big as a small orange (of which I believe you have none in England)'. Although at first critical of Dom João, Tyrawly had come to admire him, perhaps because they had susceptibilities in common. In recognition of his plenipotentiary services, the king presented Tyrawly on his departure for England with fourteen bars of gold – coincidentally the same number as the illegitimate children who embarked with him – together with three 'wives', one Portuguese: little wonder that Horace Walpole considered him 'singularly licentious, even for the courts of Russia and Portugal'. Sir Benjamin Keene, the urbane envoy from 1746 to 1749, seems to have rather enjoyed the company of what he called the 'jolly free factory', but then he was more convivial – and more chaste – than his predecessor.

Pombal in Office

After an illness during which Maria-Ana acted as regent, Dom João died on 31 July 1750. Three days later, the future Marquês of Pombal (1699–1782) took office as minister, and it was not long before Dom José left the day-to-day administration of government largely in his hands. The ineffectual thirty-six-year-old king had never shown any interest in such matters; with Mariana Victoria, he preferred the chase, playing cards or attending the opera. Pombal's urgent preoccupation was to bring some semblance of order into the machinery of government, to extract the maximum revenues from Brazil, to combat contraband trade and to prohibit the export of bullion. He created a company to supervise the export of wine in 1750, causing friction with the British shippers, and founded mercantile associations to trade with Portuguese colonies in Asia and elsewhere. Pombal was not opposed to the activities of English merchants, but having seen for himself the advantages and progress of capitalism when in London, he intended that Portugal should attain a similar prosperity, and he would put into effect any improvement by which this might be advanced.

At about this time Lisbon was getting a reputation in England for its fine climate, but few of the valetudinarians hoping for a fresh lease of life were long to survive. Among them was Henry Fielding, the ailing author of *Tom Jones*, who disembarked there in August 1754, but left his *Journal of a Voyage to Lisbon* uncompleted. Any description of the city he might have written would have been soon unrecognizable, for fifteen months later the capital was shaken to its foundations by an unprecedented earthquake.

THE LISBON EARTHQUAKE

On the morning of 1 November 1755 Lisbon was convulsed by an earthquake – the worst ever recorded in Europe – in which a large part of the capital collapsed, followed by a ravaging fire and a tidal wave which submerged the quays and overwhelmed the shipping. Perhaps as many as 30–40,000 people died in the calamity and in the following epidemics and famine. Joseph Baretti, in describing the devastated parts almost five years later, which left 'a dreadful indelible image' on his mind, stated that nothing was to be seen 'but vast heaps of rubbish, out of which arise in numberless places the miserable remains of shattered walls and broken pillars'.

The catastrophic state in which the citizens found themselves was alleviated by the presence of mind of Pombal, who ordered several vigorous measures to be undertaken without delay. Dom José and his

Court would remain under canvas in their palace garden: there would be no further talk of decamping to Rio de Janeiro, as had been mooted, which would have had a disastrous effect on morale. The tottering ruins of houses left standing in the lower town were razed and military patrols were posted in an attempt to prevent looting, but not much was saved from the wreckage and losses were incalculable. G.C. Bibiena's opera-house was destroyed only seven months after its inauguration and churches without number were consumed, among them that of the Carmelites (founded by Nun'Alvares Pereira), the ruins of which were left as a memorial. Fine libraries, including an invaluable collection of music assembled by Dom João IV, the royal archives, including ships' logs and other records of Portugal's extensive navigations and 'discoveries', many of them still secret, had been consumed in the conflagration, as had irreplaceable works of art. Wardrobes were scattered; indeed, many people survived in a state of *déshabillé*, having not yet dressed for Mass on that All Saint's Day. Immediately on hearing of the disaster, the British Parliament voted £100,000 as an earnest of their solicitude and sent out quantities of food, supplies and equipment, including pick-axes, crow-bars and spades. Apart from the capital, near the epicentre of the earthquake, other towns were severely damaged, Lagos among them, but Oporto survived physically unscathed.

The cataclysm served as a text in Voltaire's *Poème sur le désastre de Lisbonne*, the pessimism of which provoked a letter of protest from Rousseau; it was also to suggest an episode in Voltaire's *Candide*.

Pombal in Power

Pombal's draconian measures were resisted by some members of the nobility, who felt threatened, and also by the Jesuits, but inexorably he consolidated his control of every aspect of government. At the same time he set about the reconstruction of Lisbon, partly on a rectilineal plan, imposing an unadorned design to façades, in which even the heights of churches were limited to that of adjacent structures. Pombaline architecture is well exemplified in buildings flanking the water-lapped Terreiro do Paço (known as 'Black Horse Square', from the equestrian statue of Dom José). Its name was then changed to the Praça

The Marquês de Pombal in 1766, after Louis Michael van Loo

do Comércio, for commerce, in the dictator's view, was essential to the well-being of the nation and trade was a noble activity. Pombal's achievements — 'that great man, known as such to the middle and thinking classes of his nation', in the words of Jacome Ratton, a Lisbon businessman of French descent, writing some decades later — were greater than his faults. Any opposition to his energetic policies was ruthlessly suppressed, as with the so-called 'Tipplers' Revolt' against the rising price of wine in Oporto in February 1757, for which Pombal's General Company was blamed. In the September of the following year an attempted assassination of Dom José served as a pretext to execute members of the Távora and Aveiro families, further intimidating the nobility. The Jesuits were also accused of complicity, and a year later a royal edict was published by which they were expelled from Portugal and then from Brazil and her other overseas territories, and their immense wealth was confiscated. Several of the Jesuits languished in jails until 1777, as did numerous political prisoners, victims of Pombal's regime. Many others were banished.

But Pombal's progressive reforms proliferated in many fields. In 1761 slavery was abolished in mainland Portugal. Further secularization of the State took place, and any distinction between Old and New Christians was abolished. A College of Nobles was founded in 1761 to improve the education of the aristocracy, and both primary and secondary schools were established throughout the country. In the following decade, Pombal turned his attention to cleansing the Augean Stables of the University of Coimbra, rooting out residual Jesuitical influence and inaugurating faculties of natural sciences and mathematics. At the same time he attempted to control intellectual curiosity by setting up a royal rather than an ecclesiastical Censorship Board, by which certain works by such authors as Hobbes, Voltaire and Rousseau remained prohibited. Under the erudite Frei Manuel de Cenáculo Vilas Boas, who was president of the board and confessor and tutor to Dom José, the king's grandson, literature was promoted which was believed useful to the state, so the Censorship Board proved comparatively creative.

The military establishment was radically reformed in the early 1760s, largely through the efforts of Count Wilhelm von Schaumburg-Lippe, who recruited a number of British officers to assist him in the task. This had become essential after Portugal had been drawn into the Seven Years' War, lest it be invaded again. In 1759 Boscawen had defeated a French fleet off the Portuguese coast. France then demanded satisfaction from Portugal. Pombal had appealed to England. By 1761 Spain was obliged to declare war on England by a secret article in the renewed Bourbon Family Compact, and in April 1762 Spanish troops entered the Trás-os-Montes, later occupying Braganza and Chaves, and then Castelo Branco. Eight thousand troops were dispatched from England to hold the frontier, at first commanded by Tyrawly, who was then superseded by Schaumburg-Lippe, the Earl of Loudoun and General Burgoyne. Hospitals were set up at Lisbon, Coimbra and Santarém, under the superintendence of John Hunter, who was later to become a famous surgeon. By November a truce had been declared and peace was made in the following February, after which the military establishment was neglected.

Dona Maria and the Viradeira *or volte-face*

By late in 1776 Dom José became ill, and his wife Mariana Victoria became regent. Pombal had sought to introduce a Salic succession, whereby Dona Maria, their daughter (who since 1760 had been married to her uncle, who as her consort was known as Pedro III) would be excluded in favour of her son and heir, José. (Carlos III of Spain had proposed that Maria should marry his son Luis; it was to avoid this that she had been married off to her uncle.) Dom José, before becoming incapacitated shortly before his death, had expressed the wish that the Infante, an admirer of Joseph II of Austria, was found a wife without delay, and so he was married to Maria Benedita, his aunt, also a supporter of Pombal. Unfortunately, this 'advanced' couple never reigned, for in 1788 young José died of smallpox, as his mother had not permitted him to receive the recently discovered inoculation.

Dom José died on 24 February 1777. Next morning Pombal was curtly informed that he was dismissed, and soon after he was banished to his estate at the town of Pombal. There he died in May 1782, bed-ridden but retaining his clear and vigorous mind, defying his perse-cutors by arguing that he had done no more than carry out his sovereign's wishes.

Dona Maria, although she released some political prisoners, did not entirely dismantle the machinery of government set up under her father's auspices. The redoubtable intendant of police, Pina Manrique, remained in office, although some of Pombal's legislation as far as the ecclesiastical establishment was concerned was repealed. The queen promised to re-open the cases against those surviving from the Távora affair and decreed the restitution of their properties. Being excessively devout, pangs of conscience tormented her. The monopolistic companies and many of the manufactures Pombal had established were 'privatized'. The treasury, poorly administered by the Marquês d'Angeja, was soon in a parlous state, for which Pombal – naturally – was blamed. In an attempt to balance the budget, mass dismissals of workers were made and public works suspended, creating unemployment, while futile savings were made by selling off some royal coaches and emptying the royal stables (though a magnificent collection of gilded coaches still may be seen). At the same time a fortune was spent on the erection of the Basilica da Estrela in fulfilment of a vow made by Dona Maria to celebrate the birth of an heir to the throne, and it was here that she was later buried. It was not long before the epigram '*mal por mal, antes Pombal*' (evil for evil, better under Pombal) entered the language. However, there was progress in certain fields: an Academy of Sciences and a Royal Orphanage were founded in Lisbon, where street lighting was put in hand. After some delay, construction of a highway between the capital, Coimbra and Oporto was recommenced, but it was not until 1798 that a regular coach service on it was inaugurated.

In 1785 João, Dona Maria's second son, married Carlota-Joaquina of Spain. His father died in 1786, and José, heir to the throne, in 1788, both losses contributing to depress Dona Maria, whose mind became progressively unbalanced by the startling rumours reaching Lisbon from Paris during 1789. By 1791 she was subject to profound melancholy. In spite of the ministrations of Dr Francis Willis, summoned from London after treating George III, her mental condition continued to deteriorate, and by the following year she was incurably insane, although she did not die until 1816. Dom João – later João VI – governed in her name, but did not assume the title of prince-regent until 1799.

Lisbon received a number of visitors from Britain, among the better known names being Nathaniel Wraxall; William Julius Mickle, the translator of Camões's *The Lusiad* in 1776; William Hickey, the diarist; William Beckford, England's 'Wealthiest Son'; Lord and Lady Holland; Mary Wollstonecraft; young Robert Southey; John Adamson and Viscount Strangford, both admirers of Camões; while Francesco Bartolozzi was director of the National Academy from 1802 until his death. At this period too, among prominent Portuguese in cultural fields were the architects Nicolau Nasoni and Eugénio dos Santos (who replanned Lisbon after the Great Earthquake); the artists 'Vieira Lusitano', 'Vieira Portuense', Morgado de Setúbal and Domingos António Sequeira; the composers Marcos Portugal (who followed the Court to Rio in 1811) and later João Bomtempo, and the opera-singer Luisa Todi; not forgetting the poet Bocage (a 'pale, limber, odd-looking young man', whose compositions apparently 'thrilled and agitated' Beckford in 1787).

CHAPTER TEN

The Peninsular and Miguelite Wars

Resistance to French Republican Aggression

After the outbreak of the French Revolution in 1789, Portugal aligned herself with England and Spain, but maintained neutrality, to avoid invasion should France overwhelm Spain or threaten Brazil. It was not until 1793 that she signed separate treaties with her allies, and sent troops to cooperate with the Spanish fighting the French in Roussillon. Spain then sued for peace in July 1795 without advising Portugal, for which Manuel Godoy, by then virtually running Spain on behalf of Carlos IV and María-Luisa, received the hollow title of 'Príncipe de la Paz'.

Left in the lurch, and relying on Britain to protect her Brazilian trade, Portugal was able to remain in a delicately balanced diplomatic state while collaborating with England; in 1798 she sent a squadron to join Nelson's fleet in Aboukir Bay, only to find the battle of the Nile over and the French already defeated. Her ships turned back to blockade Malta, which the French had recently seized. In the previous year, warned of its presence by a Portuguese frigate, Sir John Jervis had sailed from the Tagus to decimate a Spanish fleet off Cape St Vincent (14 February 1797).

In 1801 France signed a treaty with Spain in which it was stipulated that they would force Portugal to open her ports to French and Spanish ships and close them to the English. Portugal refused, and in that May Spanish forces, led by Godoy, crossed into the Alentejo and occupied Olivenza and Juromenha in a walkover derisively known as 'the War of the Oranges'. Under pressure, Portugal agreed ostensibly to the

Franco-Spanish demands. (Despite provision in the 1814 *Treaty of Paris* for Olivenza's return to Portugal, this was never implemented.) There was then a lull in hostilities, due to the short-lived *Peace of Amiens* (1802). Britain occupied both Madeira and Goa, to protect them from likely future French attack.

TRAFALGAR

It was essential for Napoleon, still intent on knocking England out of the ring, to have Spanish naval resources for his projected invasion. In April 1805 General Junot visited the capital in a fruitless attempt to persuade the Portuguese to declare war on Britain. Only six months later, on 21 October, a Franco-Spanish fleet was virtually destroyed by Nelson off Cape Trafalgar, an event celebrated in the Tagus estuary by British ships there firing their guns all night. Basing themselves on Portuguese ports, English ships now blockaded the mouth of the Mediterranean, while Portuguese vessels protected English shipping under the guise of defending the Algarve coast from Algerian corsairs. The country could hardly stretch its neutrality any further.

On 21 November 1806 France decreed the British Isles to be 'in a state of blockade', prohibited all shipping from trading there, and threatened to intercept all shipping sailing from British colonies. The British retorted by proclaiming a 'Continental Blockade', but to impose this it was as vital for her to control Portuguese ports as it was for France if she intended to isolate the British Isles. In July 1807 France notified Portugal that if she did not support France in the conflict, now taking on more the aspect of an economic war, she would be occupied by a Spanish army; meanwhile, Portuguese shipping in French-occupied ports would be confiscated.

JUNOT'S INVASION

In mid-October 1807, before the *Treaty of Fontainebleau* had been signed by Napoleon and Carlos IV, agreeing to the partition of Portugal (the north would go to the displaced King of Etruria, the south to Godoy, and the rest to France), French troops, commanded by Junot, were already marching south-west from Bayonne towards the Portuguese frontier. Britain was unable to offer any immediate military support, but it had been agreed that the prince-regent, with the royal family, Court and government, would embark for Brazil forthwith, taking all the seaworthy vessels at hand, and escorted by Sir Sidney Smith's fleet, which had entered the Tagus on 17 November. On the 29th, with perhaps as many as 15,000 retainers, functionaries and their families, and other attendants, with their baggage, half the cash in circulation, archives, and a vast amount of treasure, the Court set sail on what was to be a long exile; it was not until 1821 that Dom João VI (king since 1816) returned to Portugal. Among the party was Strangford, the British Minister. When the famished and exhausted vanguard of Junot's army tramped into Lisbon on 30 November, it is said that the rearmost sails of the fleet could still be discerned on the horizon. Junot had lost a high proportion of his 25,000 men during his protracted advance down the Tagus valley – as ordered by Napoleon. He did not realize that although apparently a shorter route, for half its length it ran through a series of rocky defiles in an almost unpeopled wilderness providing scant sustenance for either his men or their mounts. It was ten days before Junot's rearguard entered the unresisting capital – for the Portuguese then had no army to speak of – having suffered severe privations *en route*.

By Christmas, the occupying army numbered some 10,000 men, later reinforced. In February 1808 Junot declared that the House of Braganza had ceased to reign, and that he, representing Napoleon's government, would draft a new Constitution. A Portuguese Legion under the Marquis of Alorna was raised to serve with the French: this would keep them out of Portugal. In April, Napoleon had decoyed Godoy and the Spanish Bourbons to Bayonne and dispossessed them of the Spanish crown, which he conferred on his brother Joseph Bonaparte. On hearing of this treacherous manoeuvre, on 2 May the citizens of Madrid rose in revolt against Murat's occupying force – as vividly depicted by Goya – but ever since the Tagus estuary had been blockaded by a squadron under Sir Charles Cotton, there had also been stirring against Junot's regime in Lisbon. Junot was obliged to send troops to assist Murat, for several other towns had risen against the invaders, who found it necessary to concentrate near the capital. By 6 June Oporto had proclaimed the prince-regent; *juntas* were formed, the disbanded militia was reassembled and a 'Lusitanian Legion' was mobilized under Sir Robert Wilson, together with any regular troops not under French control. Before long the whole country was in ferment – at Coimbra, the university laboratory was manufacturing bullets and powder – while envoys were sent to England to obtain urgent military support.

The Peninsular War

In July 1808 British transports were anchored off Vigo to await orders from General Sir Arthur Wellesley, who had sailed ahead to confer with Portuguese *junta* at Oporto under their patriotic bishop, the executive authority in unoccupied Portugal. Wellesley conferred also with Sir Charles Cotton, who was commanding naval forces off the coast, as to a suitable place to disembark his expeditionary force, and Mondego Bay, west of Coimbra, was decided on. Here, during the first week of August, an army 14,000 strong, later joined by a few Portuguese units, assembled and marched towards Lisbon. On 17 August they confronted the enemy at Roliça, a village just south of Obidos. It was the first action in what came to be known as the Peninsular War, for it was in the Iberian Peninsula that virtually all the fighting on land between the British and French took place during the Napoleonic era.

VIMEIRO

To avoid outflanking movements, the French pulled back from Roliça to regroup with Junot's main army, while Wellesley approached Vimeiro, nearer the estuary of the Maceira river, where he was expecting reinforcements. Here, on 21 August the enemy launched several impetuous attacks in columns on the British lines, only to be defeated. They would have been routed had not Wellesley been superseded by two senior but pusillanimous generals, who then agreed to an armistice, the so-called *Convention of Cintra* (30 August). By a humiliating clause in this, some 25,000 French troops, together with their booty, were repatriated in British transports. Wellesley (when back in London to face a parliamentary enquiry into the unpopular Convention) stated to Castlereagh: 'I do not consider myself

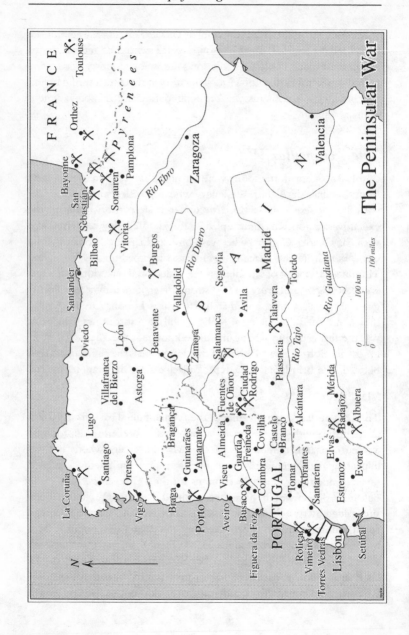

The Peninsular War

responsible in any degree for the terms in which it was framed, or for any of its provisions.' However, it did clear Portugal of French troops for several month.

In October Sir John Moore, now in command of the army, marched from Lisbon into Old Castile, having been promised Spanish cooperation, which was *not* evident. Moore little realized that Napoleon himself, after having entered Madrid, had made a forced march towards his troops, by then retiring on Benavente. Napoleon chose not to follow up his thrust, but returned to Paris, leaving Soult to see the British out of Spain. Moore's famished troops stumbled north-west via Astorga and up through snow drifts into the mountains and on to Lugo, reaching the coast at Corunna. Although fatally wounded in the ensuing battle, Moore's decision to retreat through Galicia enabled his army, although reduced in numbers, to turn on and maul Soult at Corunna (16 January 1809) before re-embarking for England in the 'Dunkirk' of its day. By late March Soult had turned south and occupied Oporto.

OPORTO LIBERATED

By 23 April Wellesley was again in command of the remaining British troops in Portugal, which together with reinforcements numbered about 10,000 effectives. On 12 May, having rapidly marched north from Lisbon, he wrested Oporto from Soult by his daring 'Passage of the Douro' and sent the French scurrying north-east back into Galicia, losing virtually all their equipment in a precipitate retreat. Any chance of their escaping east had been frustrated at Amarante by a body of troops under General Beresford's command and a Portuguese contingent under General Silveira.

TALAVERA

Wellesley now proceeded south to Abrantes and then turned east into Spain to cooperate with a Spanish army. Here, at Talavera, on 28 July he won a Pyrrhic victory against Marshal Victor. It was a 'murderous' battle – 'two days of the hardest fighting I have ever been a party to', in his words. It was after this action that he received the title of Viscount Wellington. Thoroughly disillusioned by the incapacity of this Spanish army, led by General Cuesta, who had promised but had not provided any provisions, Wellington was obliged to retire south-west into Portugal, where he set up a base hospital at Elvas. Here his men were further incapacitated by malaria, for past the walls of neighbouring Badajoz coiled the mosquito-infested Guadiana.

No serious confrontations took place during the following few months, during which General (later Marshal) Beresford, a rigid disciplinarian, was fully occupied training Portuguese troops which were then integrated into what became an Allied army. Meanwhile Wellington, who had taken note of the defensible area of hills across the neck of the wide peninsula north of Lisbon during the weeks after the battle of Vimeiro, set about the construction of a complex series of fortifications there, which would protect the capital, for inevitably the French would attempt to re-occupy that part of Portugal at some future date. These were later known as 'The Lines of Torres Vedras', for that was the main town standing immediately south of the seaward end of the twenty-five to thirty mile chain of redoubts, which were to stretch diagonally across to the Tagus itself.

BUSACO

It was not until the Summer of 1810 that Marshal Masséna marched his army west from Salamanca, and the fortress of Almeida fell to him fortuitously on 28 July. Meanwhile Wellington, having destroyed most roads north of the Tagus by which Masséna might approach the capital, awaited him behind the long ridge of Busaco, north-east of Coimbra. Here, on 27 September, the French were to suffer heavy casualties, for Masséna, undissuaded by the saner counsel of his subordinates, whom from previous experience were well aware of the risks in assaulting Wellington when in such a strong defensive position, insisted on sending his columns in an uphill frontal attack. Some 24,000 Portuguese, still largely untried recruits, had been distributed among the British divisions, and, in the words of Commissary Schaumann: 'They behaved just like the English troops, and, indeed, fought with such valour that the French believed them to be Englishmen disguised in Portuguese uniforms.' Portuguese troops were to remain an intrinsic and vital part of the Allied army for the rest of the long war.

THE LINES OF TORRES VEDRAS

Wellington had delayed Masséna long enough for his carefully prepared 'Lines' to be completed, behind which some 200,000 souls and
their livestock had been herded into what by now had become an
entrenched camp. This was part of his deliberate 'scorched earth'
policy. The French, who relied heavily on marauding, would be forced
to stray from their bivouacs in search of food and forage. In doing so,
they would be picked off by the militia, by individual peasants and
vengeful partisans, for the invaders had displayed the utmost cruelty
throughout their advance and during their previous occupation. In
Wellington's words: 'The people of Portugal are doing that which the
Spaniards ought to have done. They are removing their women and
properties out of the enemy's way, and taking arms in their own
defence. The country is made a desert, and behind almost every stone
wall the French will meet an enemy.' Masséna was dumbfounded at
seeing such a formidable barrier on approaching Lisbon for, expecting a
walkover, he had not brought any siege artillery with him, nor provisions. They 'will lose the greatest part of their army if they attack us.
They will starve if they stay much longer, and they will experience
great difficulty in their retreat,' was Wellington's evaluation, and he was
right. On 14 November Masséna retired to Santarém, where he dug in.
Wellington was astonished that the French were able to subsist there so
long, in fact until 5 March 1811. Then, on learning that the British
were expecting reinforcement, Masséna commenced his retreat, with
Wellington close on his heels. Several minor actions took place during
the following month, notably at Foz de Arouce and Sabugal. By 11
April Masséna was back in Spain, after an absence of almost ten months.
The campaign had cost him dear: his total casualties have been estimated at 25,000 men, of which only 2,000 had been killed in battle and
8,000 had been taken prisoner. The rest had met their death at the
hands of Portuguese irregulars, had deserted or had died of malnutrition
if not actual starvation. In addition, he had lost almost 6,000 mounts,
numerous guns and virtually all his wagon train. It has been said that if
the confrontation at the 'Lines' had been an actual 'battle', it would
have been celebrated as one of the most decisive ever fought as far as

British troops crossing the Tagus near Vila Velha de Ródão

comparative casualties were concerned, for the Allies had lost only a few hundred.

Having been successfully defended, Lisbon slowly reverted to a life of wartime normality, and those many thousands who had been accommodated somehow behind the 'Lines' throughout the winter now returned to their homes, too often to find them destroyed or derelict and their fields desolate. The capital continued to remain the main base of supply for the Allied army until late in the war, when ports on the Biscay coast took over.

FUENTES DE OÑORO

In an astonishingly short space of time Masséna managed to re-equip and reinforce the relic of his 'Army of Portugal', and in a desperate attempt to redeem his lost reputation he returned to fight the battle of Fuentes de Oñoro on the Portuguese frontier west of Ciudad Rodrigo (3–5 May). Failing to break through or outflank the Allied defensive line pivoted on this village, he retired, frustrated. It was to be Masséna's last battle, for Marmont replaced him soon afterwards.

The Portuguese side of the frontier in this area in particular remained the base both of Allied operations and of their winter cantonments for the next two years, with Wellington's village headquarters at Freineda. A frequent corridor for the movement of Allied troops behind the frontier were the roads which converged on the Tagus at Vila Velha de Ródão, notably during the sieges of the Spanish fortresses of Ciudad Rodrigo and Badajoz. The short winter days and long evenings were occupied in a variety of pursuits, from hunting to amateur theatricals. It is recorded that at Covilhã, when headquarters of Sir Stapleton Cotton's cavalry, 'barbarously brilliant' balls were held, the local females being passionately addicted to dancing.

FROM SALAMANCA AND VITORIA TO TOULOUSE

On 22 July 1812 Wellington inflicted a stunning defeat on Marmont's army at Salamanca and the Allies were able to enter Madrid briefly. But after Wellington's signal failure to take Burgos that October, and with other French units converging on them, the Allies retreated back to safe if not snug winter quarters west of the frontier. It was during these months that Wellington planned his great Spring offensive, which was to drive the French entirely from Portuguese soil. Some 60,000 men – 70 per cent of his army – were discreetly marched north into the Trás-os-Montes, while Wellington himself ostentatiously entered Salamanca with General Hill. Leaving Hill's few units to advance to the northeast, on 28 May Wellington rode fifty miles north-west across country, by dusk reaching the Douro at Miranda. Swung over the torrent in 'a kind of hammock', he rejoined his main force. This, traversing the Esla two days later, was in a position to outflank Joseph Bonaparte's and Marshal Jourdan's troops, by then intent on defending the line of the Duero. Continually out-manoeuvred during the next three weeks, the French were forced to retreat until they reached Vitoria, where on the 21 June they were to suffer perhaps their most crippling defeat of the war.

While the siege of San Sebastián, and the battles of the Pyrenees, Nivelle, Nive, St Pierre, Orthez and Toulouse, fought against the redoubtable Marshal Soult, are not immediately relevant to this history, one should not forget that Portuguese troops took an important part in them all. Naturally, a great deal of *camaraderie* developed between the Allies. Some weeks after peace had been proclaimed in April 1814,

The village house in Freineda occupied by Wellington during the winters of
1811–12 and 1812–13

several hundred Portuguese (and Spanish) 'soldiers' wives', unless formally married, were assembled to follow the long road home under
escort. They were followed later by the Portuguese troops, their mules
and muleteers. As one British soldier confessed: 'Many were the heavy
hearts in both armies on this occasion, for it is not easy to conceive how
the circumstances of passing through scenes of hardship, trial, and
danger together, endeared the soldiers of the two armies to each other.'

The war had laid waste large areas of Portugal, and it has been
estimated that over 100,000 Portuguese, a high proportion of them
civilians, lost their lives in the long struggle.

Constitutionalism

It was to take Portugal many years to recover from the ravages of war:
the ensuing peace treaties provided scant compensation and she
received a trifling amount in reparations from the French. The country
was deeply in debt; the maintenance of her large and now superfluous

army consumed much of her income; and the Anglo-Portuguese treaty of 1810, which allowed Britain to trade directly with Brazil at advantageous terms, had removed the mainstay of her economy. It has been said that in the immediate post-war years, notably after 1815, when Brazil was proclaimed a kingdom on equal terms, that Portugal was little more than her colony, and a protectorate of Britain. Indeed, the undisbanded military establishment remained under the command of Marshal Beresford, which caused resentment among senior officers.

Dom João VI and his Court remained at Rio until 1821, and the politicians in Lisbon had no government at hand to direct them. No wonder the intellectuals, well aware of the political changes taking place in Europe, preferred some form of Constitution. In March 1817 General Gomes Freire de Andrade, who at one time had commanded Napoleon's Portuguese Legion and was a Masonic Grand Master, led a Liberal conspiracy against the administration (in which there is evidence of collusion in government circles), which Beresford crushed with excessive severity. The general was shot for his involvement, together with a dozen of his accomplices, which hardly improved the marshal's waning popularity. Although Castelreagh urged Dom João – or at least young Pedro, his heir – to return to Lisbon and fulfil his regal duties, the advice was ignored. Meanwhile, unrest was apparent in Oporto, where in 1818 a lodge known as the Sinédrio was founded by Manuel Fernandes Tomás. Early in 1820 – while Beresford was visiting Rio – having gained support from military garrisons in the north, a provisional *junta* was set up in opposition to the Lisbon government. The Lisbon garrison joined in the liberalizing movement and a 'Constitutional *cortes*' was assembled there to draw up a democratic Constitution, by which the king would be placed in a subordinate position, dependent on his parliament. Naturally the conservative Catholic Church and the landowning nobility resisted such radical ideas. In March 1821, when the capital was illuminated to celebrate the passage of a draft Constitution, the papal Nuncio's windows were stoned and shattered for remaining unlit. The *cortes* were reassured on receiving a congratulatory message from Jeremy Bentham.

The Count (later Duke) of Palmela sailed to Rio to persuade Dom João, with his family and Court, to return home forthwith. They eventually reached Lisbon in July 1821, but Dom Pedro had been left in Brazil. (When Beresford arrived, he was refused permission to land and sailed on to England in a huff.) Although Dom João accepted the Constitution, Carlota-Joaquina, the queen, refused to do so, and was therefore confined to a palace at Ramalhão, near Sintra. From Ramalhão, the virago continued to spin a web of conspiracies with her equally reactionary brother, Don Carlos of Spain, and it was from there that the latter proclaimed against his niece Isabel II in 1833, precipitating the First Carlist War, largely fought out in the Basque provinces of Spain.

PEDRO IV

Dom Pedro chose to ignore the *cortes*'s order to return to Portugal and on 12 October 1822 he was proclaimed emperor of an independent Brazil, the loss of which Portugal was powerless to resist. In the following January the Count of Amarante pronounced against the Constitution, but although his rising in the north was subdued, four months later Dom Miguel, Pedro's brother, egged on by his mother, led another 'absolutist' revolt known as the 'Vilafrancada' – at Vila Franca de Xira, north of Lisbon – which received enough support for him to be able to suspend the Constitution. Dom João reacted to a design on Miguel's part to supplant him by exiling Miguel, who later settled in Vienna. Before he died on 10 March 1826, and in the absence of his sons, Dom João appointed a council of regency under his daughter Maria-Isabel, at the same time recognizing Dom Pedro as his successor. In spite of being head of what was now an independent state, Pedro, in accepting this and confirming his sister's regency, then announced that he would confer a constitutional Charter on Portugal similar to Brazil's. This was signed on 29 April and remained the country's fundamental constitutional text until the fall of the monarchy in 1910. Dom Pedro also confirmed his intention to abdicate in favour of his seven-year-old daughter, Maria da Glória, on condition that she marry her uncle, Dom Miguel (repeating the consanguinary formula adopted by his own mad grandmother), and that he would accept the new Charter. Saldanha, the liberal minister of war (and a grandson of Pombal) supported the Charter, but a clique of 'abolutionists' objected and, backed by Spanish reactionaries, caused trouble. To deter this the regency called on England, and a force of 5,000 men was sent out under General Sir William Clinton to the regent's aid. Tension increased after the installation of the new form of government in October 1826, for although Dom Miguel had professed to accept the Charter, incited by meddling Metternich in Vienna, he laid claim to the regency prior to any eventual marriage. Metternich even sent a mission to Dom Pedro to get his approval, at the same time suggesting that Maria da Glória be sent to Lisbon, where her presence might produce some tranquillity and unite the moderates. Pedro agreed to appoint his brother as his lieutenant on the understanding that the Austrian emperor and the king of England would ensure that he respected the Charter. Dom Miguel landed in Lisbon on 22 February 1828. Within days, there were serious disturbances there, fanned by the machinations of Carlota-Joaquina, intent on placing her younger son on the throne. This he usurped on 11 July, meanwhile having dissolved the *cortes* and convoked an assembly of his supporters, which was recognized only by the representatives of the United States and Mexico in Lisbon – all other diplomats asked for their passports. With a number of political refugees, Palmela and Saldanha took ship for England. Maria da Glória, hearing the news of the *coup d'état* while *en route*, sailed directly to England, where she was received as a queen.

The Miguelite War

On 18 May the garrison of Oporto proclaimed their loyalty to the Charter and to Dom Pedro and his daughter. As the uprising gained impetus, both Palmela and Saldanha sailed for the Douro to lead the movement, but the time was not yet ripe and with Miguelite units approaching, they re-embarked. Liberal troops assembled under the future Viscount Sá da Bandeira retired into Galicia, from where they were shipped to England to await events. Clinton's contingent was likewise recalled, lest it be thought that Britain was taking sides. However, Canning's policy of non-intervention was on the point of collapse, for the political situation had become complex. Refugees reached London with reports of executions, arrests and deportations.

Wellington's Tory government, never very liberal, but which was shortly to fall, favoured Dom Miguel. Lord Palmerston, critical of Miguelite activities, although still claiming to be a non-interventionist, at the same time was conniving at the usurper's deposition. In April 1831 Dom Pedro IV abdicated the Brazilian throne in favour of his infant son and sailed for the island of Terceira in the Azores, his base for a future invasion of Portugal. Here, Mousinho da Silveira was entrusted with fiscal reform of residual 'feudal' systems. Loans were negotiated through Mendizábal, the Spanish liberal financier. Palmerston allowed arms to be acquired and volunteers recruited, which in the following February were conveyed to the Azores in ships commanded by Captain Sartorius.

Preparations for the expedition being completed, Dom Pedro's fleet with 7,000 men aboard, sailed for Oporto, landing there on 9 July. They were isolated by besieging Miguelites, who continued to shell the city in a desultory fashion from batteries near the Serra convent, as had Wellesley twenty-three years earlier. Among those who had landed were Alexandre Herculano, the future historian, and Almeida Garrett, the future author and liberal politician. The garrison had been stiffened by a motley 'International Brigade' – largely out-of-work Glaswegians and Cockneys under the command of Colonel Charles Shaw, plus a sprinkling of Peninsular veterans. Eventually, the number of combatants increased to some 17,800 Liberals closely invested by 24,000 Miguelites. Captain Glascock, with a small flotilla, patrolled the mouth of the Douro, keeping a weather eye on British interests. Cholera raged. A soup kitchen was set up by the British Factory; dogs and cats, including Shaw's pets, became the ingredient of stews. As a parting shot – witnessed by young Joseph Forrester, later an influential figure among the British exporters – the Miguelites set fire to the warehouses of Vila Nova de Gaia and the blaze was only stopped from spreading by the resolute action of Glascock and his marines. Nevertheless, some 27,000 pipes of boiling wine gushed into the swirling Douro, turning it into a muddy red. The deadlock was broken in June 1833 when Admiral Charles Napier, who had replaced Sartorius, with the aid of the new steamships was able to defeat and capture the Miguelite fleet off Cape St Vincent. Liberal troops under the Duke of Terceira landed at Tavira and marched on Lisbon, which capitulated on 24 July. Dom Pedro entered four days later, but he had only the two major cities in his hands; his brother occupied the rest of the country. Lord William Russell, a convinced Liberal, still doubtful as to the outcome of the civil war, observed that there was little to choose between the two contestants: Pedro was 'governed by a faction of unprincipled democrats who have no more love of liberty and justice than Miguel himself'. He wondered too whether it was 'the duty of England to rescue all other nations from the consequences of their own folly': 'We are neither the tutors nor the police officers of Europe.'

The Quadruple Alliance

In September 1833 Fernando VII of Spain died, and a real danger threatened of the whole Peninsula being consumed by two concurrent civil wars. In January 1834 Palmerston proposed that the deposition of Dom Miguel, now urgent, might be followed by a general amnesty and the establishment of a Liberal government. Intervention had occurred, with Spanish troops crossing the frontier in a futile attempt to capture Don Carlos, who was animating his Carlist partisans from Portuguese soil. Within a month, on 22 April, a *Quadruple Alliance* was signed by Palmerston, the French and Spanish ambassadors (Talleyrand and the Marquis de Miraflores respectively) and the Portuguese envoy in London, which provided that all four countries would unite to expel Dom Miguel and Don Carlos from Portugal. The war in Portugal was soon over. Threatened by troops approaching from Spain and by Terceira's capture of Viseu and Coimbra, and after his defeat in an action at Asseiceira, just south of Tomar, Dom Miguel capitulated at Evora-Monte on 26 May. A British frigate took him from Sines to Genoa; he then settled in Austria, taking no further part in politics. Don Carlos escaped to London, from where, disguised, he returned to carry on his war in Spain.

Dom Pedro immediately instructed Joaquim António de Aguiar to commence dissolving the monastic orders and sequestrating their properties, which were sold off in the hope of remedying the disastrous state of the national finances, but with trifling success. The health of the thirty-six-year-old king (a congenital epileptic) further deteriorated and he died of consumption on 24 September. Maria da Glória, declared of age at fifteen, succeeded him as Maria II. On 1 December she was married to her stepmother's brother, who died within three months; and in February 1836 the young widow married Ferdinand of Saxe-Coburg-Gotha, a cousin of Queen Victoria's Prince Albert. While the *ancien régime* in Portugal may have been brought to an end, there were difficult decades ahead. Liberalism had been victorious, but it was bankrupt.

CHAPTER ELEVEN

The last Braganzas and the First Republic

The first cabinet of Maria II (1834–53) was presided over by Palmela, a diplomat of experience, whose first priority was to try to improve the parlous state of the country's finances. Demobilization had caused widescale unemployment. The seizure of ecclesiastical property – including that of the former military Orders – and the removal of Miguelite bishops from their sees, provoked a breach with Rome (until 1842). Tensions developed within the administration, partly caused by individual interpretations of the text of the Charter. The Liberals divided into two main camps, the Conservatives and Progressives. The more radical among the latter formed a faction known as 'Septembrists', after the military and popular demonstrations in Lisbon in that month in 1836. Their more moderate opponents were referred to as 'Chartists', among whom Costa Cabral was to come to the fore. A new government headed by Miguel Passos brought about some overdue educational reforms, while Sá da Bandeira prohibited the slave trade in the Portuguese possessions. Although both Terceira and Saldanha opposed the Septembrists, there was a period of confusion until a new compromise Constitution was promulgated in April 1838, which helped to provide some economic stability. Among Septembrist reforms were the institution of a civil register (of births, deaths and marriages); the division of Portugal into more manageable districts, *concelhos* or municipalities, and parishes; and the setting up of new administrative and penal codes; all of which tightened centralized control. How it was that the queen was permitted the extravagance of erecting the grotesque neo-Manueline pile of the Castelo da Pena above Sintra in a period of financial stringency, remains a mystery.

Dona Maria II in 1834 (detail) after John Simpson

Costa Cabral's too authoritarian ministry caused much antagonism, notably in the Minho where the rural population resisted paying for new roads. His sanitary regulations prohibiting further burials within churches were defied in what became known as the revolt of 'Maria da Fonte'. Order was imposed with difficulty and in May 1846 Costa Cabral resigned and left the country. His place was taken by Palmela, but in October the queen dismissed her minister and called on Sardanha to form a government. Before long, another radical revolt, known as that of the 'Patuleia', flared up in Oporto. Civil war was avoided and although Colonel Wylde, sent from London as mediator, was unable to influence Passos and Sá da Bandeira, on 29 June 1847 the *Convention of Gramido* brought about a temporary political settlement. However, within two years the queen misguidedly called on the intolerant Costa Cabral to head the administration again, which merely fomented widespread opposition. It was not until April 1851, having meanwhile antagonised Saldanha, who then brought out liberal Oporto against his authoritarian regime, that Costa Cabral definitively resigned.

REGENERATION

Saldanha introduced several modifications to the Charter by an act of July 1852 and by the application of a new electoral law. Although the franchise was still restricted to some 36,000 voters, this satisfied the more reasonable Septembrists. The two main parties in the comparatively stable government now changed their labels: the conservative Chartists to Regenerators, and the moderate Septembrists to Historicals. Almeida Garrett was appointed to office under Saldanha, which

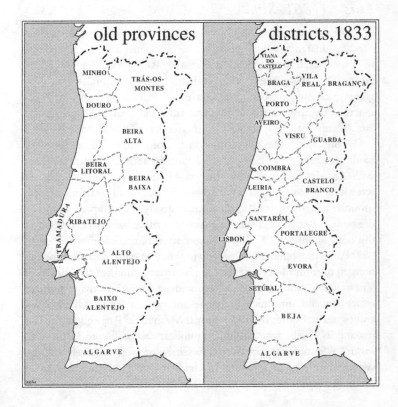

gave the impression of some cultural regeneration also. Camilo Castelo Branco may be mentioned as one of the more eminent authors in this 'Romantic' era, and Eça de Queirós at a later date.

In November 1853, having provided her consort with eight children, Maria II died in childbed, aged thirty-four. Pedro de Alcântara, her eldest son, succeeded her as Dom Pedro V (1853–61), while his father acted as regent for the next two years. In 1858 Pedro married Stéphanie of Hohenzollern-Sigmaringen, who died of diphtheria two months later. Pedro survived her by only three years, succumbing to typhoid fever in 1861, as did two of his brothers.

Luís (1861–89)

Pedro was succeeded by his brother Luís, who proved to be a model constitutional monarch, under whose aegis the major parties agreed to a system of rotation in office. At first, the 'Regenerators' were led by Fontes Pereira de Melo, who embarked on a comprehensive programme of public works: building roads, bridges and port facilities, initiating the first section of a railway from the capital to Oporto, and establishing both telegraph and cable services. The 'Historicals' were led by the Duke of Loulé (brother-in-law of Dom Pedro), at first with Sá da Bandeira, who later opposed him. In 1868 the latter, together with António Alves Martins (Bishop of Viseu), pursued a policy of reform in which the civil service was reduced, civil list salaries cut and subsidies abolished, but this did comparatively little towards balancing the budget. In the following year Anselmo Braamcamp joined Loulé at the helm. Fontes de Melo's administration remained in power from 1871 until September 1876, when the Reformists and Historicals merged to form the Progressists, led by Braamcamp and the Bishop of Viseu. They extended the suffrage and set about improving primary education and introducing changes in taxation and banking laws, among several other belated reforms. Meanwhile Republicanism was making itself felt, with the first republican being elected in Oporto. From 1879 until 1906 the two parties shared power alternately, but the system soon fell into disrepute. In October 1889 Dom Luís died, to be succeeded by Dom Carlos.

The Scramble for Africa

With the upheaval of the Peninsular and Miguelite wars and the subsequent recurrent domestic crises of earlier decades in the century,
Portugal did not give much thought to her overseas possessions.
Mozambique continued to be a port of call for shipping *en route* to Asia
and the Orient. Sá da Bandeira had endeavoured to stamp out the slave
trade between Guinea and Angola and Brazil via São Tomé and the
Cape Verde islands. In 1839 Palmerston had authorized British warships to search vessels flying Portuguese colours, if suspected of carrying
slaves; this interference caused resentment in Lisbon. Already, in the
1790s, Britain had established herself in the Cape, and now the Dutch
were settling in the interior; while ever since Francisco de Lacerda's
expedition – in the last decade of the previous century – there had been
occasional similar exploratory expeditions by the Portuguese. But with
the city of Luanda being visited by Livingstone in 1854, the southern
shore of the Bay of Lourenço Marques being occupied by a British
naval force in 1860, Stanley obtaining land on the left bank of the
Congo on behalf of Leopold II of Belgium in 1878, and the French
founding Brazzaville in 1880, Portugal had every reason to become
apprehensive of foreign designs on what she considered her rightful
possessions. The European powers thought otherwise: in their view
effective occupation of territory rather than prior discovery justified
colonial claims. Brazil and the United States of America were stronger
magnets for emigrants from Portugal, and there had been little success
in making any lasting settlements in the hinterland of Angola and
Mozambique. Partly to confirm their rights, exploratory expeditions
were sent in 1877 and 1884 respectively, led by Serpa Pinto, and by
Capelo and Ivens, which crossed central Africa, thus reviving Lacerda's
aspiration to establish Portuguese dominion right across the continent.
Britain recognized Portugal's claim to both banks of the Zaire in 1884,
but in June 1887 Lord Salisbury resisted her intention to control all land
between Angola and Mozambique. His excuse was that his government could not recognize Portuguese sovereignty in territories not
occupied in sufficient force to maintain order. In reality, Portuguese
claims cut across Britain's own interest in possessing an unbroken

swathe of territory between Cairo and the Cape. By then too, Germany had entered the 'scramble' in asserting a protectorate over South-West Africa, and the Congo had been grabbed by Leopold II of the Belgians. The friction intensified as Britain sought to extend her own sphere of influence, and came to a head as far as Portugal was concerned on 11 January 1890, when Salisbury brusquely threatened that unless Portuguese troops withdrew forthwith from the disputed areas (what is now Malawi), the British minister in Lisbon would be recalled. Such humiliating treatment from her old ally caused great indignation. The Republicans used the inevitable humiliation of Portugal as a stick with which to beat both the king and the government, and fomented a political crisis. The tension generated by this wretched episode subsided, with Britain renewing her pledge to defend the integrity of Portuguese possessions in the *Treaty of Windsor* of October 1899, signed three days before the commencement of the Boer War. Fourteen months later the British Channel Fleet visited Lisbon as an earnest of continued protection. Meanwhile, Portugal turned her attention to 'civilizing' and further exploiting the natives of her African possessions.

Carlos　*(1889–1908)*

Socialist theories were being more frequently aired during the latter decades of the nineteenth century. The drift of people from the land to the main conurbations persisted, and with it, urban discontent. While slow progress was made with industrialization, no legislation was put in hand to protect the workers; the trade unions which formed were harassed; strikes were declared illegal; attempts were made to muzzle the now more vociferously critical Press. At least, there appeared to be a gradual fall in the amount of illiteracy, which was still 69 per cent in 1910.

The first decade of Dom Carlos's reign was one of sustained financial crises. Luiz (later Marquês) de Soveral, at the Portuguese Legation in London, where he was on cordial terms with the Prince of Wales, arranged for Carlos to visit England to discuss a possible loan. In 1902 Edward VII – equally portly in appearance – made a return visit to Lisbon and agreement was entered into with regard to the repayment of debts. The volatile state of the rival political parties, which continued to scrap, and the fall of the Progressists in 1906, decided the king to ask João Franco, an authoritarian monarchist with progressive views who had previously founded a Conservative Liberal Party, to form an administration. Carlos hoped that Franco might put a brake on the drift towards republicanism, for by 1906 the Republican party had secured over half the votes in the capital. But the Republicans returned to the attack by accusing the king of having covertly received illegal advances from the Treasury, and they were excluded from the chamber. Franco then proceeded to govern by decree, which merely drove more Liberals into the Republican camp. Protests proliferated from both politicians and municipalities, and in September 1907 all the main parties joined in condemning the virtual dictatorship. Carlos then identified himself in print with his minister's policies, and although Franco promised elections the following April, the impatient Republicans conspired to stage a mutiny. On 28 January 1908 this was pre-empted, probably by a tip-off to the police, but Franco drew up a decree that exiled those implicated for crimes against the security of the State. This was sent to Vila Viçosa to receive the king's signature. Carlos then decided to return to Lisbon. On 1 February, as the royal family were crossing the Terreiro do Paço in an open landau, both Carlos and his eldest son, Luis Filipe were shot dead. Manuel, the younger brother, was slightly grazed, but the queen was not hit. No one knows if the unpopular minister was the real target, whose non-appearance had caused the assassins to fire on the king. Although two of the assailants were shot by the police, no accomplices were ever arrested, nor was any report on the crime published. It has been assumed that they were *carbonários*, activists of a secret society. The Republicans were certainly not responsible, although they showed little regret and even started a subscription for the families of the regicides.

Manuel II, 'the Unfortunate'   (1908–10)

The eighteen-year-old Manuel II had not expected or been trained to rule. A Council of State recommended that he dismiss João Franco, who went into exile. A non-party prime minister, Admiral Ferreira do Amaral, endeavoured to lead the country out of the immediate crisis, but his publication of the list of unauthorized advances to the royal family, which compromised most recent ministers of finance, hardly inspired sympathy for the monarchy (although it was the civil list rather than Dom Carlos's personal extravagance that swelled the bill). In the elections of 1 November 1908 the Republicans swept into power, but half a dozen other administrations were to enter but not dominate the political arena during the thirty months of Manuel's reign. Mutual recrimination racked the monarchical parties, which continued to bicker among themselves. Accusations of corruption were rife.

By 1910 the Republicans were strongly entrenched in the capital, and their tenets were propagated effectively among the disaffected naval establishment and the Lisbon garrison. With the pretext of celebrating the arrival of a Brazilian cruiser in the Tagus, a Republican rising had been planned for 3 October, but with the suicide of Admiral Cândido dos Reis, who had agreed to lead it, Machado dos Santos, a junior naval officer with Carbonarist affiliations seized an infantry barracks, while two rebellious warships began to bombard the royal palace of Necessidades. With few loyal troops to defend him, Dom Manuel drove off to Mafra with his mother and grandmother, and later boarded the royal yacht riding at anchor off Ericeira. Assured that any resistance would be futile, the idea of sailing to Oporto was abandoned and after reaching Gibraltar, he eventually took ship for England. Here, at Fulwell Park, Twickenham, Manuel II, 'the Unfortunate', devoted the next two decades to forming a splendid library of Portuguese books – the catalogue has been described as 'one of the few really great books ever prepared by a monarch' – which, since his death in exile in 1932, has been housed in the Braganza palace at Vila Viçosa.

The (First) Republic

In 1910 a provisional government with Teófilo Braga as president and the suave Bernardino Machado as minister of foreign affairs, set about the suppression of anything royalist, including titles of nobility. Afonso Costa, the energetic anti-clerical minister of justice, undertook the disestablishment of the Church by a Law of Separation (April 1911) and suppressed all outward forms of religious observances, intent on Portugal being a lay state. The patriarch and prelates were deposed. Although these excessive measures provoked opposition in conservative rural communities, where the still largely illiterate peasantry had long submitted to the baneful influence of the Church, they received popular urban support. In August, the first Republican Constitution was approved, and a coalition adminstration took office. Monarchists in the north of the country meanwhile fomented what became, in 1912, an ineffectual counter-revolution, after which its supporters were arrested. Workers in Lisbon, taking advantage of their right to strike, found their leaders imprisoned. Costa's Democratic Party regained control of affairs in the following year, when he effectively balanced the budget. Some progressive legislation followed, but disillusionment set in, for Costa was neither able to improve the standard of living, nor was any economic revival apparent by the outbreak of war in 1914, which ended any hope of financial stability. Costa resigned and in the following year General Pimenta de Castro was asked by President Arriaga to form a government. However, his dictatorial measures were denounced by the Democrats and in May he was arrested and banished, while Arriaga resigned. By November, Costa was again prime minister.

The First World War

Britain had undertaken to prevent any encroachment on Portuguese colonies and to protect Portuguese shipping lines as far as possible. Although Portugal had intended to remain neutral, she had already sent out reinforcements to Angola and Mozambique – both bordered by German colonies – in the expectation of frontier incidents. The Democrats then decided that the hour had come to intervene. On 24 February 1916 as many as seventy German ships anchored in Portuguese ports were seized and a fortnight later Germany declared war. Within a year, a Portuguese expeditionary force of 25,000 men (later increased to 40,000) had sailed to join the Allied lines in Flanders, where it suffered heavy losses, notably in the battle of the Lys in April

1918. (The Portuguese 'Tomb of the Unknown Soldiers' – one from Africa, one from Flanders – is at Batalha.)

SIDÓNIO PAIS

Meanwhile, a domestic crisis had developed, due to disruption in agriculture and trade – massive emigration in the previous decade and the call-up had reduced the labour available. The resultant food shortage and the disorganization and profiteering in its distribution had left some cities famished, and rioting had taken place, notably in Lisbon. Governmental opposition formed around Major Sidónio Pais, minister at Berlin until Portugal entered the war, who on 5 December 1917 engineered a military *coup*, which was strongly supported in the conservative north. Costa was arrested, President Machado was exiled and Sidónio Pais assumed the offices of both president and prime minister. As a sop to his more obscurantist followers, he allowed the exiled religious leaders to return and resumed relations with the Vatican. However much he may have been received with enthusiasm when touring the countryside, he was unable to win over an exasperated opposition and, smeared as being pro-German, was accused of failing to support the army in France. Economic difficulties mounted and the *escudo*, the new currency, lost almost half its value. In October, a disturbance in Evora was followed by numerous arrests. The prisons in Lisbon were packed with dissident Republicans. On 14 December 1918, when entering the Rossio station in Lisbon, *en route* to Oporto to set up military *juntas* to sustain his tottering regime, Sidónio Pais was assassinated by a fanatic. He had already survived an attempt on his life nine days earlier, on the anniversary of the founding of his 'New Republic'. This now collapsed entirely: there was no one to take his place.

POST-WAR CHAOS

Admiral Canto e Castro, formerly minister of marine, was elected president. By April 1919 the Democrats were back in office, but political instability continued for another seven years. Strikes were frequent and some workers organized themselves into Anarcho-Syndicalist unions. No administration appeared capable of offering a determined line of policy: four reshuffles took place in 1919 and seven in the following year. There were another five in 1921, in the October of which political gangsters (dressed as sailors) assassinated António Granjó, then prime minister, and several other eminent politicians, among them Machado Santos, a demagogue of the 1910 Revolution.

This lamentable episode temporarily moderated the political turmoil and Dr António Almeida, elected president in 1919, was the first to complete his term of office. He was succeeded by Manuel Teixeira Gomes in 1923, but the constant financial crises hardly allowed governmental stability. It was at this period that the scandal known as the 'Portuguese Banknote Case' hit the headlines. A group of swindlers using Bank of Portugal notepaper were able to trick Waterlow, the London printer, into printing 580,000 500-*escudo* bank-notes, which entered the country in the Venezuelan diplomatic bag and went into circulation via the newly floated Banco de Angola e Metrópole. Notes with numbers duplicating those already in circulation alerted the police and both series were called in. The episode hardly improved the already deplorable state of confusion then reigning.

Three unsuccessful attempts at military risings were made in 1925, but although those responsible were tried, they were acquitted. It was not until late in May 1926 that General Gomes da Costa (who had commanded troops in Flanders), after appealing to all citizens 'of dignity and honour' from reactionary Braga, was able to lead a bloodless *coup* and form a military administration, in which General António Oscar de Fragoso Carmona was responsible for foreign affairs. In the following February the Oporto garrison showed their discontent by rebelling, and 120 were killed and 650 wounded in the ensuing confrontation. Following the failure of the Monarchist General Sinel de Cordes to resolve the financial situation, Carmona – non-partisan and Catholic – became acting president of the Republic, confirmed by his election to that position in the following March. He held the position until his death in 1951, having been re-elected in 1935, 1942 and 1949. Most democratic institutions were repressed and for the next half-century Portugal was to remain bridled by a dictatorship strongly influenced by the hierarchy of the Church.

CHAPTER TWELVE

Salazar's 'New State'

António de Oliveira Salazar *(1889–1970)*

In April 1928, António de Oliveira Salazar (1889–1970), a Catholic professor of political economy at Coimbra since 1918, was offered the portfolio of finance. On accepting the post, he insisted that Carmona gave him entire control of all governmental disbursements: no other

Detail from a photograph of Salazar

minister should incur any expense without his approval. By his rigid administration of the fiscal machinery, by curbing expenditure and applying new taxes, the public debt was steadily reduced and 'miraculously' – although his book-keeping methods were suspect – Salazar was able to stabilize the currency and produce a budgetary surplus within a comparatively short time. This surplus was spread over a series of long-term projects: public works, improvements in agriculture, etc. His apparent success enabled him to overshadow any ambitious rivals, and by 1932 Carmona had appointed him President of the Council of Ministers, a position he retained until incapacitated by a stroke in 1968. Were it not that he manipulated the reins of power himself, he might well be described as an *éminence grise*, for he remained an austere, ascetic and sombre character, avoiding the political limelight.

By March 1933 Salazar had promulgated a new Constitution, which incorporated certain fundamental laws and formed the basis of his authoritarian, pro-Catholic *Estado Novo* or 'New State'. Only one political party, the 'National Union', was permitted, although, at the time of alleged elections, others were authorized. This enabled the regime to identify their opponents with ease, but they had little chance of presenting a candidate. He did not hide his contempt for the principle of a democratic vote; in the election of 1934 the number of voters going to the polls was a mere 7.6 per cent of the population, and was only 14.8 per cent thirty years later. As for the ordinary voters, Salazar wished to 'protect them from themselves', from making decisions concerning matters about which it was better for them to remain ignorant. Legislative decisions remained entirely the prerogative of the government, which condescended to be advised by a nominated Corporative Chamber. Salazar controlled the interests of employers by the formation of a series of *grémios* or Federations within the corporative system; that of employees by *sindicatos nationais* or National Unions (members of which, naturally, were forbidden to strike). The professional classes were represented through a scheme of 'Orders', all part of the apparatus of a 'corporate state'. This institutionalization of all forms of activity became a strait-jacket from which it was precarious to disengage. Anyone not complying with official directives found themselves the object of harassment or threatened with loss of employment, as in the case of dissident university professors. (Dr Egas Moniz, a neurologist who had received the Nobel Prize for Medicine in 1949, was conspicuously ignored by the government, owing to his democratic convictions, while his scientific treatise entitled *A Vida Sexual* could only be acquired by members of the medical profession in view of the ban on pornography!) Fishermen and agricultural labourers were patronizingly provided with associations and what were ostensibly communal welfare centres, in reality bodies supervising and regulating their activities.

A youth movement was set up (aping those in other dictatorships). The police, under military command, together with the *Polícia Internacional e de Defensa do Estado* or PIDE (a secret political police force) were ubiquitous and, relying on a wide network of informers, kept a close watch on all forms of dissidence. The PIDE's repressive methods, particularly when dealing with clandestine organizations, 'secret societies' (including the Freemasons, which had many adherents among intellectuals) and members of the Communist Party (which had gone underground), made it a notorious instrument of the apparatus of state, even if wielded with much less brutality than in fascist Germany. Another paramilitary arm of the autocratic system was the Security Police (PSP), which attended all public gatherings. In these insidious ways the man in the street felt insecure and intimidated. Press censorship was strictly enforced: no public protest, discussion or criticism of governmental decisions were tolerated. As Fernando Pessoa, the most eminent poet and man of letters of the period, admitted: 'I don't want to get drawn into discussions of the New Constitution and the Corporate State; I accept them both as disciplines; I keep myself clear of them because I don't agree with them.'

Additional discreditable aspects of the theocratic regime were Salazar's sanctioning the return of the religious orders and the Catholic Church's exploitation of the cult of the Virgin of Fátima. In 1917 three peasant children claimed to have witnessed visions of the Virgin. The ecclesiastical authorities, eager to reap the fruits of fervent devotion – as so evident at Lourdes – were not slow to seize on their infantile delusions by further imposing on the gullible and largely illiterate peasantry. Pilgrimages were expediently organized. Inordinate sums were spent by Salazar in erecting a monstrous basilica at Fátima, consecrated in 1953, which is little less than an affront to any instinct of veneration, well-described as a 'Spiritual Disneyland'.

Salazar supported General Francisco Franco's Nationalist revolt against the Socialist government in Spain in 1936, in which year he admitted: 'We are anti-parliamentarians, anti-democratic, and anti-liberal.' A Portuguese legion fought for Franco, with whom Salazar had periodic meetings. However, Salazar was persuaded to remain neutral both during the Spanish Civil War – even if anti-fascist troops seeking safety in Portugal were passed back to Spain, where they were inevitably shot – and at the commencement three years later of the Second World War, during which he was sympathetic to the Allied cause. Although Hitler put pressure on her not to supply countries other than Germany with wolfram, threats did not stop Portugal continuing to supply the Allies. The Allies were also allowed to establish vital bases in the Azores in June 1943 after the British Government's invocation of the ancient alliance, while Britain reciprocated by promising all possible aid should Portugal be attacked by land. Later that year – in which the country was racked by severely repressed strikes – an anti-fascist movement (MUNAF) was founded, with General Norton de Matos as president, but it soon foundered.

After May 1945, when news of the German surrender was announced, there were massive anti-fascist demonstrations and Salazar momentarily agreed to promise free elections – 'as free as in free England'. A Movement of Democratic Unity (MUD) was authorized, but as it received wide support its public meetings were suspended in October. In the following Summer, when the government applied for admission to the United Nations, MUD produced damaging evidence that would militate against their entry, for which the leaders of the movement were put on trial for 'defamation'. In 1949 Portugal was admitted to NATO, which merely confirmed that the Western Allies were prepared to accept the continuance of repressive fascist regimes in Europe as long as their stance was anti-Communist. In 1955 Portugal was accepted as a member of the United Nations, while two years later it was thought diplomatic – on account of the ancient alliance between the two countries – to concede a state visit to Lisbon of Elizabeth II,

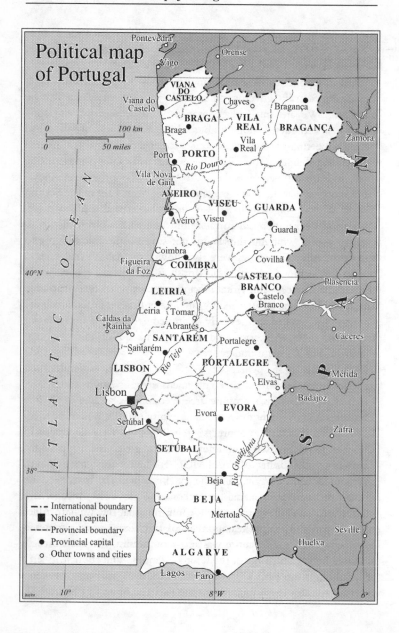

Political map of Portugal

Pontevedra
Vigo
Orense

VIANA DO CASTELO
Viana do Castelo
Chaves
Bragança

0   *100 km*
0   *50 miles*

BRAGA
Braga
VILA REAL
Vila Real
BRAGANÇA
Zamora

Porto
PORTO
Rio Douro

Vila Nova de Gaia

AVEIRO
Aveiro
VISEU
Viseu
GUARDA
Guarda

Coimbra
Covilhã

Figueira da Foz
COIMBRA

CASTELO BRANCO
Castelo Branco
Plasencia

LEIRIA
Leiria
Tomar
Abrantes
Portalegre
Cáceres

Caldas da Rainha
SANTARÉM
Santarém
Rio Tejo
PORTALEGRE
Mérida

LISBON
Lisbon
Elvas
Badajoz

Setúbal
Evora
EVORA
Zafra

SETÚBAL

Beja

Rio Guadiana
BEJA
Mértola
Seville

Huelva

ALGARVE
Lagos Faro

A T L A N T I C   O C E A N

40°N

38°

— · — International boundary
■ National capital
- - - Provincial boundary
● Provincial capital
○ Other towns and cities

10° 8°W 6°

giving Salazar's administration a nod of recognition which it scarcely deserved. In 1960 Portugal entered the European Free Trade Association (EFTA).

MATERIAL RECOVERY

After the disruption caused by the war, the government concentrated on putting the economy back on its feet. Belatedly, the infrastructure of communications was extended and modernized: new bridges spanned the Douro and Tagus (the 'Salazar Bridge', then the longest suspension bridge in Europe, was completed in 1966); and dams were constructed, dramatically increasing the output of hydro-electric power (from 260,000 kilowatt hours in 1930 to 6,840,000 in 1969). Schools, barracks, airports, harbour and ship-repairing installations, power-stations, hospitals, hotels, libraries and museums were built. Attention was given to ship-building, the creation of a national airline (TAP) in 1946, re-afforestation – too frequently by eucalyptus for paper production, which provoked criticism – and the cultivation of rice. While the manufacture of textiles remained basic, the metallurgical industries grew in importance but, due to slow mechanisation, the agricultural sector, in which 30 per cent of the working population was still employed in 1970, stagnated. Illiteracy was said to have been reduced to only a quarter of the population by 1970, but the per capita income stood at a quarter of the European average in 1973. It was no longer an essentially rural country, as substantial migration took place towards the main urban centres, where an acute shortage of housing caused the proliferation of suburban shanty-towns. No wonder Portugal still suffered the highest infant mortality rate in Europe.

In the cultural field, from 1957 the Calouste Gulbenkian Foundation had assumed the role of patron of the arts. Its museum in Lisbon – one of the first and better examples of contemporary, non-totalitarian architecture – was inaugurated in 1969. Censorship continued to be enforced and thus most authors avoided publishing anything contentious or liable to prosecution, except brave writers like Torga, who published his own anti-fascist work and suffered imprisonment. Even the publication in 1972 of *New Portuguese Letters* by three women writers was banned as an outrage to public decency, and its 'liberated' authors arrested, which only provoked counter-productive publicity. Maria Helena Vieira da Silva, the country's most prestigious artist, had left as early as 1928.

COMMUNIST RESISTANCE

Resistance to the regime took many forms: as early as 1936, Communists infiltrated the Navy and attempted to hijack three ships, with the intention of joining the Spanish Republicans; in 1947 two mechanics were able to sabotage some twenty aircraft at the Sintra air-base, only to find that a planned *coup* did not take place. In 1959 Henrique Galvão, an anti-Communist, having a decade previously complained to the National Assembly about the scandal of forced labour in Angola and gone into opposition, was imprisoned. He then escaped to Brazil, where he published an 'Open Letter to Dr Salazar', accusing the dictator of having 'intimidated and beaten into submission eight million Portuguese whom you have turned into the wretched morons who wander around to the tune of Fado, Fátima and Football . . .'.

Meanwhile, members of the Communist Party (PCP) continued to keep the political pot boiling, even if its most capable strategist, Alvaro Cunhal, remained incarcerated at Peniche. However, in January 1960, with the complicity of a sympathetic guard, he made his escape by the age-old expedient of tying sheets together. In the December of the following year another group of well-organized Communists made a more spectacular getaway by commandeering the armoured Mercedes presented to Salazar by Hitler, with which they rammed open the prison gate at Caxias. In 1961, both a cruise liner and a TAP plane were hijacked, sensational incidents which kept the predicament of Salazar's opponents before the world at large.

General Delgado

On the political front, between 1946 and 1962, after an unsuccessful attempt to assassinate Salazar in 1937, there had been several conspiracies on the part of dissidents to overthrow the regime, which felt increasingly threatened and reacted with increasing intensity. In 1948 the octogenarian General Norton de Matos endeavoured to unite the opposition and contested the presidential election, but his supporters found themselves continually harassed and he was forced to withdraw. In 1958 General Humberto Delgado, an old-style Republican, whose frequent contact with the British over the Azores bases and residence in both Montreal and Washington in official capacities during the decade 1947–57 had obviously influenced him, had put his name forward in opposition to Admiral Américo Tomás, the National Union's chosen candidate. Fearlessly outspoken, he condemned the standard of living as being one of the lowest in Europe, 'even in the category of an underdeveloped country', while it was scandalous that economic power should still be massively concentrated in the hands of a few monopolistic groups. When in Oporto, Delgado was received with far too much enthusiasm for the authorities to tolerate, and in May, on his return to Lisbon, several civilians were killed by the panicking police when trying to disperse the huge crowds awaiting him. More pitched battles in the streets of the capital were to take place between then and election day (8 June), when the farce was concluded. The government had meanwhile resorted to every conceivable device – even circulating secret instructions to the PIDE on how to control the vote – to ensure that the result of the election was 'fixed' in their favour. It was feared that the military might rise in Delgado's support and within days he was suspended from the post of director-general of civil aviation. He was dismissed in the following January, which led to his seeking asylum in the Brazilian Embassy. A series of strikes ensued and in March a military conspiracy led by Manuel Serra known as the 'Cathedral plot' – their weapons having been stored in the crypt of Lisbon's cathedral with the connivance of a merchant navy chaplain – was postponed at the eleventh hour, although some involved in the planned uprising were arrested. Serra escaped to Brazil, where he joined Delgado. After a two-year lull, in January 1962 another armed insurrection, planned by Delgado to take place at Beja, misfired. Three years later he was assassinated near Badajoz by the PIDE in collusion with Franco's police. It was young Mário Soares, in his role as lawyer to the Delgado family, who took up the case both in the Spanish courts and in Portugal, and it was he who openly accused the PIDE of being responsible for the murder.

STUDENT RESISTANCE

Long-smouldering student unrest had frequently manifested itself in minor disturbances, culminating in violent protests during the Spring of 1962, in the wake of which were inevitable prosecutions and imprisonments. Further outbreaks occurred in the 1960s, notably at Coimbra in the the Spring and Summer of 1969 (perhaps encouraged by the outcome of the Paris disturbances of the previous year). There were further clashes between university students and the police early in 1971 and again in 1972 and 1973. The universities remained a fertile recruiting ground for the revolutionary left, the more so when students found themselves conscripted into officer-training corps preparatory to military service in the colonies. This interrupted their studies and delayed the start of their careers, so many chose to continue their education abroad. Besides this brain drain, the number of emigrants from the less privileged classes escalated dramatically during the decade; those to EEC countries alone were so numerous that the total resident population of Portugal had actually declined in the late 1960s. Some three-quarters of the emigrants settled in France, and Paris became the city with one of the largest Portuguese populations after Lisbon. It has been estimated that well over 100,000 young men emigrated to avoid conscription, mostly illegally, as the government would only sanction emigration on the completion of military service.

LABOUR UNREST

Unrest was not confined to students. A slight liberalization of labour laws was followed by several waves of strikes among key unions: textile and metallurgical workers, fishermen, dockers, journalists and bank employees were among those involved. Within a few months of its formation in October 1970, some forty unions, representing many hundred thousands of workers, had become affiliated to the *Intersindical*, a federation of independent opposition unions.

From 1970, more radically subversive groups indulged in direct action. They sabotaged military installations, a warship due to sail for Africa, helicopters at the Tancos air-base; destroyed electricity pylons and cut telephone lines, etc. They would stop at nothing which might help to topple the regime.

VIOLENCE IN THE 'OVERSEAS PROVINCES'

Portugal's 'Overseas Provinces' – as they were termed after 1951 – formed an integral part of the 'New State' and continued to be administered from Lisbon. In 1970 the populations of Angola and Mozambique alone were 5,674,000 and 8,234,000 respectively. Lisbon could not stem the tide of insistent demands for decolonization. In February 1961 violence erupted in Luanda (Angola), the oldest European capital city in Africa south of the equator, led by rival nationalist elements. In that December Goa was occupied by India. In 1963 Guinea, and in 1964 Mozambique, also sought independence. Salazar intransigently refused to negotiate, with the result that guerrilla warfare broke out.

Although increasing exploitation of the natural resources of Angola had contributed to the Portuguese economy, the cost in terms of men and military material to hold down such a huge territory by force increased dramatically. Settlers were massacred; there were not sufficient military units at hand to contain the violence, and the situation was only stabilized, temporarily, by the arrival of troops from Lisbon. The colonial war intensified on three widely separated fronts and the 30,000 Portuguese troops normally deployed in Africa were increased to around 150,000. Aid was provided by other NATO countries, even if they had reservations concerning Portuguese colonial policy. War-weariness set in among the professional army and the conscripts were displaying increasing hostility towards the protracted war and militarism in general. While the hard-liners in Lisbon believed that they would ultimately win by refusing to give concessions, an increasing number of Salazar's supporters were seeking alternative political solutions, such as sanctioning progressive autonomy.

Marcelo Caetano

In September 1968 Salazar was incapacitated by a stroke and President Tomás called on Marcelo Caetano, a professor of administrative law, to take his place. His attempts to widen the basis of support for the regime by conceding limited liberalization and promising reforms in the New State only led to impatient demands for immediate democratization, which was resisted by the diehard conservatives. There was continuing economic growth, partly due to less restrictive industrial policies, which led to increasing foreign investment in Portuguese industries. It has been estimated that this rose from 1.5 per cent in 1960 to 27 per cent by 1970. Meanwhile, there had been an increase in emigrant remittances and a boom in receipts from tourist traffic, but there was rising domestic inflation also. Although more was being spent on a rudimentary welfare system, on public works, the construction of motorways and the replacement of slums by low-cost housing (the demand for which always exceeded supply), there was little sign of change in other vital respects, even if the powers of the PIDE were curbed and some of its personnel retired. Meanwhile, the parasitical functionaries of the corrupt and inefficient bureaucracy centralized on Lisbon spun their web of red tape, obstructing by their sheer bloody-mindedness any smooth operation of the machinery of state. A major disillusionment was the fact that Caetano, although extending the franchise to all literate adults, including women – it has been insinuated that this was because a recently published survey had indicated that they had a tendency to be more conservative than men – had not set up any mechanism which might allow the return of a democratic party system. So the opposition refused to contest the legislative election of 1973, realizing that seats would only be distributed to members of the National Union. The passing of a law of industrial reform was delayed by entrenched interests until 1972, which caused over forty major strikes in the following year, and so the implementation of the improvements promised was to be overtaken by events. Reactionary elements resisted proposals for reform, which might lead to economic stability, better social standards and subsequent democratization. Wilfully, they pinned their hopes on winning the African war, which would strengthen their hand, although certain militant Catholic groups were distancing themselves from others by denouncing atrocities reported to have been committed by Portuguese troops, and were actively supporting colonial self-determination.

MILITARY UNREST

Nothing much was done to bring the fruitless war in Africa to a negotiated conclusion. By 1971 the expenditure for 'defence' had reached almost 46 per cent of the budget. In September 1973 Guinea and Cape Verde proclaimed their independence, which was recognized by some sixty countries within three weeks. The situation in Mozambique was also becoming increasingly untenable. By 1974, one in every four adult males was in the armed forces, and the official figures for servicemen dying in Africa by that May were 7,674 – not necessarily killed in action – together with almost 27,000 seriously wounded. The casualty figures naturally discouraged recruitment to the Military Academy, and two decrees were issued in the Summer of 1973 in an attempt to resolve the shortage of trained young officers to carry on the struggle. These provided the opportunity for conscript officers, often graduates, to rise in rank more rapidly than professional officers, who were frequently from families too poor to provide any education for them except through the army. This bred a class grievance which merely exacerbated the already volatile situation by fomenting further demoralization and unrest among the lower ranks of the military establishment. This led to the organization at Evora that September of the Armed Forces Movement (*Movimento das Forças Armadas* or MFA).

CHAPTER THIRTEEN

The Revolution of 1974 and after

It is virtually impossible to explain in a few pages the confusing complexities and ramifications of this revolutionary period, for which the reader is referred to the detailed studies listed in the Further Reading section, but in outline the situation early in 1974 was as follows.

There was increasing resentment among officers at the demands being made on them by the politicians and 'top brass', not merely over professional grievances. Since the previous October, when a 'Coordinating Committee' had been set up by the MFA, it had received numerous messages of support from colleagues still fighting in Africa. Prominent on the committee was Major Otelo Saraiva de Carvalho, just back from Guinea. On 1 December eighty-six delegates, representing military units throughout the country, assembled at Obidos to discuss plans for a *coup d'état*. The minister of defence, soon aware of what was afoot, seemed stunned, and no immediate action was taken. General Francisco da Costa Gomes, chief of the general staff, had already expressed sympathy for the grievances of junior officers, notably captains. On 15 January 1974 General António de Spínola, the flamboyant Governor of Guinea until the previous August, was appointed his deputy. Eight days later, Spínola's *Portugal and the Future* was published, contending that only a political solution to the war was viable. On 8 March, Caetano, frequently indecisive, reacted by dismissing both Spínola and Costa Gomes (replaced by a hard-line ex-commander in Angola, General Joaquim da Luz Cunha), by arresting or transferring a number of MFA officers and demanding loyalty from all senior military commanders.

This set off a chain of events which led to a premature *coup* on 16

March, when some 200 men of the garrison at Caldas da Rainha drove to Lisbon in armoured vehicles, only to surrender to loyal troops without firing a shot. The government was reluctant to impose severe penalties on those responsible for this mutiny; such measures might precipitate a more violent military backlash. Most of the MFA leaders were still at liberty and they decided that it was vital that a concerted revolt be delayed no longer. Meanwhile, Major Ernesto Melo Antunes had been busy drafting a political programme, described by Spínola as 'primitively Communist'. During this period, for reasons of security, the MFA reduced to a minimum any contact they had made with civilian members of the opposition, with whom power would be shared once the *coup* was a *fait accompli*.

The Revolution of 25 April 1974

In the early hours of 25 April a sympathetic disc-jockey on a Lisbon radio station played a popular song entitled '*Grândola, vila morena*', which was the signal for the *coup*, meticulously organized by Major Otelo Saraiva de Carvalho, to begin. By 3 a.m. the two main radio stations were in the hands of the MFA, who called on all citizens to remain at home and on the police not to put up any opposition. By 7.30 a.m. Captain Salgueiro Maia was in the Praça do Comércio with 200 men and tanks from the Cavalry School at Santarém. They soon received reinforcements, while other units held the airport and the main roads entering the capital. There was a brief confrontation with pro-government tanks, but they held their fire and by midday had surrendered to the MFA, who meanwhile had boarded a frigate in the estuary. There was supportive intervention by the airforce. Barracks then surrendered, among them that in which Caetano had sought sanctuary before giving himself up to Spínola. Only the Directorate-General of Security, or secret police headquarters, held out, but gave in next morning after four or five people had been killed in its vicinity. President Tomás was picked up from his home by paratroopers and both he and Caetano were flown to Madeira, and a month later to Brazil. There was very slight resistance in Oporto, but within hours an euphoric atmosphere reigned in Lisbon and other cities. Red carnations were distributed to the troops and the demand for them from those of all walks of life was so great that quantities had to be flown in from Holland. Few could believe that the virtually bloodless 'Revolution of the Flowers' was over so soon: governments throughout the world were taken entirely by surprise.

A VACUUM TO BE FILLED

Immediately after the *coup*, power was exercised by a military 'National Junta', presided over by Spínola, nominated president of the Republic. However, although the MFA was able decisively to influence the course of events, few of its members had any political experience. They intended to be 'above party', but this proved an impossible ideal. Rival factions developed in the executive power struggle. The provisional government declared that civil governors would be replaced, generals and admirals who had been prominent supporters of the former regime would be forcibly retired, and political prisoners released. Immediate measures were taken to abolish the PIDE, whose compromising files were seized by the Portuguese Communist Party (PCP), and all forms of censorship. Most former institutions and associations were disbanded, together with several additional trappings of a totalitarian state. It was also stated that a diplomatic, not a military, solution would be sought to end the war in Africa. Political parties were free to form, with free elections promised within twelve months.

Several exiled political leaders returned to Lisbon, among them, from Paris, Mário Soares. He had founded a Socialist Party while resident in West Germany, with the slogan 'The people are with the MFA'. Alvaro Cunhal (the former general secretary of the PCP) flew in from Prague. A pro-European Popular Democrat Party (PPD) was founded by Francisco Sá Carneiro which, while at first closely allied to the Socialists, was to veer to the right, thus preventing the formation of a strong single centre party. Meanwhile, further to the right, arose the Centre Social Democrats (CDS), founded by Diogo Freitas do Amaral, behind which several progressive conservatives assembled, while among other groupings now pullulating was a left-wing Popular Democratic Movement (MPD).

On 17 July Brigadier Vasco Gonçalves became prime minister, while

'Otelo' – as he was popularly known – now a brigadier and with progressively ultra left-wing sympathies, was establishing a military intervention force, COPCON, which soon became almost as much a tool of reaction as the PIDE had been. Spínola was still of the opinion that the former colonies might be saved by the creation of a Lusitanian community, which would include Brazil, but the left-wing parties were adamant about giving them independence and withdrawing from them without further procrastination. This led to a showdown in late September 1974, from which the MFA radicals emerged victorious. On 30 September Spínola resigned to avoid possible bloodshed and further upheaval (there was going to be enough bloodshed in both Angola and East Timor, as it was). General Costa Gomes – nicknamed 'the cork' for his ability to float with the tide – became the new president. On 11 March 1975 a come-back on the part of Spínola fizzled out but led to arbitrary arrests of his supporters by COPCON, and the setting up of a Council of the Revolution, controlled by the more radical members of the MFA.

NATIONALIZATION AND LAND-SEIZURES

Dismantlement of former monopolies had already commenced, and the Council of the Revolution now also set about the nationalization of privately owned companies, starting with banks and insurance companies, key industries, petrol companies, many forms of transport, etc. In many cases, factories were occupied by workers, who then demanded state intervention to forestall what was alleged to be economic sabotage being practised by former managements. Previously, under the New State, an oligarchy of some forty families had held the country's economic reins and a high proportion of the industrial élite also held government posts. It has been estimated that one former conglomerate alone, owned by the De Melo family, had accounted for 10 per cent of national production and 20 per cent of Portuguese industry (including 70 per cent of the tobacco market), while the Champalimaud family had a near monopoly of the cement production.

In the countryside, notably in the Alentejo, there had long been a high proportion of *latifúndia* property, large (and often uncultivated) estates on which landless labourers found seasonal employment, amounting to over 1,000,000 hectares, or a fifth of all agricultural land owned. This, owned by 1,300 landowners (often absentees), was the object of wildcat seizures early in 1975, and was then distributed to over 150,000 peasants. It was in this area that the agricultural unions that had been formed were dominated by the PCP. Becoming progressively at odds with the authorities in Lisbon, they were starved of funds, technical assistance, fertilizers, etc. The work force was largely illiterate and their cooperatives lacked sufficient administrative experience. Indeed, the rural economy never got off the ground in the post-revolutionary period until agricultural reforms known as the *lei Barreto* (instigated by the agricultural minister of that name) were introduced in 1977, by which owners of expropriated property received some compensation. By the end of 1980, just over half the land 'illegally seized' had been returned to the previous owners and over a hundred cooperatives had been dissolved.

The Election of 25 April 1975

The polling for the Constituent Assembly on the first anniversary of the Revolution passed off without incident. The turn-out was exceptionally high, averaging 91.7 per cent. The Social Democratic Party (then known as the PPD) headed the polls in eight out of the eleven districts of the Beiras and the north, with the Socialist Party (PS) winning in Oporto, Castelo Branco and Coimbra; in the south, the PS topped the polls everywhere except in Beja, in the backward Alentejo, which was won by the PCP. During the Summer, Cunhal's Communists found themselves increasingly marginalized and their offices frequently attacked in the northern two-thirds of the country, while the MFA split up, with Otelo's COPCON on its left wing, which attempted to stop a mass meeting held by Soares's Socialists in Oporto. Soares now contradicted his former conviction: no longer were the people with the MFA. He proposed a 'government of national unity' and that Gonçalves should go. Meanwhile, in August, the more reasonable members of the MFA produced a 'Document of the Nine' (drawn up by Melo Antunes), which gained the majority support of regular officers in the three services and condemned the irresponsibility of the 'revolutionary vanguard' in imposing their political tenets on the country. He was in no way responsible for and could not condone the anti-Communist flare-up that Summer, when some fifty of their party offices were sacked or burned in the centre and north of the country.

On 27 September 1975 the Spanish Embassy and consulate in Lisbon were set alight in reaction to the execution by Franco of five militants in the previous month. In the following month the Chinese – who, together with both Russian and Cuban 'technicians', had taken advantage of the upheaval in Angola by supporting the subversive liberation movements – started to withdraw. The vacuum was soon filled by the Bakongo in the north, the Ovimbundu in the central Benguela plateau and the Mbunda in Luanda.

A state of confusion under a succession of provisional governments continued until 25 November, when Colonel (later General) António Ramalho Eanes took over anti-revolutionary operations. COPCON was disbanded and Otelo arrested, and any further drift towards possible civil war prevented. By 26 February 1976 a pact was entered into between the military and the political parties whereby the former's Council of the Revolution would remain a guarantor of democracy for another four years, legislative elections would be held two months later, followed by presidential elections. In the former, the Socialists lost slightly to the two Democratic parties, but Mário Soares was able to get a new Constitution approved by the Constituent Assembly on 2 April. In July, the austere and taciturn Ramalho Eanes took over the presidency from Costa Gomes, having gained 61.5 per cent of the valid votes in competing against three other candidates. Otelo Saraiva de Carvalho – released from detention in an amnesty – came second with 16.5 per cent. Soares's minority government presented their programme to the Assembly that August. The administration had enormous economic problems with which to contend, for the country was already suffering from the European recession which followed the Yom Kippur War of 1973. However, any immediate crisis was briefly postponed, as the economy had been cushioned by the extensive gold and foreign currency reserves hoarded by Salazar. The fact that Portugal continued to be a very considerable exporter of canned fish, wine, marble and cork was still not enough to keep her 'afloat'.

REINTEGRATING THE *RETORNADOS*

A serious embarrassment to the government was the immense task of repatriating the *retornados*, refugees (50 per cent of whom were under fifteen years of age) from the African colonies. There were perhaps as many as 800,000, mostly without financial resources – callously referred to as 'imperial flotsam' – who had to be assimilated, found accommodation, schools and employment. This total was only slightly less than the numbers which had to be absorbed by France from Algeria – and Portugal's population was five times smaller. To this figure must be added approximately 200,000 demobilized troops, for by mid-1976 the armed forces had been reduced to about 46,000 men, and also the return home of many thousand *regressados* or migrant workers who had lost their jobs due to the recession in Europe. It has been stated that as much as a fifth of the funds set aside for the relief of the *retornados* may have been fraudulently misappropriated. This caused widespread resentment and by late November 1976 welfare payments were suspended. Meanwhile, hotels and holiday accommodation had been requisitioned to shelter them, for – not surprisingly – the Revolution had caused a steep decline in the number of visitors and those seeking a secondary residence, and thus a hiatus in the speculative building of tourist accommodation on the Algarve coast. By the end of 1977 unemployment had risen to 25 per cent.

TOURISM

The 1974 'Revolution' caused a salutary check to the indiscriminate 'touristic' development of Portugal's shores. They have not been blighted to the same extent as those of Spain and are largely contained in the torrid Algarve, although still tighter control would be well-advised. More attention has and is being given to providing facilities and to the quality of facilities. In the upper reaches of the travel market the number of *pousadas* has increased throughout the country. To accommodate these, a number of buildings of historical or architectural interest were restored, among them at Amares, Guimarães, Obidos, Queluz, Palmela, Arraiolos, Crato, Evora, Estremoz, Vila Viçosa and Beja.

Admission to the European Community

On 28 March 1977 Portugal applied formally to join the EEC, but it was to take until January 1986 before the formal act of admission, signed the previous July, came into effect. Meanwhile, in January 1980, an Aliança Democrática (AD) government assumed office – a coalition of the Democratic parties led by Francisco de Sá Carneiro – the first majority administration since 1976. However, its legislations were vetoed on twenty-three occasions during that year by Eanes and the military Council of the Revolution, which was hardly conducive to political stability. It was not until Eanes had stepped down from his second term as president in 1986 that the administration passed from the hands of the military to those of civilians, although the necessary constitutional revisions did not come into effect for another three years.

Sá Carneiro was killed in a plane crash on the eve of the presidential election of December 1980. Eanes was returned as president. Sá Carneiro was succeeded as prime minister by the more malleable Francisco Pinto Balsemão, co-founder of the Social Democratic Party (PSD). Balsemão was replaced by Mário Soares in 1983, but with a minority government. Soares was succeeded by Aníbal Cavaco Silva two years later, who set about a programme of full or part-re-privatisation of almost seventy directly state-owned companies (among others) after 1989. Although some changes had already been made in the 1976 Constitution, it was not until a second revision received an absolute majority vote that these came into effect in 1989.

The presidential election of 1986 was narrowly won by Soares. The first civilian head of state for sixty years, he was to hold that office until 1996. On 1 January 1986 Portugal became a full member-state of the European Community, entry to which had been opposed only by the Communists. During its first decade as a member, Portugal received conspicuous inflows of capital from the European Union. Much of this was spent on a belated modernization of the country's infrastructure: building bridges, dams, roads and railways; in the agricultural and textile sectors, in setting up a variety of training schemes; and in improving the welfare services. By 1993 living standards were estimated at 64 per cent of the EC average, while unemployment had fallen to a

The Socialist leader Mário Soares in 1974

level which was low by EC standards. With the signing of the Schengen Accord, the land frontier with Spain could be crossed without the tedious delays and impediments formerly encountered.

In 1996 Jorge Sampaio, formerly secretary-general of the Socialist Party and mayor of Lisbon, was elected president, with almost 8 per cent more of the votes than cast for Cavaco Silva, who then retired from politics.

In 1998 the 500th anniversary of Da Gama's voyage to India was celebrated by a World Trade Fair, with the development of an extensive site in a long-dilapidated area flanking the Tagus north-east of the congested nucleus of Lisbon, and with the construction of a new bridge striding across the wide estuary to provide easier communication with the Alentejo and the main highway from Madrid which enters the country at Badajoz.

In June 1999 the Socialists just won the election for the European Parliament, but failed to gain an absolute majority in the National Assembly that October. However, the two main parties – the PS to the left and, to the right, the Social Democrats – remain firmly planted in the centre of the political spectrum and their differences are minor. Jorge Sampaio was re-elected in the presidential elections of February 2001.

Naturally, there are many areas of concern requiring the attention of the administration. On realizing what some might describe as 'political maturity', in developing her economy, and having displayed a remarkable capacity to adjust rapidly to the very different world in which she found herself after weathering the turmoil of revolution, Portugal now enjoys her well-merited place in the community of Europe. Although one of the smallest, she is one of Europe's longest-surviving independent nations and retains her characteristic individuality. One should not forget that she was also foremost, by her 'Discoveries', in expanding Europe's horizons during the fifteenth, sixteenth and seventeenth centuries. Because she established the first seaborne empire around the globe, the Portuguese language is the official language of 200 million people world-wide (156 million in Brazil alone). After English and Spanish, Portuguese is the third most widely spoken of European languages.

Notes

Notes

Notes

General Glossary

ajimece	two–light window, divided by a slender stone shaft
alcáçar	castle or fortress (from the Arabic *al-qasr*)
Almohads	a ruling dynasty of Berbers from the Masmuda tribes of the Atlas mountains
Almoravids	Berber nomads from the Sanhaja group of tribes, which were supplanted by the Almohads
anta	or dolmen; collective Megalithic grave, usually with a burial chamber and corridor; also an *orca*
artesonado	coffered wooden ceiling, often of Arabic workmanship
auto–da–fé	'Act of the Faith', the condemnation and sentence of execution, usually by the burning of heretics and crypto-Jews by the Inquisition
azulejos	tiles, usually forming painted and glazed panels, depicting scenes, designs, or floral patterns (*albarrada*)
bairro	district or quarter of a town
baixa	lower
barragem	dam of a reservoir
cabaceira	apse of a church
caciques	local political bosses
Câmara Municipal	Town Hall
capela–mor	chancel or sanctuary of a church
cartuxa	charterhouse
castro	prehistoric, usually hill-top, fortified settlement; also a *citânia*
CDS	Democratic and Social Centre Party
chafariz	public fountain, often monumental
charola	ambulatory of a centralized church, the most notable being that of the Convento de Cristo at Tomar
Christão–Novo	'New Christian' or converted crypto-Jew; also a *Converso*
citânia	prehistoric hill-settlement
claustro	cloister

comarca	adminstrative unit
concheiro	shell midden
conventus	group of towns whose inhabitants enjoyed full Roman citizenship during the early imperial era, while the capital of a *conventus* served as its judicial centre
Conversos	Converted Jews and their descendants
COPCON	Operational Command for Continent Portugal
coro alto	part of a church normally containing the choir-stalls
cortes	originally a representative assembly of the three estates of nobility, clergy and people
cruzeiro	cross, or crossing of a church
Dom and **Dona**	king and queen
EEC or **EC**	European (Economic) Community
Feitoria	'Factory' or trading agency or settlement
fidalgo	noble or gentleman
forais	charter
garum	condiment, apparently much appreciated by the Romans, prepared with decomposed salted and sun-dried fish
igreja	church; a parish church is an *igreja matriz*
Infante/a	prince/princess
janela	window
Joanino	late Baroque style in fashion at the time of Dom João V (1706–50)
Judiaria	Jewish quarter or ghetto
junta	council, usually political or military
Manuelino	characteristic late Gothic style of architecture current during the reign of Dom Manuel I (1495–1521) and later
Marrano	former derogatory name for a Portuguese Jew, or Crypto-Jew, assumed to be converted only ostensibly to Catholicism
mesquita	mosque
mestiço	of mixed blood
MFA	Movimento das Forças Armadas; the Armed Forces Movement
misericórdia	almshouse
mosteiro	monastery
Moçárabe	or Mozárab, Christian subject to the Muslims; a term extended to their architecture
Mouro	term loosely applied by the Portuguese to all 'Moors' or Muslims, from the Mauri of Mauretania
MPD	Portuguese Democratic Movement

Mudéjar	Muslim subject to the Christians; and a term extended to their architecture and decoration, often including cufic script
municipium	settlement of the indigenous inhabitants with the status of Latin citizenship, the magistrates of which were privileged by being granted the more superior status of Roman citizenship
Murabit	Arab name for the Almoravids; see above
muralha	wall
Muwahhid	Arab name for the Almohads; see above
Muwallad or *Muladi*	Christian converted to Islam
ordenança	second-line militia
paço	country house or mansion, or palace (usually *palácio*)
PCP	Portuguese Communist Party
pelourinho	stone column, sometimes ornamented, and ubiquitous in the towns and villages of northern Portugal, but seen less south of the Tagus. These emblems of feudal or municipal jurisdiction, from the steps of which the edicts of town councils were read, also served as pillories or gibbets, see p. 199 for example
PIDE	International and State Defence Police, an insidious and repressive secret agency under the Salazar regime, which frequently relied on informers
Pombalino	architectural style employed in the rebuilding of Lisbon after the earthquake of 1755, named after the Marquês de Pombal
pousada	one of a once partly state-subsidised network of hotels, often in restored buildings of architectural merit
PPD	later *PPS*, Popular Democratic Party; Social Democratic Party
praça	square or (market-) place; also a *largo*
pronunciamento	*coup d'état*, usually of military inspiration
PS	Socialist Party
quartel	barracks
quinta	country estate, or the main residence on such
retrato	portrait
sé	cathedral
serra	range of hills or mountains
solar	manor house, or the seat of an armigerous family
taifa	petty kingdom, many proliferating in the 11th century after the breakdown of caliphal authority
talha	carved woodwork, frequently *dourada* or gilded
torre de menagem	castle keep

Chronology of Major Events

BC

*c.*1100	Phoenicians active in what is now southern Portugal
*c.*750	Probable date of the foundation of Carthage
*c.*700–600	What is now northern Portugal invaded by Celtic tribes
*c.*700–500	'Tartessian' culture flourishes in the south-west of the Peninsula
*c.*600	Greek traders reach Portugal
247–41	First Punic War
218–01	Second Punic War, after which much of Iberia was dominated by the Romans. By 197, part of what is now Portugal included in the province of Hispania Ulterior (further), with the eastern half of the Peninsula being Hispania Citerior (nearer, to Rome)
154	The Lusitani revolt; Viriatus, their leader, assassinated in 139
146	Destruction of Carthage by Scipio Aemilianus
138–136	Expedition into Gallaecia under Decimus Junius Brutus, who established his capital at Olisipo (Lisbon)
72–61	Further Lusitanian raids
60	Olisipo (Lisbon) confirmed as capital by Julius Caesar
25	Augusta Emerita (Mérida) founded
19	The territory which now constitutes Portugal is 'pacified' by the Romans
*c.*16	Augustus divides the province of Hispania Ulterior into Lusitania and Baetica, while Hispania Citerior becomes Tarraconensis

AD

14–37	Tiberius emperor
98–117	Trajan (born at Italica, near Seville) emperor
117–38	Hadrian (born in Italica) emperor
171–3	Baetica raided by Moors (Mauri) from Mauretania

298	Diocletian subdivides Tarraconensis
306–37	Reign of Constantine I, converted to Christianity in 312
376	Visigoths enter the Roman Empire
385	Death of Priscillian
409	Northern Gallaecia and Baetica invaded, largely by Hasding Vandals, Alans and Suevi; Lusitania occupied by the Alans
410	Rome sacked by Visigoths
c.411	The Suevi settled between the Minho and Douro
c.417	Visigoths under Wallia invade the Peninsula and in c.429 force the Alans over to North Africa
430–56	The Suevi dominant in the western half of the Peninsula
456	Visigoths under Theodoric II, allied with Rome, enter the Peninsula, driving the Suevi to the north-west; their king, Rechiarius (448–56), defeated by the Visigoths
466–84	Reign of Euric, a Visigoth, who completed the conquest of the Peninsula; the Visigoths start settling there
507	Visigoths in Gaul toppled by the Franks at the battle of Vouillé
527–65	Justinian emperor
551–624	Byzantine enclave in southern Hispania
c.570	Birth of Muhammad (d. 632)
585	Leovigild (569–86) suppresses the Suevic enclave in Gallaecia
587	Reccared, Leovigild's successor (586–601), is converted from Arianism to orthodox Catholicism, and in 589 the Visigoths are likewise (formally) at the Third Council of Toledo
624	Suinthila expels Byzantines from southern areas of the Peninsula
647	First Arab incursions into North Africa, taking Carthage in 698
654	Reccesuinth promulgates *Forum Iudicum*, a code of laws
710	Civil war follows the death of Wittiza
711	Muslims led by Tariq ibn Ziyad invade the Peninsula from North Africa, and Portugal south of the Mondego occupied by c.716
c.722	Christians under Pelayo defeat a small body of Moors at the 'battle' of Covadonga, initiating the reconquest of the Peninsula
732	Muslim invasion of France checked at Poitiers by Charles Martel
740	Berbers revolt against Arab administration
756	Foundation of the Umayyad emirate of Córdoba by 'Abd al-Rahman I, independent of Damascus
778	A Frankish expedition into the Ebro valley led by

	Charlemagne withdraws; Roland's rearguard destroyed by Basque guerrillas at Roncesvalles
791	Oviedo established as a Christian capital under Alfonso II
c.830	Relics of St James are claimed to have been found at Compostela, and pilgrimages to the site are promoted
844	First Viking raids, repeated in 966 and 971
868	Oporto reconquered by the Christians; the area between the Minho and Douro first referred to as 'Portucale' in 883
910	Alfonso III (the Great) of Asturias deposed by his sons
914	Oviedo replaced by León as capital of the Asturian kingdom
910	Monastery of Cluny (Burgundy) founded
929	Al-Andalus proclaimed a caliphate by Abd al-Rahman III
981–1002	Al-Mansur in power at Córdoba; he sacks León in 988 and Santiago in 997
1000–35	Reign of Sancho III (the Great) of Navarre
1031	The Umayyad caliphate disintegrates into *taifa* states
1037	Castile and León united under Fernando I (1035–65)
1073	Alfonso VI king of Castile, Galicia and Portugal. His daughter Urraca marries Raymond of Burgundy, who by 1095 was also lord of Galicia and count of Coimbra
1085	Toledo recaptured by Alfonso VI of Castile, defeated in 1086 by the invading Almoravids at Sagrajas or Zallaqa (near Badajoz)
1094	The Cid seizes Valencia
1097	Raymond's cousin, Henry, given the county of Portucale and Coimbra. On his death (1112/14) his wife Teresa (an illegitimate daughter of Alfonso VI) became regent for their son, Afonso Henriques
1099	Jerusalem captured by the Crusaders
c.1099	The Almoravids settle in the Algarve (al-Gharbh al-Andalus), followed by the Almohads in 1146
1114	St Bernard founds Clairvaux
1118	Templars founded; Saragossa captured by Alfonso I of Aragón
1128	The Portuguese revolt against Alfonso VII of León, the battle of São Mamede (Guimarães) being won by Afonso Henriques
1137	Independence of Portugal (with Afonso Henriques as king) recognized by León-Castile, more formally in 1143 by the Treaty of Zamora, and by Pope Alexander III in 1179
1139	The Muslims decisively defeated at Ourique by Afonso Henriques
1146	Almohad invasion of the Peninsula from North Africa
1147	Lisbon falls to Afonso Henriques

1153	The Cistercians given land at Alcobaça, in construction between 1178 and 1223
1158	Alcácer do Sal taken; and Beja and Evora in 1162 and 1165
1158–70	Spanish military Orders of Calatrava, Santiago and Alcántara founded
1171	The Christians pushed back to Santarém by the Almohads
1189	Dom Sancho I captures Silves in 1189, but loses territory south of the Tagus the following year
1195	Dom Afonso VIII defeated at Alarcos by the Almohads
1208	The future Dom Afonso II marries Urraca, daughter of Alfonso VIII of Castile and Eleanor Plantagenet Commencement of the Albigensian crusade. Pere II of Aragón killed at the battle of Muret in 1213
1211	The first *cortes* held, at Coimbra
1212	The battle of Las Navas de Tolosa in Spain, with the Almohads defeated by united Christian armies: a watershed in the reconquest of the Peninsula as a whole (Fernando III of Castile-León takes Córdoba and Seville in 1236 and 1248 respectively)
*c.*1230	Collapse of Almohad rule in Al-Andalus
*c.*1237	Nasrid dynasty established at Granada
1239	Jerusalem lost to the Christians
1248	Seville falls to Fernando III of Castile
1267	Castile gives up all claims to the Algarve, completing territorial integration of Portugal
1270	Eighth crusade; death of Louis IX (St Louis) at Tunis
1282	Pere III of Aragón conquers Sicily
1297	Portuguese frontier with Castile endorsed by the *Treaty of Alcañices*
1311	The Templars abolished; the Order of Christ founded in 1319
1340	Dom Afonso IV, allied with Alfonso XI of Castile, defeats the Muslims at the battle of Salado
1348	Outbreak of the Black Death in Portugal
1355	Inês de Castro murdered
1367	The Black Prince, allied to Peter the Cruel, defeats his half-brother Enrique II at Nájera
1371	John of Gaunt, Duke of Lancaster, marries Peter the Cruel's daughter, Constanza and assumes title of King of Castile
1373	Lisbon sacked; an Anglo-Portuguese alliance signed
1381	Edmund of Cambridge's troops land at Lisbon
1383–5	Interregnum of Leonor Teles
1385	The battle of Aljubarrota (14 August). Juan I of Castile defeated by João of Avis, proclaimed King of Portugal as João I

1386	The *Treaty of Windsor* signed. A Lancastrian army lands in Galicia prior to a projected (but fruitless) invasion of Castile
1387	Dom João I marries Philippa of Lancaster, daughter of John of Gaunt, at Oporto
1388	The construction of Batalha is commenced
1415	Ceuta captured
1419–20	Madeira colonized
1427	Diogo de Silves sights the Azores
1434	Gil Eanes rounds Cape Bojador
1437	Tangier expedition fails
1441	Slaves from the Mauretanian coast first landed at Lagos
1445	First 'factory' on West African coast established, at Arguim
1449	Battle of Alfarrobeira, in which the Duke of Coimbra is killed
1450s	The Portuguese reach Guinea and Sierra Leone
c.1456	Cape Verde Islands discovered; settled in the 1460s
1460	Death of Prince Henry 'the Navigator', who had instigated much maritime exploration
1469	Marriage of Isabel of Castile and Fernando of Aragón, known as 'the Catholic Monarchs' after their kingdoms were united in 1479
1471	Tangier is eventually taken
1476	Indecisive battle of Toro against the Castilians
1479	Portugal cedes Canary Islands to Spain
1482	The fort of São Jorge da Mina built on the Gold Coast; Diogo Cão reaches the Congo river; the interior penetrated in the 1490s
1487–8	The Cape of Good Hope rounded by Bartolomeu Dias's expedition
1490s	The Portuguese penetrate into the interior of Congo
1492	The Spanish capture Granada; the rediscovery of 'America' by Columbus; c. 60,000 Jews expelled from Castile and Aragón take refuge in Portugal
1493	On returning from the Antilles, Columbus puts in at Lisbon
1494	The *Treaty of Tordesillas* divides the new discoveries between Spain and Portugal
c.1495	Portuguese make a landfall on Greenland
1497–8	Vasco da Gama discovers the sea-route to India
1499–1502	Newfoundland, Labrador and Nova Scotia reached by Gaspar and Miguel Corte-Real
1500	Brazil discovered by Pedro Alvares Cabral; Madagascar 'discovered'
c.1501	A fishing settlement is established on Newfoundland
1503	The Seychelles 'discovered'

1507	A fort is built at Mozambique; Albuquerque takes Ormuz
1510–15	Goa and Malacca occupied by Afonso de Albuquerque
1512	A Portuguese Factory established at Calicut
1513	Balbao discovers Pacific ocean; Azemmur, in Morocco, captured
1513–15	The Brazilian coast reconnoitred by João Dias de Solis
1514	The first Portuguese trade mission to China under Jorge Alvares
1515	Portuguese missionaries enter Benin; Albuquerque captures Ormuz
1516–56	Charles V, first of the Habsburg dynasty ruling in Spain
1518	A fort is built at Colombo, Ceylon
1519–21	Hernán Cortes conquers the Aztec kingdom of Mexico
1519–22	The surviving ship of Magellan's expedition, commanded by Elcano, circumnavigates the globe
1520	Luther excommunicated; Portuguese embassy to the Negus in Ethiopia
1525	The American coast from Newfoundland to the Chesapeake explored by Estevão Gomes (in the service of Castile)
1531	The Inquisition introduced into Portugal
1533	Fernando Pizarro captures the Inca capital of Cuzco in Peru
1534	The Society of Jesus (Jesuits) founded by Ignacio de Loyola
1537	Diu ceded to the Portuguese
1542	Portuguese missionaries at Goa
1542–3	The Portuguese reach Japan; a Jesuit mission is established there by Francis Xavier in 1549
1545	Silver discovered at Potosi
1549	A Portuguese governor-general takes up his post in Brazil
1554–8	Felipe/Philip II of Spain married to Mary Tudor
1557	A trading post established at Macão
1559	An embassy is sent to Angola
1565	Spain occupies the Philippines
1571	The Portuguese established at Nagasaki. Turkish fleet scattered at Lepanto by combined Christian fleets
1572	Camões's *Os Lusíadas* published. Massacre of St Bartholomew
1578	Dom Sebastião killed at the disaster of Alcácer-Quibir
1579	The 'United Provinces' proclaim their independence, recognized by Spain in 1609
1580	António, Prior of Crato, proclaims himself king, but is defeated by the Duke of Alba at Alcântara (near Lisbon)
1580–1640	The Castilian usurpation: the 'Sixty Years Captivity'

1581	The *cortes* at Tomar proclaims Felipe II of Spain king as Felipe I of Portugal
1588	A large part of 'the Spanish Armada' sets sails from Lisbon and is virtually destroyed
1598	*The Edict of Nantes* protects Protestants; revoked in 1685
1606	The New Hebrides 'discovered' by Pedro Fernandes de Queirós
1607 on	Dutch competition on the increase
1618	Commencement of the Thirty Years War
1620	The 'Pilgrim Fathers' sail to America
1630–54	Dutch occupation of much of the coast of north-eastern Brazil
1637	Revolt at Evora
1639	Spanish fleet defeated by the Dutch at the battle of the Downs
1640	The Catalans rebel against Castile. The Spanish governor overthrown at Lisbon and the seventh Duke of Braganza proclaimed king as João IV. Under the Tokugawa shogunate (1603–1867) the Portuguese and other foreigners are expelled from Japan (until 1852)
1641	Fall of Malacca
1642	Treaty signed with Charles I of England just prior to the Civil War
1644	Spanish defeated at Montijo
1648	The Dutch expelled from Angola. Further exploration of the Amazon basin commenced by António Raposo Tavares
1650	The Portuguese expelled from the Persian Gulf
1654	*Commonwealth Treaty* signed with England
1655	England captures Jamaica from Spain
1655–63	Loss of Ceylon and Malabar to Dutch
1659	*Treaty of the Pyrenees*: peace between France and Spain; Elvas attacked by Spain
1661	*Treaty of Alliance* with England
1662	Catherine of Braganza sails to England to marry Charles II; Tangier and Bombay ceded to England as part of her dowry
1663	Evora occupied by Spanish forces (May), who are defeated at Ameixial in June
1664	Portuguese defeat Spanish besieging Castelo Rodrigo
1665	Spanish defeated at Montes Claros (June)
1668	Spain recognizes Portugal's independence. Afonso's brother Pedro marries his former sister-in-law and becomes prince regent
1680	The Colony of Sacramento founded on the Río de la Plata
1690s	Alluvial gold found in Minas Gerais
1699	The first shipment of Brazilian gold reaches Lisbon

1702–13	The War of the Spanish Succession, Portugal siding with Britain
1703	*The Methuen Treaties* signed with Britain
1704	The Archduke Charles reaches Lisbon (March). Spain declares war on Portugal (April). Berwick advances into Portugal, but retires that July. Gibraltar captured by the British (August)
1705	The widowed Catherine of Braganza is regent after Pedro II has a stroke in January; she dies on 31 December. Portuguese take Valencia de Alcántara and Albuquerque (May). The Archduke Charles leaves Portugal in late July
1706	Portuguese take Alcántara (April)
1707	Allies defeated at Almanza (25 April)
1709	Portuguese defeated near Arronches (May)
1712	Suspension of arms in Portugal (November)
1713	*Treaties of Utrecht* signed by Britain, France, Portugal, Prussia and Savoy (April)
1714	Queen Anne dies (August), succeeded by George I
1715	Portugal concludes peace with Spain (February). Louis XIV dies (September)
1717	The construction of Mafra commenced
1720	The Royal Academy of History founded in Lisbon
1729	Diamonds discovered in Minas Gerais, Bahía, Brazil
1734	Gold discovered in Mato Grosso, Brazil
1749	The Aguas Livres aqueduct at Lisbon completed
1751	The Indians of Brazil emancipated
1755	The Great Lisbon Earthquake (1 November). Pombal in power
1758	Assassination of José I thwarted; Aveiros and Távoras incriminated
1759–60	The Society of Jesus expelled from Portugal and her overseas territories
1761	Slavery abolished in mainland Portugal
1762	Spanish declare war (May) and invade the Trás-os-Montes and Beira. Truce declared in November; peace signed in February 1763
1763	The capital of Brazil transferred from Salvador to Rio de Janeiro
1768	Captain Cook sails for Tahiti
1775	America at war with England, declares independence in 1776
1777	Pombal dismissed from office
1787	An English colony established at Botany Bay, Australia
1789	Commencement of the French Revolution
1792–1816	Regency of the future João VI, whose mother's insanity

	obliges him to govern in her name; from 1799 he acts as prince-regent
1797	The battle of Cape St Vincent (14 February)
1798	Bonaparte in Egypt; Nelson destroys French fleet at Aboukir
1801	'The War of the Oranges', in which Spain invades Portugal and coerces her to cede Olivenza
1805	The battle of Trafalgar (21 October)
1807	Portugal invaded by the French under Junot; the royal family embark for Rio. Lisbon under enemy occupation from 30 November. Abolition of slave trade in Britain; and in 1834 in its colonies
1808–14	The Peninsular War
1808	The French occupying Lisbon are defeated by Wellesley (later Wellington) at Roliça (17 August) and Vimeiro (21 August), and are repatriated after the signing of the Convention of Cintra (30 August)
1809	Sir John Moore killed at Corunna (16 January); Wellesley returns to Portugal and drives Soult from Oporto (12 May); the battle of Talavera (28 July)
1810	Masséna enters Portugal, is checked at the battle of Busaco (12 September) and his advance on Lisbon is frustrated by the Lines of Torres Vedras
1811	The French retreat to the Spanish frontier. The battles of Fuentes de Oñoro (3–5 May) and La Albuera (16 May)
1812	Ciudad Rodrigo (19 January) and Badajoz (6 April) taken by Wellington; the battle of Salamanca (22 July), and Madrid entered
1813	The French finally thrust out of Portugal itself in mid-May, followed by the battles of Vitoria (21 June) and the Pyrenees (late July); Wellington enters France (October)
1814	The Peninsular War ends with the battle of Toulouse (10 April)
1815	Congress of Vienna; the battle of Waterloo (18 June)
1822	Brazil independent. Portuguese Constitution proclaimed
1828–34	The War of the Two Brothers. Miguel, appointed regent, proclaims himself king; eventually forced to capitulate at Evora-Monte
1827	The Turkish fleet destroyed at Navarino
1833–9	The First Carlist War in Spain
1834	Maria II, 'da Glória' marries August of Leuchtenberg, brother of her father's second wife, who died within days of entering Portugal. The religious orders are expelled
1846	'Maria da Fonte' disturbances in northern Portugal

1858	Pedro V marries Stéphanie of Hohenzollern-Sigmaringen; she dies of diphtheria two months after reaching Portugal
1890	British demand evacuation of territories between Angola and Mozambique
1895	Mozambique occupied
1898	The Spanish–American War. Spain loses her remaining empire
1905	Angola occupied
1910	Carlos I assassinated
1910	Manuel II abdicates; the Portuguese Republic proclaimed (5 October)
1916	Portugal enters the First World War on the side of the Allies
1918	Sidónia Pais assassinated
1926	Military dictatorship of Gen. Gomes da Costa. Gen. Fragoso Carmona president until 1951
1928	António de Oliveira Salazar minister of finance, and 'prime minister' from 1932 to 1968
1936–9	The Spanish Civil War
1939–45	Portugal remains neutral during the Second World War, but provides the Allies with air-bases in the Azores (1943)
1958	European Economic Community becomes effective. Gen. Humberto Delgado unsuccessful in his bid against Adm. Tomás, re-elected president, and his attempted *coup* fails in the following March
1961	Goa occupied by Indian troops
1961 on	Rebellions in Angola, Guinea and Mozambique
1968	Salazar suffers a stroke (15 Sept.)
1973	The Armed Forces Movement founded (9 Sept.)
1974	Virtually 'bloodless' military revolution in Portugal (25 April)
1976	Timor annexed by Indonesia
1980	Sá Carneiro, when prime minister, killed in plane crash (December)
1986	Portugal enters the European Community. Mário Soares is first civilian Head of State for 60 years
1996	Jorge Sampaio elected president, and re-elected in 2001
1999	Macão reverts to China
2001	Portugal decriminalizes drug use

Rulers of Portugal

Kings are usually referred to as Dom. Dates in brackets indicate the year of their marriages.

Among the Visigothic kings were:

395–410	Alaric I
416–19	Wallia
419–51	Theodoric I
453–66	Theodoric II
466–84	Euric
484–507	Alaric II
554–67	Athanagild
569–86	Leovigild
586–601	Reccared I
612–21	Sisebut
621–31	Suinthila
631–36	Sisenand
642–53	Chindasuinth
649–72	Reccesuinth
672–80	Wamba
680–87	Ervig
687–702	Egica
692/4–710	Wittiza
710–11	Roderic

House of Burgundy (or Afonsin Dynasty)

Henri of Burgundy (died 1112)		–	Teresa (*c.* 1095), illegitimate daughter of Alfonso VI of León and Castile
1128/39–85	Afonso Henriques	–	Mafalda (Mahaut) of Maurienne and Savoy (1146)
1185–1211	Sancho I	–	Dulce of Aragón (1174)
1211–23	Afonso II	–	Urraca (1208), daughter of Alfonso VIII of Castile and Eleanor Plantagenet
1223–46	Sancho II	–	Mécia López de Haro (*c.* 1240)
1246–79	Afonso III	–	Matilde, Countess of Boulogne (1235)
		–	Beatriz de Guillén (1253), daughter of Alfonso X of Castile
1279–1325	Dinis,'O Lavrador' (the husbandman)	–	Isabel (1282), daughter of Pedro III of Aragón
1325–57	Afonso IV	–	Beatriz of Castile (1309), daughter of Sancho IV of Castile
1357–67	Pedro I ('the Justicier')	–	Blanca of Castile (1328), but marriage dissolved
		–	Constanza of Castile (1340), died in 1345 (with Inês de Castro from before 1345, whom he claimed to have married in 1354; she was murdered in 1355). Two of her sons married daughters of Enrique II of Castile
		–	(Teresa Lourenço, mother of the future João I, born in June 1358)
1367–83	Fernando	–	Leonor Teles de Meneses (1372), whose daughter Beatriz married Juan I of Castile in 1383
1383–5	(Interregnum)		

House of Avis

1385–1433	João I	–	(Inês Peres), whose son Afonso, born 1380, married Beatriz Pereira (1401), daughter of the Constable Nun'Alvares Pereira, and who became Count of Barcelos and 1st Duke of Braganza in 1442. Inês's daughter married Thomas Fitzalan, Earl of Arundel, in 1405
		–	Philippa of Lancaster (1387)
1433–8	Duarte (Edward)	–	Leonor of Aragón (1428)
1438–81	Afonso V ('the African')	–	Isabel of Portugal (1441)
1481–95	João II	–	Leonor of Portugal (1471)
1495–1521	Manuel I ('the Fortunate')	–	Isabel of Castile (1497)
		–	Maria of Castile (1500)
		–	Leonor of Spain (1518)
1521–57	João III	–	Catarina of Spain (1525)
1557–78	Sebastião ('the Regretted')		
1578–80	Henrique (the Cardinal-king)		
1580	António, Prior of Crato		

House of Austria (Spanish usurpation)

1580–98	Felipe/Philip II of Spain from 1556 (I of Portugal)	–	Maria (1543), daughter of João III
		–	Mary Tudor (1554)
		–	Elizabeth of Valois (1560)
		–	Ana of Austria (1570)
1598–1621	Felipe III of Spain (II of Portugal)	–	Margaret of Austria (1599)
1621–40	Felipe IV of Spain until 1665 (III of Portugal)	–	Mariana of Austria (1647)

House of Braganza

1640–56	João IV	–	Luisa de Guzmán (1633)
1656–83	Afonso VI	–	Maria-Francisca (Marie-Françoise-Isabelle d'Aumale of Savoy, 1666; but unconsummated)
1683–1706	Pedro II (regent from 1668)	–	Maria Francisca (1668)
		–	Maria-Sofia-Isabel (Maria-Sophia-Elizabeth of Neuberg) (1687)
1706–50	João V ('the Magnificent')	–	Maria-Ana of Austria (1708)
1750–77	José	–	Mariana-Victoria of Spain (1729)
1777–1816	Maria I	–	Pedro III (her uncle; in 1760)
1816–26	João VI (regent in 1792; formally from 1799)	–	Carlota-Joaquina of Spain (1784)
1826	Pedro IV (who abdicated, leaving the kingdom to his daughter, Maria)	–	Maria Leopoldina of Austria (1817)
		–	Maria Amelia of Leuchtenberg (1829)
1828–34	Usurpation of Dom Miguel	–	Adelaide-Sofia of Loewenstein-Rosenberg (1851)
1834–53	Maria II ('da Glória')	–	August of Leuchtenberg (1834)
		–	Ferdinand of Saxe-Coburg-Gotha (1836)
1853–61	Pedro V	–	Stéphanie of Hohenzollern-Sigmaringen (1858)
1861–89	Luis	–	Maria-Pia of Savoy (1862)
1889–1908	Carlos	–	Marie-Amelie of Orléans (1886)
1908–10	Manuel II ('the Unfortunate')	–	Augusta-Victoria of Sigmaringen (1913)

Republic

Presidents or heads of governments

1910	Teófilo Braga
1911–15	Manuel de Arriaga
1915	Teófilo Braga
1915–17	Bernardino Machado
1917–18	Sidónio Pais
1918–19	Adm. João de Canto e Castro
1919–23	António José de Almeida
1923–5	Manuel Teixeira Gomes
1925–6	Bernardino Machado
1926	Commander Mendes Cabeçadas
1926	Gen. Gomes da Costa
1926–51	Gen. António Oscar Fragoso de Carmona (with António de Oliveira Salazar as 'prime minister' from 1932 to 1968)
1951–8	Gen. Francisco Higino Craveiro Lópes
1958–74	Adm. Américo de Deus Rodrigues Tomás (with Marcello Caetano as 'prime minister' from 1968 to 1974)
1974	Gen. António Sebastião Ribeiro de Spínola
1974–6	Gen. Francisco da Costa Gomes
1976–86	Gen. António dos Santos Ramalho Eanes
1986–96	Mário Alberto Nobre Lópes Soares
1996–	Jorge Sampaio

Further Reading

The majority of books in this inevitably very selective and idiosyncratic list (not all of which have been read by its compiler) were published in the United Kingdom unless otherwise described. The date of publication is that of the first edition; those of reprints are not usually given, except when substantially revised. Many of the earlier works will be out of print, but the larger libraries should be able to provide copies. Although, as the titles of several imply, while primarily concerned with Spain, they also incorporate a variable proportion to Portuguese affairs. Although most categories – among which there are certain overlappings – concentrate on mainland Portugal, two refer to some of the more important books only – themselves including extensive if not exhaustive bibliographies – devoted to her discoveries and former Empire.

Travel, Topography and General Description

BRADFORD, SARAH *Portugal* (1973)

BRIDGE, ANN (LADY O'MALLEY) and SUSAN BELLOC LOWNDES MARQUES *The Selective Traveller in Portugal* (1949; revised 1967)

BRYANS, ROBIN *The Azores* (1963)

MACAULAY, ROSE *They Went to Portugal* (1946; reprinted 1986) and *They Went to Portugal Too* (1990), both inimitable

The Naval Intelligence Division Geographical Handbook, vol. 1 *Spain and Portugal* (general and physical; 1941); vol. 2, *Portugal* (1942); and vol. 3, *The Atlantic Islands* (1945), although dated, contain much interesting if quaint information

ROBERTSON, IAN *Blue Guide: Portugal* (4th ed., 1996) describes the country and its monuments in historical perspective within the parameters imposed by the series; more personal is *Portugal: a Traveller's Guide* (1992)

SITWELL, SACHEVERELL *Portugal and Madeira* (1954), urbane although uneven

Among numerous, if unequal, earlier works, are:

ANON. [J.-B.-F. CARRÈRE] *A Picture of Lisbon taken on the spot* (1809)

ANON. *The Ancient and Present State of Portugal, containing a description of that Kingdom . . . etc., by a Gentleman who Resided there some years* (1713)

BAILLIE, MARIANNE *Lisbon in the years 1821, 1822, and 1823* (1825)

BARETTI, JOSEPH *A Journey from London to Genoa* (1770; reprinted 1970, with an Introduction by Ian Robertson); earlier chapters only

BEAMISH, HULDANE V. *The Hills of Alentejo* (1958)

BECKFORD, WILLIAM *The Journal of William Beckford in Portugal and Spain 1787–1788*, ed. by Boyd Alexander (1954); *Italy, with Sketches of Spain and Portugal* (1834); *Recollections of an Excursion to the Monasteries of Alcobaça and Batalha* (1835; reprinted 1972, with an Introduction by Boyd Alexander); and ed. by Guy Chapman, *The Travel Diaries of William Beckford of Fonthill* (1928)

BORROW, GEORGE *The Bible in Spain* (1843), earlier chapters only; ed. by T.H. Darlow, *Letters to the British and Foreign Bible Society* (1911); and Ian Robertson, *George Borrow in Portugal* (in The British Historical Society of Portugal's '21st Annual Report'; Lisbon, 1995)

BOURGOING, JEAN-FRANÇOIS *Travels of the Duke de Chatelet in Portugal* (1809)

BOWDITCH, T.E. *Excursions in Madeira and Porto Santo* (1825)

BROMLEY, WILLIAM *Several years travel of a gentleman through Portugal . . .* (1702)

CARNARVON; see Porchester

'COSTIGAN, ARTHUR' [MAJOR JAMES FERRIER] *Sketches of Society and Manners in Portugal* (1787)

CRAWFORD, OSWALD *Travels in Portugal* (1875) and *Portugal Old and New* (1880), the former written under the pseudonym of 'John Latouche'

CROKER, RICHARD *Travels through Several Parts of Spain and Portugal* (1799)

DALRYMPLE, WILLIAM *Travels through Spain and Portugal in 1774* (1777)

DUMOURIEZ, GEN. CHARLES FRANÇOIS *An Account of Portugal as it appeared in 1766* (1797)

HARRISON, WILLIAM HENRY *Jennings' Landscape Annual, or, Tourist in Portugal* (1839), illustrated with plates after James Holland

HOLLAND, ELIZABETH, LADY, ed. by the Earl of Ilchester *The Spanish Journal*, (1910) also describes Portugal in late 1808/early 1809

HUGHES, TERENCE MAHON *An Overland Journey to Lisbon at the close of 1846* (1847)

KINGSTON, WILLIAM HENRY GILES *Lusitanian Sketches* (1845)

KINSEY, WILLIAM MORGAN *Portugal illustrated* (1828), a pedestrian account

LINK, HENRY FREDERICK *Travels in Portugal* (1801)

MULLER, RICHARD *Memoirs of the Right Hon. Lord Viscount Cherington* (1782)

MURPHY, JAMES *Travels in Portugal . . . in 1789 and 1790* (1795) and *A general view of the state of Portugal* (1798)

NEALE, JOHN MASON *Hand-Book for Travellers in Portugal* (1855), referred to in the

1880s as being 'not only the worst handbook in that eminent publisher's [John Murray] series – for that might still be high praise – but probably the very worst handbook that ever was printed'; a curiosity of its period

PORCHESTER, HENRY JOHN GEORGE HERBERT, Viscount, later 3rd Earl Carnarvon *Portugal and Galicia* (1836; 2nd ed. 1837)

QUILLINAN, DOROTHY (*née* Wordsworth) *Journal of a few months' Residence in Portugal* (1847)

SOUTHEY, ROBERT *Letters from Spain and Portugal* (1797) and ed. by Adolfo Cabral, *Journals of a Residence in Portugal 1800–1801* (1960)

TWISS, RICHARD *Travels through Spain and Portugal in 1772 and 1773* (1775)

General Histories

CASTRO, AMÉRICO *The Structure of Spanish History* (1954), revised as *The Spaniards: An Introduction to their History* (1971)

LIVERMORE, HAROLD V. *A History of Portugal* (1947); *New History of Portugal* (1966), more compact; and *Portugal: a Short History* (1973)

MARQUES, A.H. DE OLIVEIRA *Daily Life in Portugal in the Late Middle Ages* (Madison, 1971); and *History of Portugal*, 2 vols. (New York, 1972); and the more concise *History of Portugal* (Lisbon, 1991)

WHEELER, DOUGLAS L. *A Historical Dictionary of Portugal* (New Jersey, 1993)

Archaeology and Early History

ALARCÃO, JORGE DE *Roman Portugal* (1988) with a comprehensive gazetteer

ARRUDA, ANA MARGARIDA *et al.*, *Subterranean Lisbon* (Lisbon, 1994), a Museu Nacional de Arqueologia exhibition catalogue

COLLINS, ROGER *Early Medieval Spain: Unity in Diversity, 400–1000* (1983), and *The Arab Conquest of Spain, 710–797* (1989). Forthcoming are *Visigothic Spain, 409–711* and *Caliphs and Kings, 798–1033*

CONSTABLE, OLIVIA REMIE *Trade and Traders in Muslim Spain* (1994)

CURCHIN, LEONARD A. *Roman Spain: Conquest and Assimilation* (1991)

DAVID, C.W., ed. and trans. *De Expugnatione Lyxbonensi* (New York, 1936), concerning the capture of Lisbon from the Muslims

FLETCHER, RICHARD *Saint James's Catapult: The Life and Times of Diego Gelmirez of Santiago de Compostela* (1984) and *Moorish Spain* (1992)

GLICK, THOMAS F. *Islamic and Christian Spain in the Early Middle Ages* (1979)

HARRISON, RICHARD J. *Spain at the Dawn of History* (1988)

HILLGARTH, J.N. *The Spanish Kingdoms, 1250–1516* (1976; 1978)

JACKSON, GABRIEL *The Making of Medieval Spain* (1972), from 711 to 1492

KEAY, SIMON *Roman Spain* (1988)

KENNEDY, HUGH *Muslim Spain and Portugal: a Political Hiistory of al-Andalus* (1996)

LIVERMORE, HAROLD V. *The Origins of Spain and Portugal* (1971)

LINEHAN, PETER *Spain, 1157–1312*, forthcoming

LOMAX, DEREK W. *The Reconquest of Spain* (1978); and ed., with R.J. Oakley *The English in Portugal 1367–87* (1988), extracts from Fernão Lopes's 'The Chronicles of Dom Fernando and Dom João'

MACKAY, ANGUS *Spain in the Middle Ages* (1977) and forthcoming, *Spain: Centuries of Crisis, 1300–1474*

REILLY, BERNARD F. *The Contest of Christian and Muslim Spain, 1031–1157* (1992) and *The Medieval Spains* (1993)

RICHARDSON, J.S., *The Romans in Spain* (1996)

RUSSELL, PETER E. *The English Intervention in Spain and Portugal in the time of Edward III and Richard II* (1955)

THOMPSON, E.A. *The Goths in Spain* (1969)

WASSERSTEIN, DAVID *The Rise and Fall of the Party Kings . . . , 1002–1086* (1985)

WATT, W. MONTGOMERY *A History of Islamic Spain* (1965)

Exploration, Discoveries, Possessions and related subjects

ALDEN, DANIEL *The Making of the Enterprise* (the Jesuits) (1998)

ALEXSON, ERIC *The Portuguese in South-east Africa, 1600–1700* (Johannesburg, 1960)

BOVILL, E.W. *Caravans of the Old Sahara* (1933), revised as *The Golden Trade of the Moors* (1968)

BOXER, CHARLES R., many of whose books have been reprinted; *Fidalgos in the Far East, 1550–1770* (1948); *The Christian Century in Japan, 1549–1650* (1951); *Salvador de Sá and the Struggle for Brazil and Angola, 1602–1686* (1952); *The Great Ship from Amacon, Annals of Macao and the Old Japan Trade, 1555–1640* (1959); *The Golden Age in Brazil, 1695–1750* (1962); *Fort Jesus and the Portuguese in Mombasa, 1593–1729* (1963); *Race Relations in the Portuguese Empire, 1415–1825* (1963); *Portuguese Society in the Tropics* (1966); *The Portuguese Seaborne Empire, 1415–1825* (1969; 2nd ed. 1991); *Mary and Misogyny* (1975); *Portuguese Merchants and Missionaries in Asia, 1602–1795* (1988): as ed. and trans., *The Tragic History of the Sea, 1589–1622*, selections from the *História Trágico-Maritima* (1959); and *Further Selections* (1959, and 1968)

CLANCY, ROBERT, and ALAN RICHARDSON *So Came they South* (Sydney, 1993), the Portuguese 'discovery' of Australia

COLLIS, MAURICE *The Grand Peregrination* (1949), a biography of the 16th-century adventurer Mendes Pinto.

COOPER, MICHAEL *Rodrigues the Interpreter* (New York, 1974), Jesuits in 16th-century Japan

DIFFIE, BAILEY W. *Prelude to Empire: Portugal Overseas before Henry the Navigator* (Lincoln, Nebraska, 1960); with George D. Winius, *Foundations of the Portuguese Empire, 1450–1580* (Minneapolis, 1977)

DISNEY, A.R. *The Twilight of the Pepper Empire. Portuguese Trade in Southwest India in the Early Seventeenth Century* (Cambridge, Mass., 1978)

DUNCAN, BENTLEY *Atlantic Islands: Madeira, the Azores, and the Cape Verdes in Seventeenth-Century Commerce and Navigation* (Chicago, 1972)

GARCIA, JOSÉ MANUEL *Portugal and the Division of the World* (Lisbon, 1994)

GODINHO, VITORINO MAGALHÃES *Portugal and her Empire, 1648–88*, in the New Cambridge Modern History, vol. V (1961); and *Portugal and her Empire, 1680–1720*, in vol. VI (1970)

GUEDES, MAX JUSTO, and GERALD LOMBARDI (eds) *Portugal-Brazil: the Age of the Atlantic Discoveries* (Lisbon, 1990)

HAMMOND, RICHARD *Portugal and Africa, 1815–1910* (Stanford, 1966)

HEMMING, JOHN *Red Gold. The Conquest of the Brazilian Indians, 1500–1760* (1978) and *Amazon Frontier. The Defeat of the Brazilian Indians* (1987)

LACK, DONALD F. *Asia in the making of Europe*, vol. 1, book 1.; 'The Century of Discovery' (Chicago, 1965) essentially concerns the Portuguese

LAWRENCE, A.W. *Trade Castles and Forts of West Africa* (1963)

LEY, CHARLES DAVID (ed. and trans.), *Portuguese Voyages, 1498–1663* (1947)

LYNCH, JOHN *Spain 1516–1598: From Nation State to World Empire* (1991) and *The Hispanic World in Crisis and Change, 1598–1700* (1992)

MCALISTER, LYLE *Spain and Portugal in the New World, 1492–1700* (1984)

MCINTYRE, KENNETH G. *The Secret Discovery of Australia* (Sydney, 1977; rev'd ed. 1982), 'two hundred years before Captain Cook'

MAXWELL, KENNETH *Conflicts and Conspiracies: Brazil and Portugal, 1750–1808* (1973)

MEILINK-ROELOFSZ, M.A.P. *Asian trade and European influence in the Indonesian archipelago from 1500 to about 1630* (The Hague, 1962)

PACKENHAM, THOMAS *The Scramble for Africa* (1991)

PARRY, J.H. *The Age of Reconaissance. Discovery, exploration and settlement, 1450 to 1650* (1963)

PEARSON, MICHAEL N. *The Portuguese in India* (1987)

PINTO, FERNÃO MENDES, ed. Rebecca D. Catz, *The Travels of* (1989); and *The Peregrination of* (1992), trans. Malcolm Lowery

PHILLIPS, J.R.S. *The Medieval Expansion of Europe* (1988; 2nd ed. 1998)

PRESTAGE, EDGAR *The Portuguese Pioneers* (1937; reprinted 1967)

ROGERS, FRANCIS M. *The Travels of the Infante Dom Pedro of Portugal* (Cambridge, Mass., 1961), and *Atlantic Islanders of the Azores and Madeira* (Cambridge, Mass., 1979)

RUSSELL, PETER E. *Portugal, Spain and the African Atlantic: Chivalry and Crusade from John of Gaunt to Henry the Navigator* (1995) and *Prince Henry 'the Navigator': a Life* (2000)

RUSSELL-WOOD, A.J.R. *Fidalgos and Philanthropists. The Santa Casa da Misericórdia of Bahia, 1550–1755* (1968) and *A World on the Move: the Portuguese in Africa, Asia, and America, 1415–1808* (1992)

SAUNDERS, A.C. DE C.M. *A Social History of Black Slaves and Freedmen in Portugal, 1441–1555* (1982)

SCAMMELL, G.V. *The World Encompassed. The First European Maritime Empires, c. 800–1650* (1981)

SIMON, WILLIAM JOEL *Scientific Expeditions in the Portuguese Overseas Territories (1783–1808) and the Role of Lisbon in the Intellectual Scientific Community of the Late Eighteenth Century* (Lisbon, 1983)

SUBRAHMANYAM, SANJAY *The Portuguese Empire in Asia, 1500–1700* (1993); *The career and legend of Vasco da Gama* (1997)

TEAGUE, MICHAEL *In the Wake of the Portuguese Navigators. A Photographic Essay* (1988)

URE, JOHN *Prince Henry the Navigator* (1977)

WHITEWAY R.S. *The Rise of Portuguese Power in India, 1497–1550* (1899; reprinted 1967)

Later History

ANDRADE E SOUSA, MANUEL *Catherine of Braganza* (Lisbon, 1994)

ANON. [JOHN MURRAY BROWNE] *An Historical View of the Revolutions in Portugal, since the close of the Peninsular War* (1827)

BEAWES, WYNDHAM *A Civil, Commercial, Political, and Literary History of Spain and Portugal* (1793)

BLANSHARD, PAUL *Freedom and Catholic Power in Spain and Portugal* (Boston, 1962)

BOVILL, E.W. *The battle of Alcazar: an account of the defeat of D. Sebastian of Portugal* (1952)

BOXER, CHARLES R. with J.C. ALDRIDGE (eds) *Descriptive List of the State Papers Portugal, 1661–1780 in the Public Record Office, London* (3 vols, Lisbon, 1979–83)

BOYAJIAN, J.C. *Portuguese Bankers at the Court of Spain, 1626–1650* (New Brunswick, 1983)

BRAUDEL, FERNAND *The Mediterranean: the Mediterranean World in the time of Phillip II* (1972–3)

CHEKE, MARCUS *Dictator of Portugal: a life of the Marquis of Pombal, 1699–1782* (1938), and *Carlota Joaquina, Queen of Portugal* (1947)

CLARENCE-SMITH, GERVASE *The Third Portuguese Empire, 1825–1975: a Study in Economic Imperialism* (1985)

COLBATCH, JOHN *An Account of the Court of Portugal under Pedro II* (1700)

DAVIDSON, L.S. *Catherine of Braganza* (1908)

ELLIOTT, JOHN H. *Imperial Spain* (1963); *The Count-Duke of Olivares* (1986)

FISHER, HAROLD E.S. *The Portugal Trade. A study of Anglo-Portuguese commerce, 1700–1770* (1971)

FRANCIS, ALAN DAVID *The Methuens and Portugal, 1691–1708* (1966) and *Portugal*

1715–1808, Joanine, Pombaline and Rococo Portugal as seen by British diplomats and traders (1985)

HANSEN, CARL A. *Economy and Society in Baroque Portugal, 1668–1703* (1981)

HERVEY, AUGUSTUS, ed. David Erskine, *Augustus Hervey's Journal* (1954)

KAMEN, HENRY *Philip [II] of Spain* (1997); *The War of Succession in Spain 1700–15* (1969), chiefly concerned with the economic issues

KEENE, SIR BENJAMIN, ed. by Sir Richard Lodge, *The Private Correspondence* [1730–57] (1933)

KENDRICK, THOMAS D. *The Lisbon Earthquake* (1956), largely concerned with European reactions to the disaster rather than with the earthquake itself

MAXWELL, KENNETH *Pombal, Paradox of the Enlightenment* (1995); *The Making of Portuguese Democracy* (1995) and *The Portuguese* (forthcoming)

MUIR, RORY, *Britain and the Defeat of Napoleon, 1807–1815* (1996)

[NADA, JOHN] JOHN LANGDON DAVIES *Carlos the Bewitched* (1962), for insight into neighbouring Court life of the period

NEWITT, MALYN *Portugal in Africa: The Last Hundred Years* (1981)

NOZES, JUDITE (ed.), *The Lisbon Earthquake of 1755. Some British eye-witness accounts* (Lisbon, 1987)

PRESTAGE, EDGAR *The Diplomatic Relations of Portugal with France, England and Holland from 1640–1668* (1925)

ROGERS, FRANCIS M. *The Travels of the Infante Dom Pedro of Portugal* (Cambridge, Mass., 1961)

ROTH, CECIL *A History of the Marranos* (1932; 4th ed., 1974)

SAUNDERS, A.C. DE C.M. *A Social History of the Black Slaves and Freedmen in Portugal, 1441–1555* (1982)

SELLERS, C. *Oporto Old and New* (1899)

SHAW, L.M.E. *Trade, Inquisition and the English Nation in Portugal, 1650–1690* (1989) and *The Anglo-Portuguese Alliance and the English Merchants in Portugal, 1654–1810* (1998)

SHILLINGTON, VIOLET M. and ANNIE B.W. CHAPMAN *The commercial relations of England and Portugal* (1907)

SMITH, JOHN, MARQUIS OF CARNOTA *Memoirs of the Marquis of Pombal* (1843)

SOUTHWELL, SIR ROBERT *Letters* (1740)

TREND, JOHN BRANDE *Portugal* (1957)

WALFORD, A.R. *The British Factory in Lisbon* (Lisbon, 1940)

WHEELER, DOUGLAS L. *Republican Portugal: a political history, 1910–1925* (1978); see also under Graham

WHITE, G.F. *A Century of Spain and Portugal (1788–1898)* (1909)

YOUNG, GEORGE *Portugal, old and young: an historical study* (1917)

YOUNG, WILLIAM *Portugal in 1828* (1828)

Modern History, Economics, Politics

BIRMINGHAM, DAVID *Frontline Nationalism in Angola and Mozambique* (1992)

CHILCOTE, RONALD *Portuguese Africa* (Englewood Cliffs, 1967)

CORKHILL, DAVID *The Portuguese Economy since 1974* (1993)

FIGUEIREDO, ANTÓNIO DE *Portugal: Fifty years of Dictatorship* (1976)

FRYER, PETER and PATRICIA McG. PINHEIRO *Oldest Ally: Portrait of Salazar's Portugal* (1961)

GALLAGHER, TOM *Portugal: a Twentieth Century Interpretation* (1983)

GRAHAM, LAWRENCE S. and DOUGLAS L. WHEELER *In search of Modern Portugal: the Revolution and its Consequences* (Madison, 1983)

JANITSCHIK, HANS *Mário Soares* (1985)

KAY, HUGH *Salazar and Modern Portugal* (1970), too sympathetic to the regime

MAILER, PHIL *Portugal: The Impossible Revolution* (1977)

PINTO, ANTÓNIO COSTA *Salazar's Dictatorship and European Fascism* (New York, 1995)

RABY, D.L. *Fascism and resistance in Portugal* (1988)

ROBINSON, RICHARD A.H. *Contemporary Portugal: a History* (1979)

Military History

AITCHISON, JOHN, ed. by W.F.K. Thompson, *An Ensign in the Peninsular War: the Letter of John Aitchison* (1981)

BRETT-JAMES, ANTHONY *Life in Wellington's Army* (1972)

BROWNE, THOMAS HENRY, ed. by R.N. Buckley, *The Napoleonic Journal of Captain Thomas Henry Browne* (1987)

CHAMBERS, GEORGE LAWSON *Bussaco* (1910)

ELIOT, WILLIAM GRANVILLE *A Treatise on the Defence of Portugal* (3rd ed., 1811)

FAGEL, BARON NICOLAS *Account of the Campaign in Portugal, 1705* (1708)

FRANCIS, (ALAN) DAVID *The First Peninsular War, 1702–1713* (1975). That of the Spanish Sucession

GLOVER, MICHAEL *Britannia sickens: Sir Arthur Wellesley and the Convention of Cintra* (1970)

GREHAN, JOHN *The Lines of Torres Vedras: the Cornerstone of Wellington's Strategy in the Peninsula, 1809–12* (2000)

HALLIDAY, ANDREW *Observations on the Present State of Portugal . . .* (1812)

HORWARD, DONALD D. *The Battle of Bussaco: Masséna versus Wellington* (1965), and *Napoleon and Iberia – The Twin Sieges of Ciudad Rodrigo and Almeida, 1810* (1984)

HUGILL, J.A.C. *No Peace without Spain* (1991), devoted to the War of the Spanish Succession

JONES, JOHN THOMAS *Journal of the Sieges in Spain* (3rd ed., 1846), containing *Memoranda Relative to the Lines thrown up to cover Lisbon in 1810* (1829)

LARPENT, FRANCIS SEYMOUR *The Private Journal of Judge-Advocate Larpent* (3rd edition, 1854); reprinted 2000, with an Introduction by Ian C. Robertson

NEALE, ADAM *Letters from Portugal and Spain* (1809)

OMAN, SIR CHARLES *Wellington's Army* (1913); and *History of the Peninsular War* (7 vols, 1902–30, reprinted 1995–7, with two supplementary volumes in 1998–9)

PRESTAGE, EDGAR *Portugal and the War of the Spanish Succession* (1938)

RATHBONE, JULIAN *Wellington's War* (1984), quoting from the Duke's dispatches

ROBERTSON, IAN C. *Wellington at War in the Peninsula, 1808–1814: an Overview and Guide* (2000)

SCHAUMANN, AUGUST LUDOLF FRIEDRICH, ed. by Anthony M. Ludovici *On the Road with Wellington* (1924, reprinted 1999)

WELLER, JAC *Wellington in the Peninsula* (1962)

YOUNG, PETER and J.P. LAWFORD *Wellington's Masterpiece* (1973), the background to the Salamanca campaign

In addition to the earlier works listed above, and apart from the general histories of Southey, Napier (including the latter's *English Battles and Sieges in the Peninsula*), and Wellington's own *Dispatches*, there were numerous other contemporary narratives of the Peninsular War, many reprinted and some first published in recent years. Most of them describe actions within Portugal, and almost all are of some interest.

Little has been written in English since the 1830s concerning the 'War of the Two Brothers', or Miguelite War. Among them are:

ALEXANDER, JAMES EDWARD *Sketches in Portugal during the Civil War of 1834* (1835)

BADCOCK, LOVELL *Rough Leaves from a Journal kept in Spain and Portugal* (1835)

BOLLAERT, WILLIAM *The War of the Succession in Portugal and Spain*, vol. 1 (1870)

GLASCOCK, W. NUGENT *Naval Sketch Book* (1834)

HODGE, G. LLOYD *Narrative of an Expedition to Portugal* (1833)

KNIGHT, THOMAS *The British Battalion at Oporto* (1834)

NAPIER, CHARLES *An account of the War in Portugal between Dom Pedro and Dom Miguel* (1836)

NAPIER, PRISCILLA *Black Charlie: a Life of Adm. Sir Charles Napier, 1787–1860* (1995)

OWEN, HUGH *The Civil War in Portugal, and the Siege of Oporto* (1835)

PROCTER, DOROTHY. Charles P. Hawkes and Marion Smithes (eds.), *Siege Lady: the Adventures of Mrs Dorothy Procter of Entre Quintas* (1938)

SHAW, CHARLES *Personal Memoirs and Correspondence* (1837)

The following now rare volumes are of interest for their illustrations:

ANON. [A.P.D.G.] *Sketches of Portuguese Life, Manners, Costume, and Character* (1826)

BACLER D'ALBE, ALBERT-LOUIS *Campagne d'Espagne, Souvenirs Pittoresque*, tome II (1824)

BRADFORD, WILLIAM *Sketches of the Country, Character and Costume in Portugal and Spain* (1809)

LANDMANN, GEORGE THOMAS *Historical, Military, and Picturesque Observations in Portugal* (1818)

L'EVÊQUE, HENRY *Portuguese Costumes* (1812–14); and *Campaigns of the British Army in Portugal* (1813)

ST CLAIR, THOMAS STAUNTON *A Series of Views . . . taken during the Peninsular War* (1815)

VIVIAN, GEORGE *Scenery of Portugal & Spain* (1839)

Art and Architecture

ASSOCIAÇÃO DOS ARQUITECTOS PORTUGUESES *Arquitectura Popular em Portugal* (Lisbon, 1980, since extended), contains several hundred photographs and some English text

AZEVEDO, CARLOS DE *Baroque organ-cases of Portugal* (Amsterdam, 1972) and with Chester E.V. Brummel, *The Churches of Portugal* (New York, 1985)

BERKELEY, ALICE and SUSAN LOWNDES *English Art in Portugal* (Lisbon, 1994), a brief introduction to the subject

DELAFORCE, ANGELA *A Aliança Revisitada* (Lisbon, 1994), a Gulbenkian exhibition catalogue illustrating the artistic, scientific and intellectual relations between the United Kingdom and Portugal over the centuries; and *Art and Patronage in 18th Century Portugal* (2002)

FRANÇA, JOSÉ-AUGUSTO et al., *Arte Português* (Madrid, 1986), vol. XXX in the 'Summa Artis' series

GIL, JULIO *The Finest Castles of Portugal* (Lisbon, 1986)

GRAF, GERHARD N. et al., *Portugal roman*, 2 vols (St Léger Vauban, 1986–7)

KUBLER, GEORGE *Portuguese Plain Architecture, 1521–1706* (Middletown, Connecticut, 1972), and with Martin Soria, *Art and Architecture of Spain and Portugal and their American dominions, 1500–1800* (1959)

LEES-MILNE, JAMES *Baroque in Spain and Portugal* (1960)

LEVENSON, J.A. (ed.), *The Age of Baroque in Portugal* (Washington, 1993), a National Gallery of Art exhibition catalogue

LOWE, K.J.P. (ed.), *Cultural Links between Portugal and Italy in the Renaissance* (1999)

MURPHY, JAMES CAVANAH [sic] *Plans, Elevations, Sections and Views of the Church of Batalha* (1795)

SILVA, JOSÉ CORNÉLIO DA and GERALD LUCKHURST *Sintra: a Landscape with Villas* (Lisbon, 1989)

SITWELL, SACHEVERELL *Southern Baroque re-visited* (1967)

SMITH, ROBERT CHESTER *A Talha em Portugal* (Lisbon, 1962), a study of *talha* or gilded wood-carving; *The Arts of Portugal, 1500–1800* (1968) and *Nicolau Nasoni, 1691–1773* (Lisbon, 1973)

STOOP, ANNE DE *Demeures portugaises dans les environs de Lisbonne* (Paris, 1986; also available in Portuguese); *Palais et manoirs, le Minho*, vol. 1 (Paris, 1995) and *Living in Portugal* (1995), for their photographs

WATSON, WALTER CRUM *Portuguese Architecture* (1908), to the end of the 18th century only

Other Subjects

ALLEN, H. WARNER *The Wines of Portugal* (1963)

ANDERSON, JEAN *The Food of Portugal* (1986)

BARRETO, MASCARENHAS *The Portuguese Columbus: Secret Agent of King John II* (1992)

BEDINI, SILVIO A. *The Pope's Elephant* (1997)

BELL, AUBREY F. *Portuguese Literature* (1922; reprinted 1970, with an updated bibliography), until the end of the 19th century only

BOWE, PATRICK *Gardens of Portugal* (1989)

BRADFORD, SARAH *The Story of Port* (1978)

BRITO, MANUEL CARLOS DE *Opera in Portugal in the Eighteenth Century* (1989)

CARITA, HELDER and HOMEM CARDOSA *Portuguese Gardens* (1991)

COBB, GERALD *Oporto Older and Newer* (1966)

DELAFORCE, JOHN *The Factory House at Oporto* (1979; revised ed. 1990) and *Joseph James Forrester, Baron of Portugal, 1809–1861* (1992)

FORRESTER, JOSEPH JAMES *A Word or Two on Port Wine* (1844) and *The Oliveira Prize-Essay on Portugal* (1853)

FRANCIS, ALAN DAVID *The Wine Trade* (1972)

GALLOP, RODNEY *Portugal: a Book of Folk-ways* (1936)

HOUSBY, TREVOR *The Hand of God: Whaling in the Azores* (1971)

JACK, MALCOLM *William Beckford; an English Fidalgo* (1997); ed., and *Vathek and Other Stories: A William Backford Reader* (1993), also including non-fiction

LIDDELL, ALEX *Port Wine Quintas of the Douro* (1992)

LIVERMORE, HAROLD V. and WILLIAM J. ENTWISTLE (eds), *Portugal and Brazil: an Introduction* (1953), essays covering a variety of topics

MABBERLEY, D.J. and P.J. PLACITO *Algarve Plants and Landscapes: Passing Tradition and Ecological Change* (1993)

MAXWELL, KENNETH *The Portuguese* (forthcoming), in the 'Peoples of Europe' series

MESQUITA, VITÓRIA et al., *Frederick William Flower: a Pioneer of Portuguese Photography* (Lisbon, 1994), a Museu do Chiado exhibition catalogue

OMAN, C. *The Golden Age of Portuguese Silver* (1968)

READ, JAN *Wines of Portugal* (revised ed. 1987)

ROBERTSON, GEORGE *Port* (1978)

VILLIERS, ALAN *The Voyage of the Schooner Argos* (1951), Portuguese North Atlantic fishing

VINCENT, MARY and R.A. STRADLING *Cultural Atlas of Spain and Portugal* (1994)

Portuguese Studies, edited by the Department of Portuguese, King's College, London and published annually by the Modern Humanities Research Association, contains valuable articles, reviews and bibliographies

Mértola: a museum town (1989) by Cláudio Torres and Luís Alves da Silva, may be mentioned as representative of local guides of quality now being produced

Also of interest are several publications of The British Historical Society of Portugal (Rua Filipe Folque 2, 1069-121 Lisbon)

Historical Gazetteer

Numbers in bold type refer to the main text

Although the gazetteer concentrates on what is now mainland Portugal, Madeira and the Azores are also included, as are some places at no great distance across the frontier with Spain (marked Sp.), which have played a part in the country's historical past, such as Mérida, former capital of Roman Lusitania.

Former names – including Roman – are printed in italic. Several representative *citânias*, Roman villas, etc. not separately listed, may be visited conveniently from the centres suggested. Naturally, there are numerous minor sites throughout the country with remains surviving which may be of interest to the archaeologist and architect, but which cannot be included in what is only a selective list.

Abrantes repulsed an Almohad attack in 1179; some two hundred years later it was the headquarters of João de Avis before the battle of Aljubarrota. British troops wintered here in 1704, during a pause in the War of the Spanish Succession. In 1807 it was seized by Gen. Junot, while leading French troops into Portugal prior to the outbreak of the Peninsular War, for which facile exploit Napoleon dubbed him Duc d'Abrantes. Wellington concentrated his army here in 1809 before marching on Talavera (although he was still Wellesley until after that battle). It remained a base of the Anglo-Portuguese forces, even passing into proverb: '*Quartel General em Abrantes; tudo como dantes*' (Headquarters at Abrantes; everything as before). **113**

Alcácer do Sal (Roman *Salacia*). Once a strong Moorish fortress, it resisted capture by Afonso Henriques, who was wounded here after taking Lisbon in 1147. It was eventually occupied in 1217 by the Christians after a long siege, in which a contingent of Crusaders anchored off the estuary *en route* to the Holy Land participated. **45**

Alcántara (Roman *Norba Caesares*) (Sp., some 75km east of Castelo Branco), takes its name from *al-Qantara*, the Arabic for bridge. Built for Trajan from *c.* 105, the six arches of the immense bridge stride high across the gorge of the Tagus adjacent to what was formerly the headquarters of the military Order of Alcántara. **25, 46, 96**

Alcobaça, famous for its magnificent Cistercian abbey, of which Lady Holland remarked in 1805 that it was 'far the best and least disgusting' convent she had ever seen. The massive church was founded by Afonso Henriques *c.* 1153, after capturing Santarém. It was visited by William Beckford in 1793, but his description of the excursion to it and to Batalha was not published until 1835. Although pillaged by the French in 1810, the tombs of Pedro I and Inês de Castro survived destruction, as did those of Afonso II and Afonso III and their wives. **55, 80**

Alconétar (Sp., 40km north of Cáceres) has remains of what was a much longer Roman bridge by which the *Via Lata* crossed the Tagus. **25**

Aljubarrota, a village that gave its name to the battle of August 1385, which took place nearer Batalha, where João, Master of Avis and the Constable Nun' Alvares Pereira virtually destroyed the Castilian army of Juan I. **60**

Aljustrel (pre-Roman *Vipasca*), has copper mines known as early as the second millenia, but only exploited actively by the Romans, whose shafts descended to 120m. The extent of the surviving slag heap gives an idea of their importance.

Almeida fell twice in the 14th century during Spanish incursions and was forced to surrender to them in 1762. It has Vaubanesque fortifications which made it one of the most powerful strongholds in Portugal and it was a base of operations against Spain in 1704. In July 1810, in spite of a spirited delaying action by Gen.

Craufurd's Light Division, the French under Masséna invested the place. Colonel Cox, the commandant, was forced to capitulate shortly after the bombardment commenced, for a chance shot exploded the central magazine, reducing the castle and cathedral to a pile of rubble and killing outright 500 of the garrison. 10km due east as the crow flies, but approached from the Spanish side of the frontier, is the equally impressive fort 'de la Concepción', blown up by Craufurd to make it untenable by the French. **114**

Almourol. The castle, on its picturesque island site in the Tagus, rebuilt by the Templars in 1171, is referred to in Francisco de Moraes's mid-sixteenth-century *Cronica de Palmeirim de Inglaterra*, translated by Southey in 1807, correcting Anthony Munday's Elizabethan version of the Romance.

Alpiarça lies north-east of Santarém. At nearby Moron are earthworks identified as the military base of Decimus Junius Brutus in *c.* 138 BC, prior to marching his troops north to the Lima. **16**

Alter do Chão, of Roman foundation, with remains of baths and a restored mid-fourteenth-century castle, was probably the *Abelterium* of the *Antonine Itinerary*.

Amarante, in the deep valley of the Tâmega, here crossed by a bridge built in 1790, was the scene of fighting in April/May 1809, when the French were forced to retreat into Galicia, having lost Oporto to Wellingon. The former Romanesque bridge, erected by the local miracle-working patron of marriages, São Gonçalo (whose festival is still celebrated by the confection of phallic-shaped cakes nibbled not only by husband-hunters past their first youth), collapsed in 1763.

Arouca, remotely sited between Oporto and Viseu, contains the Cistercian convent associated with Mafalda, daughter of Sancho I, who retired here after her marriage in 1215 to Enrique I of Castile had been annulled.

Aveiro contains the former Convento de Jesus, where Afonso V's daughter, Santa Joana, spent the last few years of her life and died in 1489. Her hagiographer admired her capacity to suffer the lice bred in her chemise.

Avis was granted in 1220 to the Spanish military order of Calatrava, then to the Knights of Evora, who built the castle. Later they were known as the Knights of Aviz and of the Order of São Bento. João I was Grand Master of the Order before he ascended to the throne in 1385. **51**

Azores, The (Açores in Portuguese). A widely scattered archipelago of nine islands of volcanic origin lying some 700 miles west of the coast of Portugal, they first appeared on maps in the mid-14th century. Although visited in *c.* 1430, when sheep were landed on their uninhabited shores, they were not colonized until after 1445. There is evidence of voyages being made westward from them after 1486. In 1576 the English were given rights to trade there, but while under Spanish domination, they became the rendezvous of well-loaded galleons returning to Lisbon,

and thus attracted English attention, being raided by Essex and Raleigh. From them Grenville attacked a fleet in 1591. The island of Terceira resisted Spanish occupation in 1581, routing the disembarking troops by the expedient of sending a herd of wild cattle against them, but they were subdued two years later. Afonso VI, exiled here in 1669, was not the last to be deported to this distant location. It was from here, during the Miguelite War, that many of Dom Pedro's supporters assembled before sailing to capture Oporto in 1832. Ponta Delgada was a base for the American Atlantic Fleet during the later part of the 1914–18 war, and in September 1943 Salazar allowed the British to establish a naval base on the strategically important islands. **63, 65, 83, 92, 122, 139, 143**

Badajoz (*Pax Augusta*; Sp., 15km east of Elvas), of Roman foundation, rose to prominence as the capital of an independent principality after the breakup of the emirate of Córdoba. The battle of Zalaca or Sagrajas took place to the north-east in 1086, in which Almoravides defeated the Christians, who did not capture it until 1230. Its position on the Guadiana, near the frontier, has caused it to be besieged frequently, notably during the Peninsular War. Salazar handed back to Franco's troops – to be shot – any Republicans who had fled across the border in August 1936; and it was near here that Gen. Delgado was murdered in 1965. See also **Olivença** and **La Albuera**, 25km south-west and south-east respectively. **37, 38, 40, 43, 45, 49**

Barcelos. The last count of Barcelos having been killed at Aljubarrota, Dom Afonso, a natural son of João I, received the county on his marriage to Brites, daughter of Nun' Alvares Pereira and built a castle to guard the bridgehead. **11**

Batalha. The construction of the great 'battle-abbey' dates from 1388, in consequence of a vow made by João I prior to the battle of Aljubarrota, fought in the vicinity. The Capela do Fundador contains the double tomb of João I and Philippa of Lancaster, and also those of Henry 'the Navigator' and their other sons. **62, 79**

Beja (Roman *Pax Julia*), the capital of the Lower Alentejo, is dominated by a lofty keep, erected on remains of a Roman fort, while a Roman arch survives as the Porta de Evora. A former inmate of the mid-15th-century Conceição convent was Mariana Alcoforado, the assumed author of *Letters from a Portuguese Nun*. At **Pisões**, to the south-west, are extensive remains of a 1st-century villa. **37, 43, 45, 46, 134**

Belmonte was the birthplace of Pedro Alvares Cabral, 'discoverer' of Brazil (cf. Santarém). Nearby are remains of a *domus municipalis*, while off the road to Guarda stands the **Torre Centum Cellas**, a ruin of Roman origin fortified in the medieval period.

Braga (*Bracara Augusta*). Substantial remains exist of the main Roman station of northern Lusitania, which became the Suevic capital and fell to Theodoric II in 456. With the conversion of the Arian Visigoths to orthodox Catholicism, it grew in importance as a religious centre, although its primacy over other sees in the north-west of the Peninsula was not confirmed until almost a century after its reconquest by Fernando of Castile in 1040. The Capela dos Reis in the Romanesque cathedral contains the tombs of Count Henry of Burgundy and his wife, and of Abp Lourenço, wounded at Aljubarrota. **16, 24, 40**

On its northern outskirts is the hamlet of **Dume** (*Dumium*), site of an ancient royal palace, the priest of which was St Martin of Dume (died 579); relics of Roman occupation survive. Nearby is the late 7th-century Visigothic chapel of **São Frutuoso de Montélios**, with Lombardic blind arcades on its exterior. **31** Some 5km to the east is the hilltop sanctuary of **Bom Jesus**, with its monumental double flight of steps, constructed after 1723, embellished with Baroque chapels, fountains and statuary. **98** *The Citânia de Briteiros* (south-east of Braga) is one of the more accessible and impressive northern Celtiberian strongholds surviving, consisting of over 150 stone huts (some reconstructed) straddling a boulder-strewn hill surrounded by three defensive walls. The settlement, dating from *c.* 300 BC, was probably abandoned by AD 300. That of **Sabrosa**, a smaller but older site, is also in the vicinity. **11**

Braganza (Bragança). Celto-Roman *Juliobriga*, the high-lying capital of the Trás-os-Montes, long a provincial backwater, provided the surname to Charles II's queen, Catherine. The dukedom was created in 1442 for a

The apse of the twelfth-century church at Castro de Avelas

bastard of João I. In the upper town is the over-restored *domus municipalis*, a rare survival of Romanesque civic architecture. Tradition has it that Inês de Castro was clandestinely married here in 1354 to the future Pedro I. At **Castro de Avelas** (3km west) are relics of a 12th-century monastery. Its Mudéjar brick-built apse with blind arcading is unique in Portugal, but similar to churches at Sahagún, further east in Spain. **24**

Buçaco. The re-afforested *serra* do Buçaco (anglicized as **Busaco**) was the 'damned long hill' north-east of Coimbra where Wellington with his Anglo-Portuguese army took up an almost impregnable defensive position, against which on 27 September 1810 Marshal Masséna ineffectively hurled his columns. Within the walled State Forest surrounding the former Carmelite convent rises a former

(pseudo-Manueline) royal summer palace converted to a luxurious hotel. **114**

Caldas da Rainha, an ancient spa built around a royal hospital, established in 1486, was frequently visited by João V. It was from here that a detachment of revolutionary troops marched prematurely on Lisbon on 16 March 1974.

'Camino de la Plata' or *Via Lata*, an important Roman highway in Spain, ran roughly parallel to the present eastern frontier of Portugal. Laid out in the reign of Augustus, it extended north from Seville, and via Mérida, Cáceres, Plasencia, Salamanca and Zamora to Astorga, from which several other main roads diverted west, among them (from Mérida) via Santarém to Lisbon, and traversed rough country (from Astorga) towards Braga.

Castelo Branco was refounded by the

Templars in the early 13th century. It was attacked by the Spaniards in 1704 and 1762, and Gen. Junot sacked it in 1807.

Castelo de Vide, a spa of ancient foundation, preserves its medieval *Judiaria*. The castle successfully resisted a Spanish incursion in June 1704, but later capitulated when the Duke of Berwick threatened to put all to the sword and 'leave the women exposed to the brutality of the soldiers'. The Portuguese dumped their remaining gunpowder in a well, and in the following year the castle was seriously damaged by an explosion. There are numerous megalithic remains in the area, and hill-top **Marvão** rises some 12km south-east.

Chaves, with keys (*chaves*) as its canting device, was the Roman spa of *Aquae Flaviae*, and later a Suevic centre and seat of Bishop Flavius Hydatius. An important frontier fortress opposing Spanish Verín, it fell to the French early in 1809, but was recaptured, when some 1,200 troops were forced to surrender. **24** The Tâmega is crossed by a Roman bridge of twelve visible arches, built in 79–104, partly by the 7th Legion. It is commanded by a castle, the keep of which is on Roman foundations. At **Outreiro Seco**, some 4km north, is a Romanesque church preserving features of interest, while several hundred metres of Roman road may be seen in the vicinity.

Cintra; see Sintra.

Ciudad Rodrigo (Sp., 68km east of Guarda), an important Spanish frontier fortress, was founded in 1150, besieged by Wellington in January 1812 and retains a fine 12–13th century cathedral. It is convenient for visiting **Fuentes de Oñoro**, Fort Conception, **Freineda** and **Almeida**. **116**

Coimbra (*Aeminium*) took its more recent name from neighbouring **Conimbriga**, from which its Visigothic kings and bishops migrated after 468. It was re-conquered by Fernando I of Castile in 1064, and from 1139 until 1385 was the capital of Portugal, having supplanted Guimarães. Its university was not definitively established here until 1537, while from 1567 Coimbra was one of the three seats of the Inquisition in Portugal. It was sacked by Masséna after the battle of Busaco. Santa Cruz, founded in 1131 but rebuilt in the early 16th century, contains the tombs of Afonso Henriques and his son Sancho I, reinterred here in 1520. In the walled upper town, the Casa de Sub-Ripas was traditionally the scene of the murder of Maria Teles, who had married the eldest son of Inês de Castro. Below the former Bishop's palace (flanked by the church of São João de Almedina, on the site of a mosque) is a Roman *cryptoporticus*. The adjacent Sé Nova was the Jesuit church until the suppression of that Order in 1759.

Across the Mondego lie Santa Clara-a-Velha, silted up by floods, in which Inês de Castro was first buried, before being translated to Alcobaça. The mid-17th-century hilltop convent-church of Santa Clara contains the original tomb and silver shrine of St Isabel (died 1336; wife of Dom Dinis). **15, 21, 35, 41, 42, 46, 53, 59, 66, 99**

Condeixa a Velha. The pre-Roman site of **Conimbriga** (from *c.* 800 BC), was an important Roman station on the road from Lisbon via Tomar to Braga, until superseded by Coimbra after its sack by the Suevi in 468. The triangular walled site, between two gorges and fed by an aqueduct, consists of a large villa, several baths, a Flavian forum overlying one of the Augustan period, a temple, a buttressed *palaestra*, etc., finds from which are displayed in the site museum.

Covilhã, a textile centre, long reputed for its brown woollen blankets, was a cavalry base during the Peninsular War, when dances, described as 'barbarously brilliant balls', were got up to enliven the long winter evenings. **47, 93**

Crato, with two Roman bridges close by, was from the mid-14th century the headquarters of a branch of the Hospitallers known as the Order of Crato. The last of its Grand Priors was Dom António, a bastard of the Infante Luiz and Violante Gomes, who in 1580 was a rival to Philip II of Spain in his claim to the Portuguese throne.

Elvas, strategically sited opposite **Badajoz**, was recaptured from the Muslims in 1230. Although one of Portugal's strongest frontier fortresses, it capitulated to the invading Spaniards in 1580, but resisted retaliatory attacks after 1644. It was then strengthened by

The *pelourinho* at Elvas

Vaubanesque defensive works, among them the outlying fort 'de Lippe', named after the English-born German count who reorganized the Portuguese army in the 1760s. It was an important British base during the Peninsular War, notably before the sieges of Badajoz in 1811 and 1812. The hilltop Moorish castle, with a later keep, was built on Roman foundations. A good example of a dolmen may be seen at **Barbacena**, 15km north-west. **90**

Esposende is only of interest for the number of Iron Age sites and megalithic remains in its vicinity, and an extensive medieval necropolis partly covered by dunes. (The local tourist office should provide detailed directions.)

Estói. On the site of the 2nd–6th-century Roman villa of **Milreu** are remains of 3rd-century baths and a temple converted into a Paleo-Christian basilica.

Estoril. This resort was popular with British valetudinarians, and has been the residence of miscellaneous monarchs and pretenders in exile, among them Carol of Rumania, Umberto of Savoy and Juan de Borbon.

Estremoz is dominated by the hilltop keep of its royal palace, rebuilt by João V after an explosion in 1698. Isabel, the 'Rainha Santa', wife of Dom Dinis, died in the former palace in 1336. The Count of Ourém, while entertained here in 1380 when finalizing secret negotiations between Richard II and Dom Fernando, contrived to make Dona Leonor, Fernando's not-so-saintly queen, pregnant.

Evora, Celtic *Ebora*, was awarded the title *Liberalitas Julia* by Julius Caesar. An early bishop attended the Council of Elvira in 300. Reconquered by Geraldo Sem Pavor, it became an important Christian bastion against the Muslims, and is still encircled by 14th-century walls. After the accession of the House of Aviz in 1385 it was frequently a royal residence. João II had his over-mighty brother-in-law, the Duke of Braganza, beheaded here in 1484. A Jesuit university was established in 1559, which survived for 200 years until suppressed by Pombal. Here in 1637 occurred the first serious revolt against the Spanish occupation of Portugal. The town was brutally sacked by the French in 1808 and a period of decline followed, its population falling to a mere 5,000. In September 1973 the 2nd–3rd century Roman temple was a rendezvous of disillusioned junior army officers who were to bring about the bloodless Revolution in the following April. Pedro Fernandes de Queirós, the 'discoveror' of Australasia, was born here in 1563. **10, 21, 43, 45, 66, 79, 90, 147**

Evoramonte, with a restored castle of 1306, was where Dom Miguel signed the convention of May 1834 ending the futile Miguelite War and abandoning all further claim to the throne.

Faro (Roman *Ossonoba*). Little remains of the Roman town, on the forum of which the present cathedral was built. It was taken from the Muslims by Alonso III in 1249. In 1596, when under Spanish rule, it was pillaged by the Earl of Essex, who sacked up a library of indigestible theology and presented it to the

Bodleian Library, Oxford, a generous gesture from a Cambridge man. The Roman villas at **Estói** and **Vilamoura** are conveniently close. **21, 22, 50**

Figueira de Castelo Rodrigo preserves some fortifications, south-east of which, beyond the 13th-century Cistercian convent of Santa Maria de Aguiar, is the Casarão da Torre, relic of an imposing Roman temple.

Figueira da Foz, an important fishing port and now a resort at the mouth of the Mondego, was where Wellington disembarked his expeditionary force in August 1808 prior to marching south towards **Roliça** and **Vimeiro**.

Freineda lies not far south of Castelo Bom, on the road between **Guarda** and the Spanish frontier near **Fuentes de Oñoro**; see also **Almeida**. The balconied granite house opposite the village church served as Wellington's spartan residence during two successive winters (1811–13), while his headquarters' staff was dispersed in neighbouring villages. Here too, with his huntsman Tom Crane, were kennelled a pack of hounds, with which he would regularly hunt.

Freixo de Espada à Cinta is said to take its curious name – 'ash-tree of the girt sword' – from the gesture of Dom Dinis, who here encircled a tree with his sword-belt when founding the frontier fortress. It was the birthplace of Jorge Alvares, the navigator and chronicler of Japan (in 1547). **76**

Fuentes de Oñoro (Sp.) lies 17km south-east of Almeida and just across the frontier. It was here, in the granite-walled alleys of the older village, that the French under Masséna – intent on restoring his tarnished

reputation after their disastrous retreat from the Lines of **Torres Vedras** – lost the battle (3–5 May 1811) which Wellington referred to as 'the most difficult one I was ever concerned in and against the greatest odds'. In the vicinity are 'Fort Conception' (cf. **Almeida**) and **Freineda**.

Guarda, a cathedral town of strategic importance due to its command of the upper valleys of the Mondego and the Zêzere, was founded in 1197 by Sancho I as a frontier guard against the Muslims. It was a base of Wellington's operations in 1811–12. At adjacent **Póvoa do Mileu** are slight remains of a Roman villa. **47**

Guimarães contends with Braga for the title of 'cradle of the Portuguese monarchy'. In 840 Alfonso II of León convened a council here; Henry of Burgundy made it his court in 1095 and his son Afonso Henriques may have been born here. An alliance with England was signed here in July 1372 prior to the *Treaty of Windsor*. The hilltop castle has been reconstructed and the *paço* of the Dukes of Braganza has been tastelessly over-restored. **40, 42**

Idanha-a-Velha, *Igaeditania*, although probably of pre-Roman origin, gave the name *Egitana* to the Swabian and Visigothic centre which was the seat of a bishopric from 596 until 1199, although sacked by the Muslims some time before the latter date. The village takes up only part of the original walled enceinte. A medieval tower stands on the podium of a Roman temple, and Roman remains collected in the vicinity are preserved within a restored Paleo-Christian basilica. Both a ruined baptistry and bishop's palace may be seen, and a Roman bridge spans the little river Ponsul. **21, 47**

Lagos succeeded Roman *Lacobriga* (the site of which may have been at adjacent Monte Molião) and was not reconquered from the Muslims until 1241. After this, defensive walls were built, parts of which survive. It was a base for exploratory expeditions initiated by Henry 'the Navigator', and African slaves were formerly auctioned below the custom house. It was a port of assembly for Dom Sebastião's ill-fated Moroccan campaign, shortly after which it became the capital of the Algarve, until 1755, when it was laid in ruins by the Lisbon earthquake. Boscawen defeated a French squadron off the coast here in 1759.

Lamego, probably Roman *Lamaecum*, an old episcopal city standing high above the south bank of the Douro, was reconquered in 1057. During the summer of 1811 a train of Wellington's heavy artillery was hauled up from the river here and then across country towards Almeida. In the vicinity are the Visigothic basilica of **São Pedro de Balsemão**, dating in part to the 7th century. **31** Some 15km south-east is **São João da Tarouca**, part of the first Cistercian monastery in Portugal, containing the tomb of Dom Pedro (died 1354), Count of Barcelos and a bastard of Dom Dinis. **35, 98**

Leiria was long contested before its eventual reconquest. The first *cortes* in Portugal at which the Commons were represented was assembled here

by Afonso III in 1254. It was later a residence of Dom Dinis, but only became an episcopal city in 1545. A restored royal palace dominates the town. **42, 51**

Linhares. Formerly *Leniobriga*, the hilltop village of ancient origin on the old road skirting the north flank of the Serra da Estrela, was once the seat of a Visigothic bishopric.

Lisboa, anglicized as **Lisbon**, the capital of Portugal, its conurbation with a population approaching two million, extends along the north bank of the broad estuary of the Tejo (or Tagus). In 1760 Joseph Baretti wrote that 'to range about such a wide scene as this metropolis and its neighbourhood, gives certainly much satisfaction to an inquisitive pair of eyes': it is as true today. Phoenician *Olisipo* was occupied by the Romans in 205 BC, after the Second Punic War, and under Julius Caesar it became the *municipium* of *Felicitas Julia*, an important city of Lusitania. In 409 it was occupied by the Alans, and then in succession by the Suevi and the Visigoths, until overrun by the Muslims in 714. The latter were not definitively ousted until 1147 after a siege by Afonso Henriques, aided by a contingent of Crusaders (cf. Oporto). Subsequently, Gilbert of Hastings was consecrated bishop. Portuguese discoveries in the 16th century brought enormous wealth and exotic cargoes to the city, and it has been argued that had Philip II of Spain, when forcibly annexing Portugal in 1580, taken heed of his advisors and made Lisbon his capital rather than Madrid, the future history of the Peninsula might have been very different. His *armada* assembled here, and after its destruction Drake and Norris made retaliatory but abortive attempts to sack the place. Lisbon proclaimed its independence from Castilian domination in 1640. English merchants were given additional privileges after 1654 and established a *feitoria* or 'Factory' here. In 1662 Catherine of Braganza set sail from Lisbon to marry Charles II, further cementing Anglo-Portuguese friendship, and retired here in 1693. It experienced a further period of opulence during the reign of João V. On 1 November 1755 the city was devastated by an earthquake. Rebuilding on a more regular plan was put in hand by the Marquês de Pombal, but it was not for several decades that Lisbon again flourished. In November 1807 the royal family set sail for Brazil in the face of French invasion, but Junot's occupation lasted less than nine months, when his troops, defeated at Vimeiro, were repatriated by the Convention of Cintra. The port remained the base of British operations throughout the Peninsular War, defended by the 'Lines' of Torres Vedras. It was frequently the scene of unrest during the Miguelite War and later in the 19th century. By 1910, two years after Dom Carlos had been assassinated there, the monarchy was overthrown and replaced by a Republic. During the Second World War, as a neutral city strategically commanding sea lanes, it had the reputation, deservedly, of being 'a nest of spies'. In the 'Revolution' of 25 April 1974 the lead given by the capital was followed by the rest of the country, since when Lisbon has again prospered, although the Chiado was scarred by fire in August 1988.

São Vicente de Fora contains the tombs of the majority of the Braganza dynasty from João IV to Manuel II, including Catherine of Braganza. In **Santa Engracia**, begun in 1682, and the national pantheon since its belated completion in 1966, are the cenotaphs of Vasco da Gama, Afonso de Albuquerque, Nun' Alvares Pereira, Henrique 'the Navigator', Pedro Alvares Cabral and Luis de Camões.

Lapped by the Tagus is the spacious **Praça do Comércio** or 'Black Horse Square', from which Catherine of Braganza sailed for England, and João VI, when regent, sailed to Brazil at the commencement of the Peninsular War. Not far to the east is a Military Museum. In the western suburb of **Belém**, which saw the departure of Da Gama's fleet, stands the **Jerónimos** monastery, containing the tombs of Manuel I, João III, Dom Sebastião, Henrique (the Cardinal-king) and Alexandre Herculano (died 1877), the historian. Adjacent is the **National Archaeological Museum** and, close by, the **Naval Museum**, beyond which is the characteristic **Torre de Belém**. North of the centre are the **Gulbenkian Museum** and, off the Campo Grande, the modern building of the National Archives, still known as the '**Torre do Tombo**', and the **Museu da Cidade**, devoted to the history of Lisbon. **24, 25, 34, 39, 44, 46, 50, 70, 71, 72, 102–3, 107**

Lorvão has a convent founded in the

12th century containing the 18th-century silver tombs of two daughters of Sancho I, who had been abbesses there.

Madeira, the main island in a group of five volcanic islands lying about 575 miles south-west of Lisbon, was rediscovered in c. 1418. A landing was made on the thickly forested island, the first colonists cutting the timber from which it takes its name. **Funchal**, the capital, was raised to the dignity of a city in 1508. Sugar-canes and Malvoisie or Malmsey vines were introduced and the production and export of 'Madeira' became largely a British preserve from 1658, when their first consul was appointed; the names Blandy, Cossart, and Leacock are among those later ubiquitous. It was the first port-of-call of both Anson and Cook on their voyages of 1740 and 1768 respectively. During the Napoleonic wars it was occupied by Hood's fleet and British troops. In 1852 its vineyards were ravished by the oidium, and by phylloxera in 1872. Funchal was shelled by a German U-boat in 1917, when three vessels were sunk. **63–7, 73, 78, 109**

Mafra. The immense conventual palace was erected in fulfilment of a vow made by João V on the birth of an heir, and its construction, regardless of the crippling expense, took place between 1717 and 1735. It accommodates a church, hospital, royal suite and a huge library. Byron, who condemned the pile in general as an example of 'magnificence without elegance', was asked by the monks 'if the *English* had *any* books in their country'. **98**

Marco de Canaveses. Nearby, at **Freixo**, was the Roman walled town of *Tongobriga*, under excavation since 1980. Baths, dwellings, cisterns, a forum, cemetery and numerous artefacts are in the process of being uncovered.

Marvão, straddling a rocky outcrop of the range known to the Romans as *Herminius minor*, has been fortified since remote antiquity. Its castle commands extensive views, with the Torre (1991m), in the Serra da Estrêla and the highest peak in Portugal, visible to the north-west. The museum displays Paleolithic artefacts found in the district. In the valley below stood Roman *Ammaia* (São Salvador de Aramenha), of which little survives.

Mérida (*Emerita Augusta*) (Sp.; 70km. east of Badajoz), was founded in 23 BC as a settlement for survivors (*emeritus*, a veteran) of Augustus's Cantabrian Wars, and it became the capital of the province of Lusitania. It flourished under the Visigoths, but surrendered to the Muslims in 713, from whom it was reconquered by Alfonso IX in 1230 and presented to the Order of Santiago. It never regained its former importance and the peripatetic Catholic Monarchs did not bother to visit the place during their progresses through the kingdom. Among Roman remains are the **bridge** of 64 arches spanning the Guadiana, the **aqueduct** ('Los Milagros'), a **hippodrome**, **amphitheatre**, and **theatre** (over-restored), **temple of Diana**, **triumphal arch** and **Alcazaba**. Notable also is the **Roman museum. 17, 20**

Mértola (Roman *Julia Myrtilis*), founded in remote antiquity, became one of the four *municipia* of Lusitania. It was in Suevic hands until occupied by the Muslims from 712 to 1236. Spectacularly sited above the Guadiana (the Roman *Anas*, and Arabic *Wadi-Anas*), it is dominated by its castle, below which stands the battlemented Igreja Matriz, a converted mosque retaining its *mihrab*. A tombstone from Mértola dated AD 525 displayed the horseshoe 'Moorish' arch, confirming that it was used in the Peninsula long before the invasion of 711. Three small museums well display artefacts from the Roman, Paleo-Christian and Muslim eras. **43, 50**

17km east lies **Mina de São Domingos**, with copper mines – an extension of those at Tharsis and Río Tinto – exploited from the time of Augustus to that of Theodosius and rediscovered in 1857 by a British company.

Miranda do Douro, long an isolated frontier post overlooking the rapids of the Douro, was the seat of a bishop from 1545 until 1782. In May 1762 it was attacked by the Spaniards, when its castle blew up, killing some 400 people. In late May 1813 Wellington, having ridden from Salamanca, was slung across the gorge to inspect his Anglo-Portuguese army of 60,000 under Gen. Graham, secretly assembled in the vicinity, which was to outflank the French near Zamora at the start of the brilliant offensive manoeuvre culminating only three weeks later in Wellington's great victory at Vitoria. **117**

Monção was founded by Afonso III and fortified in the 17th century to defend the south bank of the Minho. It was referred to as Monson at the turn of the 18th century by English factors who settled there to export its wines. Ruins of a castle survive, and the Romanesque church preserves the tomb of Deuladeu Martins, who held the Spanish at bay in 1368 by the expedient of throwing them loaves to show how well supplied the defenders were. In 1658 it resisted a Spanish attack for four months before capitulating on advantageous terms.

Monforte (north-west of Elvas), near which is the Roman villa of **Torre de Palma**.

Monsaraz. The fortified hilltop village, reconquered by Geraldo Sem Pavor in 1167 and given to the Templars, later passed to the Order of Christ. In 1381 it may have been sacked by the unpaid English archers of Edmund of Cambridge. There are numerous megalithic remains in the vicinity, for the best approach to which enquire at the tourist office at Reguengos de Monsaraz, 17km. west.

Montemor-o-Novo retains a Moorish castle rebuilt in the late 13th century. A native of the town was Juan de Dios (St John of God; 1495–1550), of Jewish lineage, and the founder of the Order of Charity, who devoted his life to the care of captives, foundlings and the sick.

Montemor-o-Velho was the birthplace of the navigator Diogo de Azambuja in *c.* 1456, who is also buried there; in *c.* 1510 of the traveller and chronicler Fernão Mendes Pinto; and also of Jorge de Montemayor, the poet and pastoral novelist, in 1519. It was eventually reconquered in 1034. Its castle once contained a royal palace. **35**

Obidos, an ancient, picturesquely walled town, was taken from the Muslims by Afonso Henriques in 1140. The castle was built by Dom Dinis. Santa Maria contains a painting by Josefa d'Ayala, born in Seville, but usually referred to as Josefa 'of Obidos', who died here in 1684. The museum contains a maquette of the Lines of Torres Vedras.

Oliveira do Hospital formerly belonged to the Hospitallers. Some Roman masonry is apparent in the area. At neighbouring **Bobadela** (Roman name unknown) stands a Roman triumphal arch, and relics of an amphitheatre may be seen also.

Olivença/Olivenza (Sp.) lies 25km south-west of Badajoz. Until occupied by the Spaniards in 1801 it was a fortified Portuguese frontier town, displaying several Manueline features, but it was never returned to them despite provision to do so in the 1814 *Treaty of Paris*. **108–9**

Some distance north-east, via Valverde, is the Roman villa of **La Dehesa de la Cocosa**. 17km east of Valverde lies **La Albuera**, site of the sanguinary battle fought on 16 May 1811 between Allied troops commanded by Beresford and the French under Soult.

Oporto; see **Porto**.

Ourém, Vila Nova de is dominated by a restored bastioned castle in which Sancho II's queen was held captive by a band of barons in 1246, very likely with her connivance.

Ourique gives its name to a battle – probably no more than a raid by Afonso Henriques into Muslim-occupied territory – said to have taken place in its vicinity in July 1139, but it is now thought that Chão de Ourique, near Santarém, was the more likely site. Nearby, survives the rectangular walled enclosure of a Luso-Roman camp, the **Castro dos Palheiros**.

Paços de Ferreira, near which is the impressive **Citânia de Sanfins**, an extensive Celtic settlement dating back to the 6th century BC. It remained inhabited until the 4th century AD. The site museum is in the valley near the ascending road.

Palmela is commanded by a hilltop castle taken from the Muslims, which in 1288 became the headquarters of the Portuguese Order of São Tiago (St James). One church – the other, on the site of a mosque, was destroyed in the 1755 earthquake – contains the tomb of Jorge de Lencastre (died 1551), a son of João II and the last Grand Master of the Order. **51**

Peneda-Gêres National Park; see **Portela do Homem**.

Peniche, a fishing-port, lies on a rock-bound, flat-topped peninsula, the strong defences of which, when in Spanish hands, were attacked unsuccessfully in 1589 by both Drake and the Prior of Crato. In 1809 Gen. D'Urban, perhaps with the recent drama of Corunna in mind, suggested that it was perfect 'for the Embarkation of the British Army, should it ever be necessary to do so in the Face of the Enemy'. Under Salazar, its *Fortaleza* was used as a political prison.

Pombal, a market-town with a castle founded *c.* 1174 by Gualdim Pais, gave a title to the '*Gran Marquês*', Sebastião José de Carvalho e Melo (1699–1782). In 1777 this dynamic if dictatorial statesman – the name Pombal, dovecote in English, belied him – retired here in disgrace on the accession of the reactionary and priest-ridden Dona Maria I. His remains were first buried in Nossa Senhora do Cardal. The place was sacked in 1811 by the French retreating from before the Lines of Torres Vedras. **100–7**

Ponte de Lima, Roman *Limia* or *Forum Limicorum*, is picturesquely sited on the south bank of the Lima. On reaching the river Decimus Junius Brutus had difficulty in persuading his troops to cross, for having trudged already across Iberia, they had assumed it must be Lethe, the River of Oblivion. As Lemici, it was the birthplace in 394 of the Suevic annalist Hydatius. English archers helped João I to capture the place in 1385. Near the ancient bridge (of which five Roman arches survive), a riverside market has been held since 1125.

Portalegre, capital of the Alto Alentejo, and an episcopal city since 1545, was besieged in 1299 by Dom Dinis during the dynastic feuds of that period, and was attacked by the Spanish in 1704. It was a British base during part of the Peninsular War.

Portela do Homem. Near this northern entrance of a Roman road between Braga and Astorga, referred to in the *Antonine Itinerary*, is the most extensive concentration of miliary columns or Roman milestone surviving in the Iberian peninsula. For precise details of their position, apply to the tourist office in Gêres, approached from the N103, leading north-east from Braga.

Portimão. It was here in July 1189 that a force of Crusaders, including some English led by Sancho I, landed to besiege Silves.

Porto, *O porto*, the port, and anglicized as **Oporto**, is the second city of Portugal. With its sprawling suburbs, it has a population approaching one million. The first settlement, referred to as *Portucale* as early as 456, grew up around the Pena Ventosa, rising above the steep north bank of the Douro, here crossed by ferry to the site of the Roman *castro* of *Cale*, probably a strengthened Lusitanian fort. In the 6th century a church was built on the commanding height. The town was recaptured definitively by the Christians in 982, and in 1147 a fleet of Crusaders landed here before sailing south to assist Afonso Henriques in capturing Lisbon. In 1387 João I and Philippa of Lancaster were married in the cathedral, and their fourth son, Henry, 'the Navigator', was born here in 1394. Porto became progressively associated with the English, although their interest in exporting the wine of the upper Duoro valley, known as 'Port', did not mature for another three centuries. The Lisbon earthquake of 1755 did not affect Oporto physically and most of the several mansions built to embellish the city by Nicolau Nasoni, who died there in 1773, have survived. The French under Soult occupied the place in March 1809, but on 12 May, taken by surprise by Wellington, whose troops had been surreptitiously ferried across, they were forced to flee precipitately. In 1832–3 the city, its defences partly manned by a motley 'International Brigade' (largely Glaswegians and Cockneys), was besieged by Miguelite forces for some eighteen months. The latter eventually retreated, after blowing up and setting fire to the *armazéns* or wine-lodges in transpontine **Vila Nova da Gaia**, when some 27,000 pipes of wine flowed into the Douro, turning its swirling waters a muddy red. During the later 19th century Porto flourished, becoming a stronghold of Liberalism and the base of opposition to several reactionary regimes. In 1878 the first Republican deputy was elected there. It is now the hub of the largest industrial and commercial complex in the country, providing some 60 per cent of the national revenue.

'To walk about this city is, I assure you, rather a violent exercise, not one street in it being on a level excepting that where the most part of the English inhabit', is how 'Arthur Costigan' described the city two centuries ago. Little has changed in this regard as far as the maze of lanes in the older, formerly walled, enceinte is concerned, where continuing restorations have not destroyed its character. The vertiginous **Ponte de Dom Luís I** was erected by Eiffel in 1886. The Rua do Infante Dom Henrique (formerly the Rua Nova dos Inglezes) is flanked by the **Feitoria Ingleza** or Factory House of the British Association, designed by Consul Whitehead, completed in 1790, and since then the main stamping-ground of the British establishment, so long influential in the wine trade. Nearby is the rebuilt '**House of Henry the Navigator**', traditionally his birthplace and, at a lower level, the quayside **Praça da Ribeira**. Some distance north of the centre is 12th-century **São Martinho da Cedofeito**, founded on the site of the Suevic king Theodomir's conversion from Arianism to Orthodoxy in the mid-6th century. **53, 61, 66, 93, 113, 119, 122**

Porto de Mos is commanded by its 13th-century castle, built on a Roman site, which was captured by Afonso Henriques in 1147. It was here, in August 1385, that the Portuguese army heard Mass before the battle of Aljubarrota, fought not far to the north-west. It was remodelled as a palace in the 15th century, of which the richly decorated balcony – similar to that at Leiria – is preserved.

Queluz. The Rococo palace, the entrance courtyard of which was designed in emulation but in miniature of the Cour du Marbre at Versailles, was built for the Infante Dom Pedro in 1747-52 and – after the experience of the 1755 earthquake – single-story extensions were added. Beckford, who attended a hushed fête held in its formal gardens, embellished with topiary and *azulejo*-lined canals, recalled the sensation of horror at hearing the agonizing wails of Maria I, who thus exhibited her incipient madness. **99**

Río Tinto, Minas de (*Tharsis* (Sp.; south of Aracena on the Serpa–Seville road) lies at the centre of one of the oldest copper and silver mining districts in the world, which extends west towards Minas de São Domingos (see **Mértola**). Exploited by the Tartessians, then the Phoenicians and Romans until *c.* 400, they were broken up by the Visigoths and remained practically derelict until 1725. The main place of export of its ores was Huelva (*Onuba*) in Spain.

Roliça, a village within a horseshoe of low hills, gave its name to the first engagement of the Peninsular War in which the future Duke of Wellington saw action, on 17 August 1808. The French, under Delaborde, were obliged to retire to avoid being outflanked by the two wings of the British army advancing south from Obidos towards the mouth of the Maceira river, where reinforcements were landing. **111–18**

Sagres, a small windswept resort and fishing-port, preserves a house claiming to have been occupied by Henry 'the Navigator', but this – 'remote from the tumult of people and propitious for the contemplation of study' – was more certainly nearer Cape St Vincent, further west. It was sacked by Drake and further damaged in 1755. It was here that Prince Henry is said to have founded an influential school of navigation, set up an observatory and died in 1460. After this the place decayed and the centre of maritime studies was transferred to Lisbon. **62, 64–5 Cape St Vincent**, the barren south-western extremity of Europe, the Roman *Promontorium*

Sacrum, takes its present name from the legend that relics of the martyred saint were brought here in the 8th century, and then, guided by a pair of ravens, were miraculously translated to Lisbon in 1173. Several naval battles were fought nearby: in 1693, when Rooke defeated Tourville; in 1780, when Rodney attacked a Spanish fleet; another Spanish fleet was scattered by Jervis and Nelson in 1797; and in 1833, when a Miguelite squadron was routed by Sir Charles Napier. **108, 122**

Santarém (*Scallabis*), on a commanding height above the Tagus, was dignified by Julius Caesar with the title *Praesidium Julium*. It derives its present name from Santa Iria, a nun of Tomar, martyred in 653, whose body was washed ashore on the bank of the Nabão. As *Shantariya* it was a Muslim stronghold from 715 until finally recaptured in 1147 by Afonso Henriques, who founded Alcobaça in gratitude. Being near **Almeirim**, a favourite royal summer residence, it was frequently the seat of the *cortes* in the 14–15th centuries. Dom Dinis died here in 1325 and in 1557 the murderers of Inês de Castro were executed here. The place was sacked by Masséna when retreating from before the Lines of Torres Vedras; in 1833 it was the last stronghold of the reactionary Miguelites. In the church of Graça is the tombstone of Pedro Alvares Cabral (died *c.* 1526; cf. Belmonte), discoverer of Brazil. São João de Alporão, now a lapidary museum, contains the tomb – preserving a tooth only – of Duarte de Meneses (died 1464), a governor of Alcácer-Quibir. **15, 39, 43, 44, 46, 53, 149**

Santiago de Caçem lies on a hill-slope dominated by a ruined Moorish castle rebuilt by the Templars. On a neighbouring height are the extensive remains of Roman *Mirobriga Celticum*, partly excavated, built on the site of an *oppidum* in occupation since the 8th or 9th century BC. **15**

Serpa, thus also known to the Romans, was not finally reconquered from the Muslims until *c.* 1232, and not resettled – due to the territory being disputed by the Castilians – until 1297. Within stretches of wall are a ruined castle, a huge *nora* or Moorish chain-pump and an aqueduct. **50**

Setúbal, an important commercial and fishing-port, with nearby shipyards, was long famous for the export of salt extracted from the adjacent flats of the Rio Sado. It takes its present name from *Cetobriga*, the Celtic *oppidum*, probably of Phoenician foundation, the site of which was once assumed to be at **Tróia**, on the far bank of the estuary. This was overwhelmed by a tidal wave in the 5th century, where fish-salting tanks have been excavated. The present town, which suffered severely in the earthquake of 1755, was founded in the 12th century and it was here that João II married Leonor de Lencastre in 1471. It was then familiarly known to English sailors as 'Saint Ubes'. Among its defences was the Castelo de São Filipe, erected by Philip II of Spain to cow the locals and protect the place from English attack. The spiralling cable-like columns and rope-like ribs in the apse of the Igreja de Jesus, begun in 1494, are characteristic of the Manueline style. **15**

Silves, as *Shalb* or *Xelb*, was the capital of the Muslim kingdom of Algarve, possessing a port and shipyards and, according to Idrisi, was of fine appearance with well-furnished bazaars. It became the centre of Ibn Qasi's revolt against the Almoravids in the mid-12th century, and in 1189 was sacked by Sancho I after a three-month siege, but not definitively reconquered for another sixty years. A decline set in with the silting up of the river and it suffered in the 1755 earthquake, being described a century later as 'one of the most desolate and deserted places in Portugal'. It contains the remains of a huge Moorish castle and – built on the site of a mosque – a dark red sandstone cathedral, sacked by Essex in 1596. **32, 43**

Sintra, the attractions of which have often been praised in poetry and prose, lies on the northern slope of its bosky *serra*. Some time before 1415, João I set about enlarging a former royal residence to palatial proportions, of which two oasthouse-like chimneys are the most conspicuous features; and it was here that he decided on the Ceuta expedition of 1415. In 1578 Dom Sebastião held his last audience here before setting out on his disastrous African crusade. Afonso VI spent his last impotent years in the palace, where he died in 1683. **39, 45, 125**

Tavira was once assumed to have been Roman *Balsa*, but this is now thought to be further west, near Luz. Reconquered from the Muslims in 1239 and raised to the rank of city in 1520, it later declined with the silting

An early 16th century view of the Royal Palace at Sintra

up of the port, and remains a characteristic and comparatively unspoilt town in the Algarve. **50, 122**

Tomar is commanded by the former castle of the Knights Templar. Gualdim Pais, Grand Master of the Order, may have already founded Santa Maria dos Olivais (in which he was buried) on lower but less defensible ground on the left bank of the Nabão near the Roman site of *Sellium*, where remains of the villa of Nabancio have been excavated. From the medieval town, in which is a restored 14th-century synagogue, a road winds uphill to the huge Convento de Cristo. The papal suppression of the Templars in 1314 was only nominally enforced in Portugal and Dom Dinis replaced it by founding the Order of

Christ, its headquarters being established at Tomar in 1356. Henry 'the Navigator' was Grand Master from 1417 until his death in 1460. In 1492 it passed into the hands of Dom Manuel, who set about extending the dependencies. Its decline dates from 1580, when Philip II was proclaimed king of Portugal there; while during the Peninsular War it was sacked by Masséna's troops. **21, 45, 51, 79, 83**

Torres Vedras, once a royal residence and the birthplace in 1436 of Eleonor of Portugal (who married the Habsburg Emperor Friedrich III and died at Wiener Neustadt), gave its name to the famous 'Lines' secretly constructed across the neck of the broad peninsula on which Lisbon stands. These comprise two main bands of

Tomar. West window of the Convento de Cristo church

hill-top redoubts – many still extant – erected on Wellington's instructions during the year prior to his retreat from Busaco in October 1810. Manned by some 30,000 militia and Anglo-Portuguese troops, they held Masséna's army at bay until early the following March, when sheer starvation forced the demoralized French to retreat back to Spain, losing virtually their entire baggage train. For the battle fought athwart the frontier two months later, see **Fuentes de Oñoro**. Nearby is the walled Chalcolithic settlement of **Zambujal**, in occupation between *c.* 2500 and 1700 BC. **9**

Trancoso was the venue in 1283 of the marriage of Dom Dinis and Isabel of Aragón. A Spanish army was routed here in 1385, and two years later, John of Gaunt concluded negotiations here for his daughter Catherine of Lancaster to marry the future Enrique III of Castile in return for a large indemnity in money and the surrender of his own claims to Portugal.

Tui/Tuy (Sp.), of ancient origin, formerly *Tudae* or *Tude*, and a capital of King Witiza in *c.* 700, stands on the right bank of the Minho opposite Valença and retains a 12–13th-century cathedral. Some 30km to the west, straddling Monte Tecla, above the estuary opposite Caminha, are the extensive remains of the Celtic *citânia* of **La Guarda**. 24

Valença do Minho, now dominated by a modern viaduct spanning the river, also crossed by a bridge of 1885 constructed by Eiffel, retains a characteristic enceinte enclosed within 17th-century ramparts facing the Spanish frontier fortress of Tuí. Until rebuilt in 1262, the Roman town was known as *Contrasta*, but apart from sustaining two minor sieges by the Decembrists in 1837 and a decade later, it has seen little action, and its walls are thus in a perfect state of preservation.

Via Lata; see **Camino de la Plata**

Viana do Castelo, a fishing-port and resort on the estuary of the Lima, where an English *feitoria* had been established by 1700, from which they exported the wines of the Minho before moving to Oporto, retains several buildings of interest. Above the town stands the Celtic *citânia* of **Santa Luzia**. Abp. Bartolomeu dos Mártires of Braga, who attended the Council of Trent, and was buried here in 1590, was an indefatigable visitor of his diocese, penetrating into its wildest fastnesses where certainly no bishop had ever been seen before. It is recorded that he once met a procession of villagers chanting 'Blessed be the most Holy Trinity and her sister the most pure Virgin', much to his consternation.

Vila do Conde, a fishing-port at the mouth of the Ave, defended by a 17th-century fort, is dominated by the huge convent of Santa Clara, begun in 1777. It was founded in 1318 by Afonso Sanches, a bastard of Dom Dinis, who with his wife is buried in the adjacent church, as is Brites Pereira, daughter of Nun'Alvares and the wife of the first Duke of Braganza.

Vila Formosa, south-west of Crato, retains an imposing six-arched Roman bridge over the Seda, which formerly carried the Roman road from Mérida to Santarém and Lisbon. 25

Vila de Frades. The Roman villa near here, known as **São Cucufate**, is an imposing structure of brick-vaulted rooms preserving early mural decoration. It was later converted to monastic use, remaining so until the 16th century. In an idyllic setting, the site continues to be excavated.

Vilamoura (north-west of Faro), preserves the extensive remains of the important Roman villa of **Cero da Vila**, which have survived vandalization by local farmers.

Vila Pouca de Aguiar has a Roman bridge and medieval castle on the site of a Roman fort at nearby **Pontido**. Also in the vicinity, further east, at **Três Minas**, are relics of Roman gold mines.

Vila Real, now the largest town in the Trás-os-Montes, was granted royal rights by Afonso III in 1271. Diogo Cão, the first navigator to reach the mouth of the Congo, was born here in 1482. In 1832 the reactionary Count of Amarante established the headquarters of an insurrectionary movement here prior to the *pronunciamento* at Vila Franca de Xira against the Liberal government of the time. **Sabrosa** (some 20km south-east) was the birthplace of

Fernão de Magalhães (Magellan) in *c.* 1480.

Vila Real de Santo António, at the mouth of the Guadiana, was run up in 1774 by Pombal near the site of Santo António de Arenilha, possibly of Phoenician origin, but engulfed by the sea in *c.* 1600. The new town was laid out on a grid plan at ruinous expense, for the ashlar used in its construction had been transported from Lisbon, after which stone quarries were 'discovered' in the neighbourhood. To the north was Roman *Baesuris*, now **Castro Marim**, with a huge castle, the first headquarters of the Order of Christ before its transfer to Tomar.

Vila Velha de Ródão (south-west of Castelo Branco) was long an important crossing point of the Tagus, notably during the Peninsular War, when on Wellington's main line of lateral communication between Guarda and Elvas. Many of the rupestrian paintings in the area have been submerged by the higher water-level of the now partly dammed river.

Vila Viçosa, dominated by its bastioned castle, which was the original *solar* or seat of the ducal family of Braganza, was briefly Edmund of Cambridge's headquarters in the Anglo-Portuguese campaign of 1382. The Paço Ducal is mainly 17th century. It was here that the future João IV received the first overtures of the nationalist party, which were to bring about his accession in 1640. Catherine of Braganza was born here two years earlier, while Dom Carlos passed his last night here before his assassination in Lisbon in 1908. In the

neighbourhood took place the battle of **Montes Claros** (June 1665), in which the Count-Duke Frederick of Schomberg, with a British contingent, defeated the Spaniards under the Marquès de Caracena.

Vimeiro was the site of the battle of 21 August 1808 fought shortly after the engagement at *Roliça*. Wellington's reinforcements had disembarked from their transports at the mouth of the Maceira, adjacent, and his small but disciplined army took up defensive positions in the neighbouring hills to await Gen. Junot's troops marching from Lisbon. Superior firepower from their extended lines caused havoc in the massed French columns, which were driven back repeatedly. Gen. Kellermann proposed a truce shortly afterwards, known as 'The Convention of Cintra' (see Sintra), to which Wellington was forced to agree by elderly superior officers. They had landed to supersede him after the battle had commenced and preferred the Convention to risking further action in spite of the fact that the French had been defeated. 111

Viseu, capital of its district and an episcopal city of ancient origin, is traditionally associated with the last stand of Viriatus against the Romans in 139 BC, and with the burial in 711 of Don Rodrigo, the 'Last of the Goths', in São Miguel do Fetal, although there is no historical foundation for either claim. Alfonso V was killed when besieging the place in 1028, and it was not reconquered for another thirty years. It was the birthplace of Dom Duarte (João I's eldest son) in 1391, possibly of the artist Vasco Fernandes, better known as 'O Grão Vasco', in 1475, and in 1496 of João de Barros, a chronicler of Portuguese conquests in Asia. Earthworks north-west of the centre probably defended a Roman camp of *c*. 61 BC, not that of Viriatus. **35**

Details of *pousadas* may be obtained from responsible travel agents via Interface International, 203 Sheen Lane, London SW14 8LE; Marketing Ahead, 433 Fifth Avenue, New York 10016; Portuguese National Tourist Offices; or direct from Pousadas Portugal, Avenida Santa Joana Princesa 10, 1749–090 Lisbon (tel.: 351 21 844 20 01; fax.: 351 21 844 20 85/7; e-mail: guest@pousadas.pt; Internet: www.pousadas.pt). As welcome is the promotion of 'Turismo de Habitação', the providing of agreeable accommodation in private homes – largely in the northern part of the country – established by TURIHAB, Praça da República, 4990 Ponte de Lima (tel.: 351 58 94 27 29 or 351 58 74 16 72).

Index